THE ULTIMATE ENCYCLOPEDIA OF
CATS
CAT BREEDS
& CAT CARE

THE ULTIMATE ENCYCLOPEDIA OF

CATS

CAT BREEDS
& CAT CARE

Alan Edwards

Veterinary Consultant:
Trevor Turner, B.VET.MED., M.R.C.V.S.

LORENZ BOOKS

This edition is published by Lorenz Books

Lorenz Books is an imprint of Anness Publishing Ltd
Hermes House, 88–89 Blackfriars Road, London SE1 8HA
tel. 020 7401 2077; fax 020 7633 9499
www.lorenzbooks.com; info@anness.com

© Anness Publishing Limited 1999, 2003

This edition distributed in the UK by The Manning Partnership Ltd, 6 The Old Dairy, Melcombe Road, Bath BA2 3LR; tel.
01225 478 444; fax 01225 478 440; sales@manning-partnership.co.uk

This edition distributed in the USA and Canada by National Book Network, 4720 Boston Way, Lanham, MD 20706; tel.
301 459 3366; fax 301 459 1705; www.nbnbooks.com

This edition distributed in Australia by Pan Macmillan Australia, Level 18, St Martins Tower, 31 Market St, Sydney, NSW
2000; tel. 1300 135 113; fax 1300 135 103; customer.service@macmillan.com.au

This edition distributed in New Zealand by David Bateman Ltd, 30 Tarndale Grove, Off Bush Road, Albany, Auckland;
tel. (09) 415 7664; fax (09) 415 8892

A CIP catalogue record for this book is available from the British Library

Publisher Joanna Lorenz
Project and Contributing Editor Gilly Cameron Cooper
Designer Michael Morey
Photographer John Daniels
Production Controller Wendy Lawson
Editorial Reader Hayley Kerr
Indexer Dorothy Frame

Previously publshed as *The Ultimate Cat Book*

1 3 5 7 9 10 8 6 4 2

Contents

Introducing the Domestic Cat

Despite its obvious liking for comfort and human company, the domestic cat has many of the same characteristics as its wild relations. It shares the lithe muscularity of a body built for stalking and hunting and a fine-furred pelt with the big roaring cats of jungle and savanna. In fact, there are smaller wild species that have at times left their feral state to cohabit with humans. At this level, the boundaries between wildness and domesticity remain fluid.

For although the domestic feline appears to have a smaller brain than its wild counterpart, if forced by circumstance, it can quite easily revert to the free-roaming, independent life of a wild predator.

◆ FACING PAGE ·
The European wild cat looks as though it might be related to the domestic tabby cat, but its wariness and untamed character are quite different.

◆ LEFT
The modern Bengal breed is a cross between a domestic cat and the wild Asian leopard cat (*Felis bengalensis*).

JOURNEY FROM THE WILD

Members of the cat family Felidae range from the great, roaring cats such as the lion and tiger to the small domestic cat. They are separated into different genuses (family sub-divisions), not because of their size, but because of differences in their anatomy. These enable members of the genus *Panthera* to roar, while the small cats in genus *Felis* cannot do so. There is a third genus for the cheetahs because they have non-retractable claws. Early in the 1900s there were more than 230 different species of cat in the family as a whole, but now there are fewer than 30. Many became extinct because cats have always been hunted and killed by humans for their fine pelts.

ORIGINS OF DOMESTIC CATS

There is a close relationship between the wild and the domestic cat, but it is uncertain which wild sub-species of the *Felis* (small cats) genus actually made the leap into domesticity. Wild cats are widely distributed and vary considerably in appearance and habits. Northern cats,

♦ LEFT AND BELOW
The European wild cat (*left*) was thought to be the ancestor of today's domestic cat because of its tabby markings, but this is now considered unlikely because of its instinctive wariness of people. The more likely contender is the African wild cat (*below*).

for example, developed dense, almost woolly coats, while in warmer, southern climes, a fine, body-hugging fur was the norm. Experts ended up with three major contenders for the ancestor of the domestic cat: the European wild cat and its Asian and African equivalents.

For many years, the Europeans believed that it was their wild cat (*Felis sylvestris sylvestris*), which is still found in localized parts of the Scottish Highlands and northern continental Europe. Their assumption was based on the cat's colouring and tabby

markings that are common in non-pedigreed cats of today. However, even if the young offspring are reared by humans, they remain very wary, and do not abandon their wild behaviour patterns. This inherent anti-social streak makes them unlikely to have been inclined towards domestication.

On the other hand, the African wild cat (*F. sylvestris libyca*), which still survives in Africa, western Asia and southern Europe, not only has the same number of chromosomes as the domestic cat but is relatively

CAT ANCESTRY

The wild ancestors of today's domestic cat were among the first carnivores that evolved during the late Eocene and early Oligocene periods of pre-history over 35 million years ago. But it was another family of carnivores, the dogs, Canidae, that became the first animal companions of human beings. Stone Age man took advantage of the dog's superior sensory

```
                    CLASS MAMMALIA
        ┌──────────────────┴──────────────────┐
  ORDER HERBIVORA                        ORDER CARNIVORA
   (Herbivores)                            (Carnivores)
                                    ┌──────────┴──────────┐
                                 Family Felidae
                                    (Cats)
        ┌──────────────────┬──────────────────┐
    Panthera              Felis            Acinonyx
 (roaring cats)       (small cats)      (cat with
 including lion, leopard,                non-retractable
   tiger, snow leopard,                    claws)
  jaguar, clouded leopard
                                            cheetah
        ┌──────────────────┴──────────────────┐
  Felis manul              Felis sylvestris libyca (African wild cat[3])
  Manul[2]                 Felis sylvestris sylvestris (European wild cat[1])
              and many other small cat species
```

1 May have bred with the early domesticated cats that reached Europe
2 A possible ancestor of longhaired cats
3 The most likely ancestor of most domestic cats

powers to help him hunt, and this provided a sound basis for an ongoing relationship. It was not until people graduated into a more settled agricultural way of life that cats became part of the domestic scene.

Small feline skeletons have been found in Stone Age archaeological sites, usually with the remains of other small wild animals such as badgers, which suggests that the cats were killed for their meat or pelts. The first evidence of cats actually living in some tentative relationship with humans was found in a New Stone Age site in Jericho in the Middle East, dating from about 9,000 years ago. However, it is unlikely that domestic cats, living in a relationship with humans similar to that of today, emerged until around 3,500 years ago in ancient Egypt.

✦ ABOVE LEFT
The leopard is in a different genus from the small cat not because it is bigger, but because the anatomy of its larynx enables it to roar.

✦ RIGHT
Every member, big and small, of the cat family is built to be an efficient killer. The tiger, the largest of the *Panthera* species, is one of the most powerful predators of all.

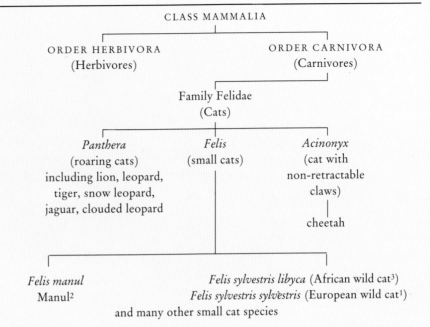

The lion is another roaring cat of the genus *Panthera*. However, it is quite clearly in the same family as the domestic cat, with its flexible, muscular body, a typically short, rounded head, and large eyes.

The cheetah is in a separate genus because it has non-retractable claws. However, it is closely related to the puma (also known as the mountain lion or cougar), which can retract its claws.

◆ LEFT
The golden fur of today's Abyssinian is ticked with a darker brown – very similar to that of the African wild cat from which it is probably descended.

sociable. Both this sub-species and the Asian desert cat (*F. sylvestris ornata*) often live on the outskirts of human settlements and are fairly easily tamed. Significantly, remains of the African wild cat have been found in caves lived in by ancient man, and it is generally accepted as the ancestor of most of today's domestic cats. *F. sylvestris libyca* (abbreviated to *F. libyca*) is, in fact, very similar to the Abyssinian breed of today – lithe, long-faced with large ears, and with a ticked, or agouti (dark-tipped) tan coat.

THE PATH TO DOMESTICATION

Our ancestors may simply have hunted and killed these cats, both as a food source and for their pelts. However, as humans were developing an agrarian society based on crops that would have attracted rodents, it is also possible that the kittens were tamed and used to control pests. This would also have been in the cat's interests – keeping the scavenger population under control provided a regular concentration of well-fed prey.

In 1865, Francis Galton, a British scientist who specialized in the study of heredity and intelligence, defined the essential qualities of the early domestic animal. It would need to be useful, easy to tend, able to breed freely, and above all (in the case of the dog and cat, for example), be comfort loving and have a liking for humans. There is also a hypothesis that the process of domestication from wild, savage feline may have been accelerated by genetic mutation. Genes, the building blocks for a living creature, include patterns for behaviour as well as the size and general conformation of the adult. A fault in the genes that control behaviour patterns could, at some time, have created a cat that was

◆ LEFT
The African wild cat (*Felis libyca*) is still found today in the wild in Africa, western Asia and southern Europe. It does not seem to be intimidated by people and often lives near human settlements.

coat qualities that resemble those of the modern domesticated cat. It also seems that in such cross-matings, the genetic trait for domestication in one sub-species can strongly affect a more savage temperament in the other. The most recent example of this is the domestic cross with *F. bengalensis bengalensis* (Asian leopard cat) to produce the pedigree variety known as the Bengal. Successive generations enhanced the domesticated qualities of this new breed. (The registration organizations for pedigreed cats in some countries, notably the Cat Fanciers' Association in the United States, do not recognize this breed or any other developed from cross-matings of domestic cats with wild cats, although the Governing Council of the Cat Fancy in the United Kingdom does.)

temperamentally unwilling to leave a juvenile (kittenish) dependency state. This, coupled with a ready supply of food from the human farmers, created an environment in which the mutual advantages of domestication were explored. The kitten-cat gained warmth, comfort and a secure environment in which to breed, and its offspring were valued as an ongoing supply of rodent exterminators. This made the spread of the genetic fault creating the socially valuable domesticated cat inevitable.

The domestication process may well have been accelerated as the African wild cat spread from warm southern and eastern regions and cross-mated with its northern European relation. It has been found recently that cross-matings of these sub-species produce animals with

♦ LEFT
The Asian leopard cat (*Felis bengalensis bengalensis*) is a wild species that has been crossed with a domestic cat to produce a new pedigree, the Bengal.

✦ LEFT
Ancient Egyptian murals depict cats well settled into domestic life. This one has tabby stripes on its back – the most common fur pattern that is also seen on the African wild cat.

✦ BELOW
A mummified cat discovered in an Egyptian tomb dating from between 1000 and 332 BC. More than 300,000 cat mummies were discovered at one archaeological site in 1890.

MEDITERRANEAN REFINEMENT

Compared with the dog, the domestication of the cat is relatively recent. It probably occurred only 5–8,000 years ago, compared with the dog's 50,000-year relationship with humans. During excavations of the 8,000-year-old human settlement of Khirokitia in Cyprus in 1983, a single feline jawbone was found. Cyprus has never had endemic wild cats, so it is possible that this cat was a domestic animal. The proximity of Cyprus to Africa suggests that it could have been related to the African wild cat *F. sylvestris libyca*.

However, overwhelming evidence points to ancient Egypt as the first area in which the cat was elevated to a role beyond that of rodent exterminator. The cat established a niche for itself in ancient Egypt as

✦ BELOW
This polished bronze statue of Bastet, the cat goddess of ancient Egypt, dates from the 6th century BC and stands 34cm (13½in) high.

early as 3500 BC. Wall paintings in tombs built at the time of the New Kingdom (1560–1080 BC) depict the cat as being part of daily Egyptian life. On the death of a household cat, Egyptian families went into deep mourning, shaving off their eyebrows as a sign of their grief.

The cat was also revered as a symbol of fertility. Bastet (also known as Bast and Pasht), daughter of the sun god Re, or Osiris, and goddess of

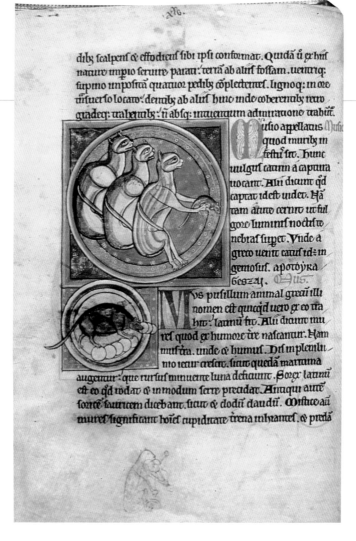

◆ RIGHT
◆ RIGHT
A cat is featured in a 13th-century bestiary (a book of beasts). Although widely feared and reviled at this time, cats were still useful mousers, and in England, were protected by the Church to some extent.

fertility, was originally depicted as a lion, but later assumed the shape of a small cat. It is from her name that the word puss is thought to derive.

In 1890, archaeologists discovered more than 300,000 cat mummies buried in an underground sanctuary dedicated to Bastet at Ben Hassan. Beside the cat mummies were mummified mice – food for the cats' journey into the afterlife. Cats were also domesticated in the Far East in ancient times, probably around 2000 BC. They may have arisen from the Asian desert cat (*F. sylvestris ornata*) and be the forebears of the longhaired domestic cat.

TRADE WITH ROME

The domesticated cat in the West spread with the expansion of the Roman Empire. Romans smuggled

◆ BELOW
By the time this cat was depicted in a 14th-century bestiary, the cat population was declining due to persecution. This helped the rodent population spread, and with it the virus that carried the Black Death through Europe.

cats out of Egypt and took them to their northern conquests, where they were used to control rodents. Cats also enjoyed some degree of veneration by the Romans. The 1st-century BC Greek historian Diodorus describes an incident in which a Roman charioteer in Alexandria, who ran over and killed a cat, was stoned to death by an angry mob.

Monks travelling to the Far East took cats with them, where they would have bred with the Asian domestic cats. The earliest domestic cat bone discovered in Britain dates back to between AD 10 and AD 43, before the Roman conquest. In Chelmsford, England, Roman roof tiles impressed with cats' paw prints have been found.

MEDIEVAL IMAGE CRISIS

The Romans saw the cat as a symbol of liberty. It was with the fall of the Roman Empire that the cat lost popularity. Earlier beliefs were adapted to fit in with the cat's gradual loss of image. The northern goddess of love, Freya, for example, had always

been depicted surrounded by cats, but later became a frightening witch whose cats were the denizens of hell. For around 700 years after the first millennium, throughout Europe the cat was often associated with witches and evil. In the town of Metz in France, hundreds of cats were burned alive on the second Wednesday in Lent, as a ritual sacrifice of witches.

In parts of the post-Roman world, the cat disappeared completely from the archaeological records. Luckily, in Britain it was still highly valued as a mouser, and until the 10th century – the beginning of the Middle Ages – it enjoyed some protection from the Church. However, in continental Europe, its fur was used to line and decorate garments, including the trimmings on the gowns of lawyers. In times of famine, cat flesh was added to the soups and stews of hungry farming folk.

✦ ABOVE
Persian cats were among the first exotic breeds to be developed in the West, their popularity boosted by the enthusiasm of European royals such as Queen Victoria of England.

✦ BELOW
The Maine Coon Cat was a valuable mouser in the north-eastern United States, and was a major winner at America's first cat show in Madison Square Garden, New York in 1895.

A NEW ERA

From the 1600s, the cat did once again find some favour as a domestic pet. The French Cardinal Richelieu was known to like cats, which he had with him while he worked. A French harpist left a large part of her fortune to her cats, together with instructions that they be properly cared for. By the 1700s, cats were sometimes featured in portraits of the Romantic era as favoured companions, and the poet Thomas Gray wrote his *Ode on the Death of A Favourite Cat Drowned in a Tub of Goldfishes*. There was even a cat fair held in the city of Winchester, England in 1598.

However, it was not until the 1800s that serious interest was taken. Country fairs in the United States included exhibitions of Maine Coon Cats from the 1860s. A cat show proper, with Maine Coons featuring strongly, was held in Madison Square

+ RIGHT
+ RIGHT
Domestic cats now outnumber dogs as favourite pets. In the United States the cat population is around 56 million compared with 54 million dogs, in Britain, 7.5 million against 6.7 million.

Garden in New York in 1895. The first British cat show – with benched cats in individual pens – was held at London's Crystal Palace in 1871. It was organized by the writer and notable cat artist Harrison Weir. The early shows were inspired by a growing interest in the glamorous pedigreed breeds. It became necessary for some sort of registration body to record the parentage of the cats, and to set some sort of standard that would list the desirable and undesirable traits for each breed. This was the role of the National Cat Club, founded in the United Kingdom in 1887, which marked the beginning of the cat fancy as it is known today. Harrison Weir was its first president.

Local clubs and clubs for specific breeds were soon formed. Today, there are active cat fancies in most countries, recent additions being Russia and Malaysia. At the early

+ ABOVE
The Turkish Angora of today is very different from its late-19th-century ancestor that, together with a Persian cat, founded many of the modern longhaired cat breeds.

shows, the main varieties seen were Persian longhairs, domestic shorthairs, Siamese, Foreign Blue (now known as Russian Blue), Manx and Abyssinian. During the 1900s, as travel became easier, wealthy enthusiasts imported cats from other countries and different breeds quickly spread across the world. Breeding suffered a setback during the world wars, and some breeds, such as the Abyssinian and Russian Blue, nearly became extinct. From the late 1950s, the cat fancy and knowledge of genetics grew, and many new breeds and colour varieties within breeds were developed.

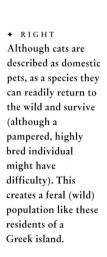

+ RIGHT
Although cats are described as domestic pets, as a species they can readily return to the wild and survive (although a pampered, highly bred individual might have difficulty). This creates a feral (wild) population like these residents of a Greek island.

Choosing the Right Cat

Many households are entirely suitable for a cat, or even a companionable pair of cats, but it is important to consider the effects a cat will have on the household. Although they are known for their independence of character, cats do need care and attention. A normal, healthy cat may live for fourteen years or more, and you need to consider whether you can stand such a long-term responsibility and commitment. Cats may all be roughly the same size and shape, but they vary a great deal in temperament, interests and needs. Before you buy a cat, it is wise to look at your lifestyle and home, and consider the type of cat that will happily fit in with it.

✦ FACING PAGE
Ragdoll kittens like these will grow into calm, good-natured adults that enjoy comfort and should adapt happily to an indoor lifestyle.

✦ LEFT
A lively Ocicat may not be of the ideal temperament to be confined to an indoor life.

WHY CHOOSE A CAT?

The cat's adaptability and independence make it a very practical pet for the modern working household. Cats do not have to be taken for walks; they self-clean and self-exercise. Some can happily adjust to a life spent totally indoors in a high-rise apartment. Depending on their character (and breed type if they are purebred), they can also learn to live with other domestic pets. For many people, though, it is the beauty of the cat that is so alluring. A cat on watch at a window, on the prowl or playing in the garden, or simply as a soothing, sleeping presence, is a graceful and rewarding, easy-care asset to the home and family.

THE RIGHT CAT

The choice of cat depends very much on personal preference for a particular type of cat, for long or short fur, or a particular coat colour and pattern. A

✦ ABOVE
Cat and bird, as well as dog and cat, are legendary enemies, but it need not be so. Cats can be persuaded to live harmoniously with other domestic pets.

✦ LEFT
A pair of farm kittens on an old tractor wheel look irresistible. They may grow up to be much-loved pets, but will probably also earn their keep as valuable mousers.

◆ RIGHT
A purebred cat with a pedigree will cost considerably more to acquire than a non-pedigreed animal, and caring for it may be a lot more time-consuming.

major determining factor is how much you want to spend. At the top end of the price scale are cats whose parents and grandparents can be traced through long pedigrees back to the late 1800s. At the other end of the scale are unplanned litters of non-pedigreed cats which may be picked up for free. In between are cross-breeds – a random or deliberate result of a mating between different breeds, or the unplanned mating of one pedigreed partner with a non-pedigree. At a fraction of the cost of a true pedigree, you could have a cat with the aristocratic qualities of its purebred mother and the resilient health of its father, or vice versa.

Size is not an issue. Unlike dogs, domestic cats do not vary greatly in size – there is no feline equivalent of the Great Dane or the tiny Chihuahua. Living-space restrictions do not generally present a problem as cats are very adaptable. Allowances need to be made for some active breeds, but most cats can settle into a small apartment as happily as into a large house.

THE PEDIGREE OPTION
Buying a purebred dog from a reputable breeder has long been accepted. However, it is only comparatively recently that interest in pedigreed cats has become established. Until about 30 years ago, there was a scarcity of breeders and, with the exception of Blue Persian and Siamese breeds, pedigreed cats were not readily

◆ ABOVE
Feral cats can be picked up for free on many a Mediterranean island, but they need particularly careful medical attention.

◆ BELOW
The non-pedigree from a known background is cheap and likely to be balanced of character and sturdy of health.

available. This situation has been radically redressed by the cat fancy (the world of pedigreed cats) being much more active in its publicity. The showing and breeding of cats with a known ancestry has become a popular hobby, making a much greater range of breeds available.

A key advantage of buying a pedigreed kitten from a reputable breeder is that there are safeguards woven into the transaction.

OFF THE STREETS
Cats that have been abandoned by their owners, or that have been born on the streets, carve a life for themselves as strays. They revert to a feral (wild) state, form colonies with other cats, and breed prolifically. It is perfectly possible to adopt a stray or feral cat you have found on the streets. One might even adopt you. However, they have been exposed to a host of infections and diseases, so thorough medical examination and inoculation is particularly important. You will also need to spend more time with a stray to help it bond with you and adjust to a settled way of life.

LONGHAIR OR SHORTHAIR?

Having a longhaired cat requires you to set aside some time every day to groom it, to keep the coat free from tangles and matting. At the other extreme, the almost hairless Sphynx cat needs extra care as it is very susceptible to temperature change and skin problems.

If you are living in a hot, humid climate, a longhaired cat (even if it sheds its cold-weather coat) is not a wise choice unless it is to live in an air-conditioned home. The coat of a Sphynx does not adapt at all to climatic changes, and the cat would need to be kept in a centrally heated environment in cold winters.

If you are allergic to cats, it will probably make no difference whether you have a longhair or a shorthair. Most human allergies to cats are due to the proteins in the scurf (dander) or in the dried saliva covering the hair.

◆ ABOVE
The Maine Coon Cat is a breed with a semi-longhaired coat, which will not need as much extra care as the long fur of a Persian cat.

◆ BELOW
The fur of the Devon Rex cat is fine and wavy and can be so delicate in places that it is broken just by the cat's own grooming. Grooming should be with a very soft bristled brush.

◆ LEFT
A sleek Oriental Shorthair with an easy-care coat will need extra grooming from its owner only if it is being prepared for a show – or for pleasure.

◆ RIGHT
This Persian cat has a splendid long coat that requires a lot of attention. If it lived in a hot climate, however, it would not develop such a full "show" coat.

FUR TYPES

Longhair: soft guardhairs up to 12.5cm (5in) long

Semi-longhair: soft guardhairs varying between 5cm (2in) and 10cm (4in) long

Shorthair: maximum about 5cm (2in) long

Hairless: suede-like coat with no guardhairs

Curly hair: short, soft, often delicate fur with rippled effect

Wirehair: short, bristly coat

BODY TYPES

Cobby: short-legged, stocky body; round, flattish face with small ears, such as the Persian

Muscular: sturdy, medium to compact build; medium length legs and tail; round face, medium ears, such as the American Shorthair

Oriental: long, lithe body; long, slender legs and tail; wedge-shaped face; large, pointed ears, such as the Siamese

GENDER AND AGE

If cats are neutered (altered), there is little difference in behavioural terms between a male and a female. However, a neutered male may be a little more indolent than a female. If you already have a cat in your home, it may be worth going for the opposite sex in your new cat. The established resident is more likely to defend its territory aggressively against a cat of the same sex.

Once sexual urges have been quelled by the neutering process, cats are likely to exhibit their true breed characteristics more strongly. The Siamese cat's attachment to its owner is accentuated, for example, and the Persian becomes even more placid and comfort-loving.

Male cats are generally larger than females. On average, a full-grown, neutered male cat tends to be a little heavier than an entire male, with an average weight of between 5 and 7.5kg (10–15lb). Females are usually about 1kg (2.2lb) lighter. The largest pedigreed variety is the Maine Coon Cat from the north-eastern United States. Male Maine Coons have been

◆ RIGHT
A kitten will adapt to your lifestyle more readily than an older cat, simply because it has not yet fully developed its mature character.

known to reach about 10–12.5kg (20–25lb) in weight. The smallest, or most dainty breed is the Singapura (the "drain cat" of Singapore) at about 2.7kg (6lb), but breeders take care to make certain that their cats fall within the minimum weight range to ensure successful breeding.

◆ ABOVE
Male cats are usually bigger than their female equivalents, although if they have been neutered (altered), they may be a little more indolent.

CHOOSING AN ADULT CAT

It can be easier to give a new home to an older cat than to a kitten. This is especially so if the cat is obtained from a major welfare source which has carried out rigorous health checks. (With a kitten from a private home, the onus of the initial health checks is usually left to you.) An older animal will be more settled in its ways and certainly have an established temperament. A poor temperament due to the cat coming from an environment where it was unhappy, can improve with changed circumstances, but you do not have the fresh start you would have with a kitten. Male cats that have only recently been neutered (altered) may carry some battle scars from their fighting days, but this is a purely aesthetic consideration.

◆ RIGHT
Although the Singapura may have evolved into one of the smallest breeds because of its tough background on the streets of Singapore, it is a sturdy animal.

◆ ABOVE
Deciding to take in an adult cat that you have found in a cat sanctuary or home may save the animal from being humanely put to sleep, and it will soon learn to be content in its new, welcoming environment.

CHOOSING THE RIGHT CAT

WHERE TO FIND A HEALTHY KITTEN

It is essential to choose a healthy kitten. One picked up from the street should be approached with caution.

Despite the pro-neutering campaigns of welfare agencies, unneutered (unaltered) cats do roam freely. This, together with the rapid maturation of the cat, makes it possible for a four-month-old to become pregnant, resulting in the next generation. Such kittens may not be physically strong, they may have been separated from their mother too soon, and are unlikely to have had any veterinary attention or inoculations. Diseases such as feline influenza and feline enteritis can strike a very young kitten and kill rapidly. In addition, feline immunodeficient diseases (feline Aids) may be present.

ACCEPTABLE FREE GIFTS

Some owners allow their cats to have one litter before neutering, and then offer the kittens "free to a good home". They may ask searching questions about your ability to look after the kittens well. Take this in good grace, for these are people who want the best for their kittens.

✦ ABOVE
These two farm kittens probably come from a long line of good hunters. Their strength is largely dependent on the physical well-being of their mother and her ability to rear them successfully until weaned.

✦ LEFT
A kitten is hand-fed using a syringe and a special formula milk, as the mother has either died or is unable to take care of her litter.

✦ ABOVE RIGHT
The weight of the hand-reared kitten is checked daily. It needs to gain about 9g (⅓oz) a day, and to be kept constantly warm.

CAT HOMES

If you want to give a home to an unwanted cat or kitten, go to a welfare agency or humane society. There are several big, well-known national organizations as well as many smaller charities that cater for homeless or unwanted cats.

Cats are not usually released to a new owner until they have been given a veterinary check, but the organization may not have had the time or resources for full investigations. This is particularly the case with feline immunodeficiency disease or feline Aids, the test for which is quite expensive. However, coats are routinely checked for parasites and fungal conditions, and the usual vaccinations are often given.

The main welfare organizations usually do investigate thoroughly, including blood-tests to ensure feline

◆ ABOVE
A tiny stray kitten may not be very strong or healthy as it was probably abandoned by its mother too soon – and the mother herself is unlikely to have been in top condition.

Aids and leukaemia are not present. In addition, once an animal has been chosen, they visit the home of the prospective new owner to ensure that it is suitable. Such attention to detail means that they may charge for the kitten, which may make the potential owner think twice before buying. But whatever the cost, it is certainly less than the cost of bringing a stray in dubious condition to peak fitness.

Some pet shops offer kittens for sale only after the necessary veterinary checks and inoculations have been done. However, for the kitten, the stress of leaving its mother, being in the shop, and then being sold on to yet another new environment within a very short time can set them back developmentally. By law in the United Kingdom, kittens must not be sold under six weeks of age. If they appear tiny, it is wise not to purchase.

◆ RIGHT
The last kitten left in a pet shop pen may look appealing, but think carefully before you buy. Will it have picked up parasites from other animals in the shop? Did it have the right medical checks and inoculations before it was put up for sale?

WHERE TO FIND A PEDIGREED CAT

Some breeders advertise in local newspapers. This is a rather hit-and-miss source as there are no guarantees that they are reputable. Some unscrupulous breeders produce kittens of the most popular breeds purely for profit. They may show little concern for either the future welfare of the offspring, or for the breed as a whole.

A far better idea is to ask at your local veterinary surgery or clinic for information on those in the area who specialize in various breeds. Often, if one breeder has no kittens available at the time you want one, he or she will recommend another. Some breeders operate on a large scale and have big catteries, while others are "front parlour" breeders, who may be interested in breeding from just one pet queen. Either can be a good source; the best way to find out about them is by recommendation via a vet

or a local breed club. It is also valuable to visit cat shows well before you actually buy. Here you will find enthusiastic owners and breeders who will explain the advantages and disadvantages of their favourite breeds and let you know of available stock. Find out about cat shows from one of the specialist cat magazines.

◆ ABOVE
The charms of a pedigreed kitten are displayed by these two White Persians. If you want information about where to buy cats like this, the best place to start is the breed club.

◆ BELOW
The Supreme Show is where you can see the best examples of all the pedigreed breeds in the United Kingdom. There are cat shows in most countries at breed club, local and national levels.

VISITING THE BREEDER

Some breeders house their animals in an outside cattery, others within their homes. A reputable breeder will not hesitate to allow a prospective owner to visit. The advantage of the house-reared litter is that the kittens are socialized earlier. They have greater contact with day-to-day noise, humans and perhaps other animals such as dogs. On the other hand, the disinfection and restricted contact routine of a first-rate cattery reduces the risk of disease and infection. Kittens from a good cattery will be handled and socialized, but this process cannot be as complete as if they were raised within the home. Beware of the unscrupulous cattery owner rearing kittens solely for financial gain. Conditions can often be substandard.

Usually, you need to make an appointment to see and select from a litter of kittens, but it is also possible to book a kitten in advance of delivery if you are drawn to a particular cat. By visiting the breeder, you can assess the general environment and conditions in which the kittens have been brought up in the first few vital weeks of their lives. If you ask the right questions and see the rest of the litter, the mother, and possibly the father, you will be able to build up a complete picture of the kitten's heritage – its breeding line; how long its relatives have lived; how big it is likely to grow; what it will look like as an adult. In addition, you can lay the foundations of an ongoing relationship with the breeder, who, if reputable, will be available for advice and help in the years to come.

A pedigreed kitten will not usually leave its breeder's home until it is twelve to fourteen weeks old. By this time it should be properly house-trained, inoculated and used to being handled. If it has been brought up in a family environment, it may already be happy with dogs and children. But if it has not been in an ideal environment, it may have difficulties bonding with a new owner. In this case (and with a non-pedigreed kitten only) it may adapt more easily if it is taken away at seven or eight weeks.

A kitten ready for handing over to a new owner should have been gently weaned and introduced to a suitable diet of fresh, canned and dry foods. It should have been registered with one or more of the many registering bodies worldwide and the registration documents and pedigree should be ready to take away. There may also be a health insurance policy that lasts about six weeks – enough time to let the new kitten settle into its new home.

The cost of a pedigreed kitten depends very much on the breed; seek guidelines from the individual breed clubs. It is possible to spend a great deal of money on rare, new varieties while the well-established, popular varieties are less expensive. Kittens of show quality are priced more highly than those of lesser quality.

♦ BELOW
Kittens being prepared to leave their breeders for a new home. If they have become used to a friendly family environment from birth, they should settle down quickly.

SELECTING A HEALTHY ANIMAL

A kitten from a responsible breeder will have had trips to the vet for inoculations against cat flu, feline infectious enteritis, and possibly chlamydia and feline leukaemia. It will have been wormed and its coat will be free from parasites (such as fleas) and fungal lesions (ringworm).

The queen passes on natural immunity to the diseases to which she is herself immune, through colostrum (first milk) during the kitten's first few days of life. This immunity is effective until the kitten is six to ten weeks of age, when it must be replaced by the artificially acquired immunity provided by inoculations. Before the age of eight or nine weeks, it is best not to interfere with the immunity acquired from the mother.

It is not advisable to take the kitten home before inoculations start if you have other cats. They might be carriers of feline diseases to which the mother of the kitten is not immune

◆ ABOVE
You may be tempted to buy both of these kittens. They have grown up together so are likely always to be friendly. They will enjoy playing together – and you will enjoy watching them. Make sure both are neutered, however!

◆ BELOW
At nine weeks old these non-pedigreed kittens could be taken from their birth home. However, some cat associations recommend they are left until 12 weeks, after the first vaccination course has finished.

and against which, therefore, the kitten has no protection. The certificate from the vet confirming first or complete vaccination carries with it the important implication that the cat is in good health – otherwise the inoculation would not have been administered.

WHAT TO LOOK FOR

The prospective owner can make his or her own immediate checks when selecting a kitten. If you are able to view the entire litter, look for the individuals with evenness of growth and solidity of muscle tone. Male kittens may already be showing a larger skeletal frame than the females. The kittens will be heavy for their size, and their spines should be well-fleshed and not feel ridged and bony.

If you see the litter shortly after feeding, the kittens will probably be sleepy, but if they are inclined to play, you can assess sociability. Frightened,

unsociable kittens rush to hide and show fear and displeasure with trembling, bad language or claws – or maybe all three at once! The sociable but sleepy kitten purrs and almost certainly demands that its tummy is tickled. The playful kitten in good health has stamina and a spring in its step. It is alert and may already be displaying intelligence and leadership in play. Rather than you doing the choosing, a particular kitten may well choose you, inviting you to play, and ending up going to sleep on your lap.

The kitten's nose leather should be naturally slightly warm and a little damp. It should not be hot and dry, or have any discoloured discharge from the nostrils. Breathing should be deep and natural with no rasping or snorting. Eyes should be clean and bright with no discharge, tears, staining or redness. The mouth should show nice light-pink gums with no furring to the tongue or ulceration. Ears should be clean and free of wax.

COAT INDICATORS

Clean kitten fur has a lively feel with a warm, naturally wholesome scent, with no evidence of parasites, rough patches or lesions. The most common ectoparasite is the flea, which leaves gritty, granular droppings. Typical sites for these droppings are just above the base of the tail, between the shoulder blades, under the chin and in the armpits. Excessive infestation of fleas may cause a lack of liveliness, and also indicate that the animal may be worm-infested.

Signs of worm infestation are commonly a staring, harsh coat and a bloated abdomen. In severe cases, the kitten may show signs of anaemia and

✦ ABOVE
This Chocolate Silver Tabby Ocicat not only has fine tabby markings, but his clear, bright eyes suggest he is in peak health.

diarrhoea. Check under the tail for staining or signs of soreness, which indicate diarrhoea.

CHECKING AN ADULT CAT

The health check for the older cat is much the same. You need to check that male cats have been neutered (altered). If this has happened recently, they may show some battle scars, but this will only affect their appearance. The most likely place for wear and tear to show is in the mouth. Teeth may be missing or broken, and the gums may show signs of disease, but this can be treated by your vet, who may advise home dental care.

Whatever the age of the kitten or older cat you are thinking of buying, however sweet and charming it is, if you have any doubts about its health, and especially if you have other cats, do not take it home with you.

✦ BELOW
A confident stride, intelligent interest and a perky tail indicate that this 15-week-old Ocicat is a cat of sociable, playful character.

Creating the Right Environment

The domestic life is one in which a pet cat can feel secure in the knowledge of where the next meal is coming from. If you also provide an exciting and stimulating environment in which it can rest comfortably and where there are opportunities to climb and play, your cat will be a well-adjusted and rewarding companion. The financial outlay of buying the right equipment for your cat may seem high, but it is the first step in ensuring it leads a contented life.

◆ FACING PAGE
Cats may be independent and perfectly able to survive without humans, but as this ginger cat shows, they adapt well to a warm home and loving care.

◆ LEFT
A non-pedigreed cat sports his new flea collar.

SETTLING IN

Acquiring a cat should not be contemplated on a whim but with an awareness of the animal's continuing needs throughout its life in your home. Thoughtful preparation and planning before a new cat arrives is essential if the transition between old home and new is to be stress-free for both you and your pet. A cat needs time and space in which to adjust, and will settle down more easily, too, if all the right equipment is there when it arrives.

FORWARD PLANNING

This will be a new and strange environment for your cat, so before you collect it, check its diet with the breeder or cattery so that you know what it likes to eat and drink and can have some food ready.

The journey itself may be the first time in a kitten's short life that it has no other feline company. Even an older cat can be disorientated. While

travelling, talk to the animal in a calm voice. Do not be tempted to let it out of its carrier (in a car, for example) unless you have a companion with you who can restrain it.

THE ARRIVAL

A new arrival is a novelty and family and friends will want to be introduced, to stroke and play with the cat, especially if it is a kitten. This exciting time makes particular demands on

◆ **TOP**
The first sortie in the new home. The cage should be kept to hand so that the kittens can be put back in it until they become used to their new environment, and any other animals in the home can be surveyed from the safety of the pen.

◆ **ABOVE**
A young ginger cat has settled happily in the cat basket. A favourite blanket brought with it from its first home is an additional comfort.

◆ **LEFT**
A Siamese half-breed kitten explores the new home. It is important to let kittens explore in their own time, but supervision is advisable in case they become stuck or locked in a cupboard.

EQUIPMENT CHECKLIST

Not all the following are essential; those that are, are in heavy type.

◆ **bed and bedding**

◆ **litter and litter tray (pan)**

◆ **2 food bowls**

◆ **water bowl**

◆ **carrier**

◆ collar

◆ harness and lead

◆ identity tag

◆ cat flap

◆ RIGHT
Gradual, supervised
introductions over
the course of a few
weeks have enabled
this Irish Wolfhound
and Chinchilla to
feel at ease with each
other. However, such
close proximity
would not be
advisable with a
pet mouse!

◆ BELOW RIGHT
Kittens will quickly
seek out the most
comfortable places to
relax; if you do not
want them in your
bed, you need to
keep the door shut!

children who, without realizing the implications, may treat the new animal like a toy. However, try to make sure there are not many people around when the new arrival is introduced. It is tempting to rush straight into the living room and let the cat out of the carrier. Instead, take it immediately to where its litter tray (pan), sleeping space, food and water bowls are going to be permanently positioned. Such items are part of a familiar routine, which will be comforting. A drink and a little food may be all that is wanted.

EXTENDING TERRITORY

A kitten will want to explore and take in all the new sensory experiences of this new environment. It must be allowed to do this in its own time, and if that means that it wants to scurry about under a kitchen cupboard, out of sight, so be it. Eventually it will emerge and continue its exploration. Allow the kitten to do this at leisure. However, supervision is wise, in case it becomes locked in a cupboard or stuck on a high shelf. Handle the cat calmly and gently. Over-enthusiastic handling

can be very disorientating and may bring out the defence mechanisms. Being bitten or scratched does not endear anyone to a new pet, but from the kitten's point of view it was probably justified. By all means stroke the cat as it passes and talk to it. The reassurance of the human voice helps bridge the gap between old and new

homes. When a new cat is tired, it will probably find its bed on its own and it should be left to sleep undisturbed. Cats and kittens sleep more than any other mammal on a daily basis and, for a kitten, adequate sleep maintains and encourages the assimilation of food and enhances correct growth.

If you already have another cat or a dog, confine the new arrival to a small area at first – or even a cage – so that it can get used to where its food, water and litter are in peace, and the animals can adjust to one another in their own time. A cage in the kitchen or living room will provide security for the new arrival and quickly allow it to adjust to any other animals in the household and vice versa.

If you have a baby in the house, it is a good idea to put a cat net over the pram or cot. A cat is unlikely to harm the baby, but could be attracted to a warm, sleeping body and may want to curl up alongside it.

HANDLING AND HOLDING YOUR CAT

If you watch a mother cat, you will see how she picks up a tiny kitten by taking hold of the loose skin at the back of the neck and gently lifting. The kitten then demonstrates one of its inborn reflexes, which is to curl up into an apparently lifeless ball. It will not move until its mother puts it down. This loose skin, which becomes far less apparent as the kitten grows, is the scruff or nap. The action of picking up a cat in such a way is called scruffing. While it is possible to lift your cat in this way, scruffing should normally only be considered if absolutely necessary – if instant control is required, for example, when the cat is at the veterinary surgery. For less flexible adult cats especially, it can be an unnerving experience, particularly as they freeze when scruffed.

It is far better to pick up your kitten or cat by placing one hand under the chest, supporting the backside with the other hand and then lifting. In this way the animal feels completely secure, with no limbs left dangling. This total support technique is essential if you are holding the cat for any length of time. As you and your cat become more confident, you can try different holds. Avoid tucking the cat under your arm with its body, back legs and tail dangling like a ragdoll. This leaves most of its weight unsupported and puts a great strain on the internal organs. Many cats do not like being held for too long, and should be gently let down if they start to wriggle.

◆ LEFT
An established resident cat has become accustomed to a new arrival, and the two now provide extra warmth for each other.

◆ RIGHT
Avoid surprising the cat when you are about to lift it. When it is relaxed, support the top of the hind legs with one hand and the chest with the other.

◆ FAR RIGHT
When holding or carrying a cat, keep the back end and legs supported. If the cat starts to wriggle, let it down gently; never force it to be held against its will, unless it is necessary.

BEDS AND BEDDING

During the initial settling-in period, a new kitten or cat should be able to settle down within easy reach of both litter tray (pan) and water. A simple cardboard box placed in a draught-proof spot with an old pillow and blanket is ideal. Then, if there are accidents, or if the cat's bedding becomes parasite-infested, everything can be burnt and little is lost.

Acrylic bedding is widely available, hygienic and easily laundered. Woollen materials, particularly if knitted, are not suitable as claws may become caught. Some cats seem also to be addicted to wool-sucking and chewing and this can cause congestion in the throat or digestive system.

Once the new arrival has settled in, you may want to provide a permanent bed. This can be made of wicker, moulded plastic or padded fabric, but it must be easy to wash and disinfect. Any bedding should be changed regularly. Very soon a collection of cushion beds, old jumpers, carpet-covered houses and other oddities will be adopted. Place these strategically where the cat likes to sleep at different times of the day.

◆ ABOVE
A cat is not fussy about the design of its bed. The advantage of a cardboard box is that if it becomes soiled or worn out, it can be easily replaced.

◆ LEFT
The owner's bed is often a favourite spot, especially if it has comfortable quilts and cushions.

◆ LEFT AND RIGHT
There is now such a range of pet beds available that you can choose one to match your decor. Whether you go for an enclosed, draughtproof and portable model or an open version, the easy-to-wash factor is the most important consideration.

LITTER AND LITTER TRAY (PAN)

A kitten or cat needs access to a litter tray (pan) if it is not able to go outside when it wants to. The tray may become redundant once a kitten is fully immunized and has learnt to use its cat flap into the garden, although it is preferable to encourage your cat to stay in at night. Even when very young, kittens are inherently clean and will not soil their bed. If a cage or crate is being used during the settling-in period, it should be large enough to contain a litter tray.

There is a wide range of products available, from basic plastic trays to covered models with entrance flaps and filters to minimize odour. The key

◆ LEFT
The most important consideration when buying a litter tray (pan) is that it should be easy to clean. Use a scoop to remove faeces independently, rather than changing all the litter in the tray every time.

point about litter trays is that they must be easy to clean, and tough enough to withstand frequent washing and disinfecting. They should also be in a position that is easy to clean. Toxoplasmosis is an infection that can

scrape the litter over any faeces deposited, which is does instinctively. Sawdust, woodshavings, cinders, ash and newspapers are not advised; nor are some pine-wood products that can be irritants.

◆ BELOW
The ultimate litter tray (pan) is not only draughtproof and private for the coy cat, but helps contain odours.

be shed in a cat's faeces without the cat showing any signs of disease. It is, however, a hazard to humans, especially pregnant women. Disposal of faeces less than 24 hours after passing and regular cleaning of litter trays with plenty of water and detergent is effective in the control of toxoplasmosis. Some household products contain ingredients, which, although fine for use in the home, can be toxic to cats. The staff at your vet's should be able to advise on these.

LITTER OPTIONS
The various litter products available should be acceptable to the cat, reduce odour and absorb urine. It should also be easy for the cat to

◆ ABOVE, LEFT TO RIGHT
Clay, wood and paper-based litters: some are highly absorbent, others are superfine and form clumps when wet.

◆ ABOVE
Kittens are instinctively clean. This feral kitten was abandoned by its mother and when a litter tray (pan) was provided, automatically began to use it after being shown it once.

FEEDING EQUIPMENT

If you already have perfectly suitable dishes, special purchases may not be necessary. The most practical choices are made of hard plastic, ceramic or stainless steel. All equipment should be easy to clean and disinfect. Discard cracked or chipped ceramic bowls, as germs may be harboured in the cracks. Once any container, new or old, has been allotted to the cat, it should not be used for anything else. Many people feed their cats in the kitchen; if there are dogs around, it is also likely that the cat is fed on a

TOXOPLASMOSIS

Toxoplasmosis affects many animals but cats are the only ones that shed the parasite in their faeces. This only happens for a short time after the cat has become infected and the faeces are only infectious after 24 hours or more. In most cases there are no visible signs of disease or illness in the cat. The infection is carried in the cat's faeces and in 24–48 hours can pass on to humans. Unless their immune system is not functioning properly, humans contracting the infection are unlikely to become ill, but if a pregnant woman is infected, there is a 40 per cent chance that her baby will also be infected. Of these infected babies, 15 per cent may spontaneously abort or acquire some abnormality.

✦ Wear gloves when gardening in an area frequented by cats

✦ Cover children's play areas, such as sand-pits, when not in use

✦ Empty litter trays (pans) on a daily basis and clean regularly with plenty of water and detergent

✦ Use a separate set of feeding equipment for the cat and do not use it for humans; clean regularly

✦ ABOVE, LEFT TO RIGHT FROM TOP LEFT
The cutlery for serving the cat should be exclusively for this purpose; plastic lids to cover unfinished tins prevent the food from drying up and the smell from spreading; a simple plastic bowl; a metal bowl; a plastic combined water and food bowl; an automatic feeder.

working surface. In either case it is especially important to maintain strict standards of hygiene to guard against the risk of toxoplasmosis (see box). The feeding area must be easy to clean and disinfect regularly. This is also important for the cat because it has a highly developed sense of smell and will reject food that has become tainted and hardened. For the same reasons, put down fresh water at least once a day. A closed-off eating area is advisable if you have crawling babies or toddlers.

For the busy owner whose lifestyle makes feeding the cat at regular times uncertain, automatic food bowls with timer switches are available. The cover automatically lifts to reveal food at pre-set times. A water bowl is kept topped up with water from a reservoir, but you do need to remember to change the reservoir frequently.

✦ RIGHT
It is more hygienic to put your cat's food on the floor rather than on a working surface where food is prepared for humans.

CARRIERS

It is essential to buy, rather than borrow, a cat carrier. You will need it not only to bring the cat or kitten home, but also for visits to the veterinary surgery – and anywhere else for that matter. Any visit to the vet will quickly reveal that very many owners have great faith in their pets' ability not to escape! They arrive with all sorts of contraptions for carrying their cats; sometimes with nothing at all to restrain an animal which may be in pain, very frightened and invariably highly stressed.

SIZE CONSIDERATIONS

Do not be seduced into buying a sweet, kitten-sized carrier; consider the future and purchase accordingly. That

◆ ABOVE
Large cat carriers provide plenty of room for your cat and can double up as pens for the settling-in period. They are, however, awkward to carry.

◆ LEFT
A top-loading wicker basket which could double as the cat's permanent bed.

cute little fur-ball is going to turn into a considerably larger adult. A carrier of around 30cm x 30cm x 55cm (12in x 12in x 22in) should last into the cat's adulthood. For an extra-large male, it might be wise to go to the next size up. Cats prefer to be in a fairly snug environment if they are experiencing a rare and disturbing event such as travelling, but they do need to be able to turn around and stretch out a little. They also like to be able to see out so that they feel a little less trapped.

If the journey is going to be a long one (over an hour or two), have a carrier that can take a small litter tray (pan) as well as clip-on water and food bowls. However, if you are likely to have to carry the cat very far, for example, when attending shows, remember the larger the carrier, the more awkward it is to carry. Strained shoulders and backs are not uncommon among exhibitors.

◆ BELOW
An easy-to-clean plastic container that might
cause loading and unloading difficulties.

◆ BELOW
A collapsible cardboard carrier that can be
dispensed with after being used to carry an
infectious animal.

◆ BELOW
An easy-to-clean plastic container that might
cause loading and unloading difficulties.

WHAT IS AVAILABLE

Basic cardboard carriers, preferably
coated with plastic, are bought
flatpacked, and, when assembled, are
suitable for transporting a sick and
possibly infectious animal, as they are
inexpensive and can be burnt after use.
However, they are not suitable for
more regular use as they cannot be
cleaned and disinfected effectively, and
are not durable. Traditionalists choose
wickerwork baskets, which come in
various shapes, and usually have
leather straps and a handle. These are
attractive and could double as the cat's
permanent sleeping quarters – at least
the cat would be less likely to panic if
travelling in its own bed.

Openwork wire baskets, especially
with the wire covered with white
plastic, have veterinary approval
because they are so easy to disinfect
and the cat is easily visible. The top
opening is secured by a separate rod
pushed through rigid loops. Moulded
plastic carriers with strategically
placed ventilation holes are available in
a great range of designs, are easy to
dismantle for thorough cleaning, and
reassembling is no problem either.
Clear moulded plastic (Perspex)
carriers with airholes are a less
worthwhile investment as the plastic
tends to crack and degrade over time.
If carried in sunlight, its occupant can
quickly overheat.

The most practical designs are
those with top access; they are less
stressful both for cat and handler. The
cat can be grasped from above and
removed without a struggle. With a
front-loading carrier, the often
frightened animal has to be recovered
from the back of a tunnel. It can also
be difficult to put the cat back inside.

◆ BELOW
If you want your cat carrier to look distinctive
or decorative, you could paint it with an
appropriate design.

COLLARS, HARNESSES AND LEADS

A collar is not necessarily merely decorative. A tag may be attached to it so that the cat can be identified if it gets lost or injured. An identity tag may be a simple engraved disc or a screw-topped cylinder containing a roll of paper with the cat's name, owner's address and telephone number, and sometimes the vet's emergency number. Magnetic tags that allow your cat exclusive entry to its cat flap can also be fitted on collars.

Most collars come with a bell which rings when the cat moves and will reduce the death toll among garden birds and other potential hunting targets. Some collars are impregnated with an anti-flea substance, but keep a careful check on your cat when you first put one on it, as they can cause an allergic reaction. Signs of irritation around the neck or eyes are the main indications of allergy. A flea collar should never be combined with any other form of flea control.

Collars have two main disadvantages. If worn continuously, as they should be if they are carrying any form of identification, they will damage the fur around the neck,

✦ BELOW
A soft collar with a bell attached will help you find your cat, and will drastically reduce its hunting successes by warning birds of its presence.

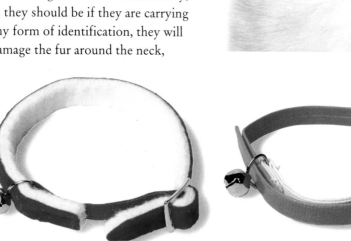

✦ ABOVE
A soft, padded flea collar with a bell and an elastic section. Flea collars should only be used on cats over six months old. They may cause an allergic reaction in some cats.

✦ ABOVE
A soft leather collar with the all-important elastic section. Any collar you buy should have this, for if the collar is caught the elastic will stretch, allowing the cat to escape unharmed.

✦ ABOVE
Fabric collars, which can be cut to size without fraying, are useful for kittens and small cats. They are cheap enough to be changed regularly, or even to have a selection of different colours.

especially that of longhaired cats. This can be unsightly and is considered unacceptable by many exhibitors; although most show judges realize the reason for any marks around the neck, they may still penalize the cat. Secondly, there is always the fear that the collar can become caught when the cat is hunting in trees or shrubs. However, if it is made of soft leather, suede, or soft fabric and has an elasticated insert, this will stretch if the collar catches, and the cat will be able to free itself. The collar should always be adjusted so that it will slip over the cat's head in an emergency, but not loose enough to allow the front leg to slip through and the collar to lodge under the armpit, which could cause injury.

GOING FOR A WALK

Cat leads are only necessary if you intend to take your cat for walks or if you are taking it to a strange house and need to keep it under control. Some cats actively enjoy this, particularly Siamese. It is not unusual to see this breed travelling on public transport on a lead. However, most cats are naturally resistant to wearing any such controlling apparatus and will fight against it, especially if they become frightened. To take them on a bus or train on a lead rather than in a carrier is foolhardy under any

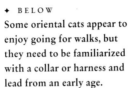

circumstances. If the cat panics, it could either become tangled and hurt itself, or escape. If a lead is worn on a more suitable outing, it should be no more than 1m (3ft) long, and have a fitted harness rather than a collar for attachment. This not only allows more control and comfort, but is more secure. Cats are great escapologists, however, and even the most carefully fitted harness may prove insecure.

Introduce your cat to a harness and lead as early as possible. Put the harness on first by itself, and just for a short time each day. After you have done this for a few days, attach the lead for a short time, several days running, but just leave it trailing. When the cat seems relaxed about the lead, try walking it, first indoors for brief spells, then in the garden, and then in a street where the cat can get used to traffic and people, but do not overdo it!

◆ LEFT
Magnetic tags double as a means of identity and a "key" to enable the wearer to go through its cat flap.

◆ BELOW
Some oriental cats appear to enjoy going for walks, but they need to be familiarized with a collar or harness and lead from an early age.

◆ LEFT
Identity tags can be simple metal discs engraved with the owner's name and telephone number, or an information-packed barrel containing the owner's address and the vet's address and emergency telephone number.

EXTRAS AND TOYS

Play for a young cat is just as essential for its well-being as it is for a human child. It is particularly important for the owner to play with the cat if it is the only one in the household. Through play, muscles are exercised and conditioned, the brain is kept alert and the eyes bright. And if the owner joins in, it strengthens the bond between the feline and its adopted human family.

At the very least your cat should have a scratching post, which it can be encouraged to use instead of the furniture and soft furnishings. A cat will naturally use surfaces such as the bark of a tree to sharpen and control the length of its claws – they are its main means of defence, and also provide grip when climbing. You can make an indoor scratching post yourself by binding a stout fence post with heavy-duty sisal string or cotton rope, and attaching it to a suitable base. A strip of old carpet is an alternative, but this is not as effective for the cat, as it frays quickly, creates a great deal of fluff, and needs to be

renewed regularly. If you do not mind your cat equipment taking over the home, feline climbing frames of varying size and complexity are readily available. Some are over 2m (6ft) high, with circular supports covered in sisal rope, carpet-covered perches, houses and barrels. They are likely to be found at cat shows, or through advertisements in specialist cat magazines and larger pet stores.

PLAY WITH A PURPOSE
A cat's play is orientated to the hunting process. When a cat swoops after a leaf in autumn, that leaf is an imaginary bird. The ping-pong ball just visible behind a chair leg is a mouse to be stalked, pounced upon and batted around. The screwed-up paper hurled into the air, caught and thrown away to be chased and sent flying again, is being

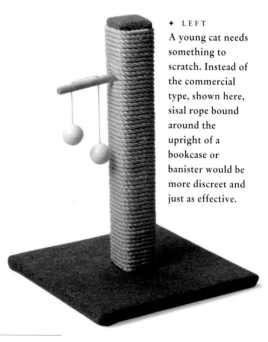

◆ LEFT
A young cat needs something to scratch. Instead of the commercial type, shown here, sisal rope bound around the upright of a bookcase or banister would be more discreet and just as effective.

◆ ABOVE
Being ten months old does not mean that this youngster has grown out of shredding curtains for fun.

◆ BELOW
Kittens enjoy playing with someone, especially if they are an only cat; they will soon become bored playing on their own with a ball.

◆ LEFT
The perfect combination for a family cat –
company, care, attention, and a game that seems
to be tailor-made for cats. Be careful of any
electrical connections, though.

hunted. Even in an apparently sterile
environment, a cat will find a scrap of
paper, a lost button, or a shadow to
play with. However, do be careful of
everyday household objects like the
odd button or needle and thread.
Swallowed thread can do even more
damage than a needle as it cheesewires
its way through the bowel.

Do check that any cat toys you buy
are reasonably solid. Some cheap
imported toys may have small plastic
bits that could fall off and be
swallowed. Some plastic materials that
are safe for children can be toxic to
cats. All that is needed can be found in
the home: paper scrunched into a ball
and thrown by the owner for retrieval
up and down the stairs; a paper
"butterfly" tied to a piece of string
and dragged around for the cat to
chase, or suspended from the back of
a chair to bat. Some cats are
particularly fond of hide-and-seek.
For group play, nothing is better than
the great game of the ping-pong ball
rolled around the carpet between
family members and friends, and
pursued by your cat.

◆ BELOW
A clockwork mouse is a poor
substitute for the real thing, as
it has to be wound up, but it is
less messy for
the owner.

◆ RIGHT
You will probably need a continuing
supply of replacement balls as they are
constantly being batted out of sight.

◆ ABOVE
Cats are nature's most efficient predators: a
fabric mouse filled with delectable catnip may
not last long in the grip of this young Ocicat.

◆ RIGHT
Here's a soft, friendly chap to dig your claws
into. Let's hope the bear's eyes are well secured
so that the kitten does not swallow them.

Care at Home and Away

A cat instinctively knows its physical limits; it can also, through learned behaviour and training, avoid potentially dangerous situations. The wise owner strikes a balance between giving the cat the freedom it needs, being aware of the dangers it could face, and protecting it from them.

◆ FACING PAGE
A mother introduces one of her kittens to the outside world. She will teach it survival and hunting skills.

◆ ABOVE
A well-cared-for ginger and white non-pedigree is completely relaxed at home and away.

CONTROLLING A CAT'S TERRITORY

If you live in an apartment block or in a busy urban environment, or your cat is frail or a valuable pedigree, it is perfectly feasible – and acceptable to most cats – to keep it indoors all the time. In some parts of the United States, vets actively recommend this for cats in urban environments.

Because of the balanced pet foods now available, modern cats do not need to go out to supplement their diet by hunting. Outdoor exercise is also unnecessary, as long as the owner provides toys and plays with the cat.

Although cats are nocturnal by nature, it is really unwise to allow much-loved pets to stay out at night. Train them to stay in from an early age and make sure there is always a clean litter tray (pan) available. This training also ensures that they are equally happy if kept indoors for long periods.

The outdoor cat's tendency to roam and exposure to the dangers of traffic, fighting and infection from other cats, can be reduced at a snip – that is, by being neutered (altered). The sex-drive of a calling queen or an active

♦ ABOVE
A Burmese is attracted to the outside world. Some cats are freedom-loving and do not like being kept indoors.

♦ RIGHT
A ginger kitten has taken over the best armchair. An indoor cat needs plenty of toys and active input from its owner if it is not to become bored and substitute the upholstery for a tree.

THE MAKING OF AN INDOOR CAT

The consultant, a breeder of Maine Coon Cats, does not let his cats out until they are well over six months old – two to three months after they have been neutered (altered). The cats are trained to litter trays (pans) and so, when they are eventually let out, it is not long before they rush back in to use their usual toilet facilities. Because they are neutered (altered), their hunting and roaming instinct is greatly curtailed and they seldom stray beyond their familiar garden.

♦ LEFT
A Persian has the comfort-loving temperament suited to an indoor life, and its long coat is easier to care for inside.

tom cat will override any considerations for road safety. The unneutered male cat can hunt over an area of about 11km (7 miles). His desexed counterparts will probably exercise territorial rights over maybe 200m (240 yards) at most.

DANGERS IN THE HOME

There are dangers even for the cat that is kept indoors all the time. Those who live in high-rise buildings should erect netting across open windows and around balconies. The defences can be camouflaged by plants. Even within the house, cats should be allowed access to heights only if they are considered safe. A specific danger area is a staircase with openwork bannisters from which a kitten could launch itself into space – not necessarily landing on its feet. Kittens should be supervised as they explore.

THE ALLURE OF MACHINES

The warmth, the smells and the movement of washing and drying machines attract a cat's attention. Always make sure that the appliance's doors are kept closed when not in use. Before you turn the machine on, check that there is no cat curled inside. The smell of food in a fridge is also enticing. At least if it were to be inadvertently incarcerated, a cat would survive there for some time, as long as there was sufficient air available. It would not, however, survive for long in a freezer. Fifteen minutes would probably be long enough to cause irreversible hypothermia.

PLAYING WITH FIRE

Burns and scalds sustained by cats exploring the source of interesting food smells are not unusual and are sometimes very severe. Cats have been known to dance across the hot rings of an electric cooker, badly damaging their paws.

Electric cables are potential playthings, so make sure no wires are loose or exposed, and if you spot your cat chewing them, conceal the cables beneath a carpet, or cover them with a catproof material such as thick, loose rubber or plastic tubing. A cat will nose around drawers and boxes packed with interesting oddments – but here too, are potential dangers such as pins and paper clips. Tasty, pingy elastic bands may be fun to pick at and chew, but could cause choking and suffocation, and the same goes for lengths of wool or cotton, or plastic film. Cats are also attracted to olives, the stones of which are just the right size to become stuck in a feline throat. Open fireplaces should always be guarded, even when a fire is not lit, for cats like climbing up chimneys and may become stuck or break a limb, or at the very least emerge soot-covered. Electric and gas fires can be equally dangerous. One cat owner was faced with a fire in her living room and some very frightened kittens, after the combined weight of the litter of kittens toppled a highly flammable chair against the bars of a gas fire.

♦ LEFT
A very cosy scene for mother and kitten – however, open fires should always be kept guarded unless you are in the room to keep an eye on your cat.

♦ ABOVE
The washing machine has just been turned off and is still warm, making it a possible spot to curl up in for an undisturbed sleep.

♦ ABOVE
The deliberate leap from the table is well within this cat's capability, but a kitten could hurt itself if it fell or jumped from such a height.

ACCESS TO THE OUTSIDE WORLD

It always used to be common practice to put the house cat out at night, so that it could carry out its rodent extermination duties, and to avoid mess in the house. Effective rodent control and the availability of litter trays (pans) have made this unnecessary. Now a cat's freedom is more likely to be dependent upon human work patterns. However, unless you have pedigreed cats which you keep for exhibition and show, or your living space necessitates an indoor lifestyle, you can allow your pet various degrees of access to the outside world.

Some cats automatically confine their territories to the back garden. Others may develop an awareness of the traffic in their area, and avoid rush hours, for example. However, it is difficult to be sure of their abilities, and even quiet streets can be dangerous because of the occasional,

unexpected vehicle. For these reasons, and the risks of territorial fighting and exposure to infection, it is worth exercising some form of control over your cat's freedom to roam.

♦ ABOVE
A Brown Burmese selects a high vantage point from which to survey the surrounding territory.

♦ LEFT
A cat will soon learn to use its cat flap with confidence. The flap swings shut when the cat has passed through.

CAT FLAPS

Cat flaps are cat-sized windows that are fitted about 15cm (6in) from the base of a door. The most practical design is one that is gravity-loaded so that the door automatically closes after entry or exit, and with a clear plastic window so that the cat can look through it before venturing outside.

Flaps are a boon to the indoor/outdoor cat that is not afraid of operating the flap and whose owners are not always home to obey the cat's every whim. They allow both cat and owner a degree of independence from each other. The main disadvantage of cat flaps, particularly when there is no such feline control, is that neighbours or feral cats will soon learn to use them, particularly if delicious food is known to be available on the other side of the flap. This could lead to disease or infection being brought into the home, or territorial fights, or both. One way of overcoming this is to have an electronically operated flap that allows entry only to cats wearing the appropriate collar and gadgetry – usually in the form of a magnetic tag that doubles as an identity tag.

Alternatively, you can allow your cat limited freedom, and, for example, lock the flap at night when you are unable to keep an eye on unwanted visitors. It is useful to buy a flap that can be locked to prevent your cat from going out at certain times, or other cats from coming in. Your cat will soon become used to whatever routine you set.

When you introduce your cat to the cat flap, spend some time encouraging it with your voice and showing it how the door works. Put the cat on one side and call encouragingly from the

✦ RIGHT
A tom cat prepares for his nocturnal prowl.
Many of the small rodents that cats hunt are
active as night falls, and this also seems to be a
prime time to look for a mate.

other. After a few tries, it will know exactly what to do by itself. However, it is not unusual for some cats to steadfastly refuse to use a flap – particularly if the flap was introduced after the cat. The same goes for flaps on covered litter trays (pans).

OUTDOOR CONFINEMENT

Indoor living can be safely supplemented by a secure outdoor area. Areas of a garden can be fenced in with wire or plastic mesh like a fruit cage, or a purpose-built shed or pen can be provided. Climbing plants can be trained to cover the sides to soften the appearance, but take advice on which plants to choose – some are poisonous to cats.

A pen can be constructed in the garden or as an extension to the house (with access via a cat flap). It should be sturdy in structure with wire or plastic mesh stretched between a solid wood frame, and roofed. Features

could include a covered shelter and an outdoor play area with logs, shelves and playthings to keep the cats amused. Such pens are commercially available. In extreme cases, or with very small areas, whole gardens are secured around the perimeter to prevent cats from escaping and, more importantly,

other cats from getting in. You can make a framework of stout posts to a height of say 3m (9ft) and attach wire netting between them. If the netting is loosely fitted the cat will not be able to climb up it and there will be no need to roof in the top. The base of the wire should be buried or well secured.

✦ ABOVE
A lithe hunter like this Brown Burmese will be
a joy to watch in your garden.

✦ RIGHT
Cats are often attracted to the shelter and
warmth offered by parked cars, so always check
beneath your car before you drive away.

✦ FAR RIGHT
Cats enjoy fresh air and sunshine from the
safety of an outside pen.

IN THE GARDEN

To watch a cat move and play in a garden is a source of delight, but there are dangers. Cats can swim, but are not generally renowned for their ability in this area, and there are cases of accidental drowning each year. The simple solution in the case of a garden pond, stream or swimming pool, is to cover the water with very fine mesh or to erect a barrier to make the area inaccessible to the cat.

Cats do have a wonderful righting ability which enables them to almost invariably land on their feet when falling from a height. However, vets regularly see cats that have been badly injured as a result of falls. If a cat lands on an unyielding surface, it is likely to injure itself if the fall is more than 3–4m (9–12ft), which is equivalent in height to the first storey of a house. The same applies if they fall out of trees. The most common problem with cats climbing is that they become absorbed in either hunting or exploring and end up on a branch too small to turn around on and escape.

♦ LEFT
Thirst, reflections and goldfish are all good reasons for cats to be interested in water. They are not renowned for their swimming skills, however, and a net over the garden pond is worth considering.

♦ BELOW
Another sticky situation for an exploratory kitten. At this stage of their development, adventurous kittens should be supervised.

This is when the rescue services are called in. Discourage habitual climbers by placing wire netting around the base of favourite or particularly dangerous trees. However, the determined feline may just look for another tree.

♦ LEFT
When maturity and wisdom have taken the place of adventure and curiosity, a garden can be a great place for sunning and relaxation.

This kitten is in danger. Curiosity has led it to explore beyond its limits to a narrow perch where its leg could become stuck, or from which it could fall.

A broken pane of glass in the garden shed spells danger for this cat. If it attempts an escape through the hole, it could cut itself badly. The lesson for the owner is to carry out repairs promptly.

TRAPPED

Apart from harbouring dangerous substances, garden sheds and garages can become prisons from which there is no escape. A brief period of captivity will not do a cat too much harm. A cat can survive for 10–14 days without food and almost as long without water, provided the ambient temperature is not too high, but the resulting

INSURANCE

Compare the cover and terms of several companies that specialize in animal insurance before you make your decision. The owner of a valuable cat may want to insure against loss, death or theft, in order to reclaim the cat's value. More general policies cushion the owner against the cost of veterinary bills in the event of accident or emergency, injury or disease, but do not cover initial injections, neutering or standard booster inoculations. The annual premium depends upon the level of cover selected and upon the insured animal's medical history. Deciding whether or not to insure is a matter of balancing what can be a fairly steep monthly or annual premium against your ability to pay any sudden, costly vet's bill. The alternative, as with any insurance cover, is to have your own contingency account to cover emergency expenses.

Cat breeders sometimes issue basic health insurance cover notes with kittens. Cover starts from the date of sale and is usually valid for six weeks. After that, the new owner can continue with the same policy or seek another one.

dehydration and starvation may have serious consequences for the proper functioning of kidneys and liver. Such a physically challenged cat is then prey to secondary infections it would normally easily shake off. If you have not seen your cat for a while, check in cellars, cupboards, tool sheds and garages, in case it is trapped. Before you go away, make sure your cat is there, and that a neighbour (or the person looking after the cat) has access to the house, and any sheds or garages.

◆ BELOW
A farm kitten has found a warm, sunny spot to sit in. Let's hope there are no nasty nitrates or rat poison lying around!

◆ BELOW
This terracotta pot looks safe enough – as long as it does not topple over, and there are no dangerous substances left inside.

◆ BELOW
A cat has taken over the greenhouse. It was allergic to tomatoes, so the plants and all potentially dangerous substances were removed before the cat moved in.

THE RISK OF POISONING

A cat enjoys exploring and takes an interest in dark, small places where danger can lurk in the form of toxic substances. A cat can occasionally be poisoned by eating or drinking poison, by indirect absorption from eating a poisoned animal, or, more commonly, by licking poison deposited on the fur or paw pads. Similarly, these substances can be absorbed through the skin itself, particularly through the paw pads.

It is vital to keep household cleaning agents in cupboards with catproof doors, and antifreezes and weedkillers safely locked away in garages and tool sheds. Always read the labels of such products carefully; if there are warnings of the danger of the contents to children, they are likely to be bad for your cat too. Although a cat is not likely to choose to drink a bottle of paint-stripper, it could knock

over a bottle containing some. If a toxic substance is spilled on a surface where a cat is likely to tread, mop it up thoroughly. If you are decorating, keep the cat out of the room. Even the smell of modern decorating materials can affect some cats.

Some of the preparations used to keep garden pests at bay are particularly lethal, as they are spread around the garden. Your cat might eat the bird that ate the slug that took the slug pellet, or it just might lick its pads on to which a slug pellet has adhered. So check the contents of any weedkillers, slug bait or growth enhancers and opt for the environmentally friendly varieties. Even these may carry a warning

♦ ABOVE RIGHT
The mouse that this young cat is playing with could carry toxins picked up at an earlier point in the food chain.

♦ RIGHT
A robust ginger non-pedigree is seeking out some greenstuff to supplement his diet. Most cats instinctively avoid potentially poisonous plants.

regarding domestic pets, and some cats have particular reactions to some substances that are safe for the majority, so keep alert.

Cats usually instinctively avoid the plants which are poisonous to them. However, indirect poisoning could possibly occur if the cat were to eat a bird or a small rodent that had fed on such a plant. Cats do eat grass and other herbage to provide minerals and vitamins, and to act as emetics to get rid of fur balls, for example. Outdoor cats are free to choose their own greenstuff and, because of their normally fastidious nature, seldom make mistakes by taking a mouthful of a toxic plant. Seeds of grasses that are beneficial to cats are marketed, and can be grown indoors. If you do have an indiscriminate plant chewer, avoid having plants that could be dangerous in the house and garden. A garden centre should be able to advise on what these are.

GOING AWAY

Most cats are probably happier to stay in their own homes when owners are away, and there are organizations that will arrange for people to move in and care for your pets. However, this service can be expensive if only one animal is involved. Most people arrange for friends, neighbours, or relatives to live in or to come in regularly to feed and check on the cat. This can sometimes present problems as cats are great individualists, and even if they appear friendly with the sitter when the owners are present may adopt a different view when they have left. In such a situation, a cat might become stressed and stray. It is wise to have a few practice runs and leave the cat for a few days before

risking a two-week break. There is usually no problem with indoor cats, or with outdoor cats that are able to continue coming and going via a cat flap. However, this can be an added worry for the carer, who may prefer the cat flap to be securely locked during the owner's absence. Cats used to freedom might be very keen to escape if suddenly confined in this way. Do make sure, before you leave, that the person who is to look after your cat knows where the cat is and has the keys to all the places to which the cat might have access – the house, the garage, plus any outhouses. Always leave your contact telephone number, and the address and telephone number of your vet, including the emergency service. Discuss responsibilities before you go to ensure that what needs to be done is absolutely clear. Leave written instructions if necessary.

BOARDING OUT

If you decide not to have someone looking after your cat at home, ask your vet for approved local catteries (many veterinary practices have boarding facilities of their own), or ask friends for first-hand recommendations. Do make arrangements well in advance of your departure, as the best boarding catteries may be booked up for months ahead. It is a good idea to visit the cattery before booking to see if the environment and atmosphere will suit your cat. Most prefer you to make an appointment beforehand. There are also questions a boarding cattery

✦ ABOVE
Food, water and a clean litter tray (pan) are not all a cat wants when its owners are away. Cuddles and games are also important if your cat is not to feel lonely.

✦ LEFT
Being home alone while the owners are away does not present too much of a problem for this cat. It has the freedom of the house, a cat flap for access to outside, and a reliable neighbour to call in and feed it.

BOARDING CATTERY CHECKPOINTS

Points to check on your preliminary visit to a cattery:

✦ are there individual runs?

✦ are the runs and houses inside or outside, and are they are adequately heated?

✦ are the pens sheltered, clean and safely out of the reach of dogs if they are taken in too?

✦ are the beds and bedding disposed of or thoroughly disinfected for each new resident?

✦ are the feeding bowls sterilized between residents?

✦ do the staff seem happy, bright and animal-loving? Do they have any qualifications?

✦ is there plenty for your cat to watch?

✦ do the runs have appropriate sneeze gaps between them? Are the partitions impervious?

✦ are there climbing posts permanently available?

✦ how often are the cats visited during the day?

✦ are the kitchens clean?

✦ is there access to a vet at all times?

✦ ABOVE
This boarding cattery has outside pens. If you have an indoor cat, will it be happy and warm enough here?

✦ LEFT
On your preliminary visit to a cattery you could check other residents to see if they look contented.

owner will ask of you, most importantly whether the cat is in good health and has up-to-date vaccination status. The cattery should have details of your vet's name, address and telephone number, and your own contact address and telephone numbers while you are away. You will be asked for details of special dietary requirements for your cat, and will need to sign a consent form regarding appropriate treatment in the case of illness, and your acceptance of any necessary veterinary bills.

✦ RIGHT
Check there is enough sneezing distance between one pen and another, just in case one inmate develops an infection.

TRAVELLING TIPS

If you anticipate regular travelling with your cat – to shows, for example – it is worth introducing travelling at an early age. Any length of journey can be very stressful for a cat, and you should try to create as secure an environment as possible within the carrier. Some cats – especially Siamese – can complain loudly throughout a journey: they are distressed because they feel trapped. This can be very distracting for the driver. A vet can administer a tranquillizer, but this should be avoided if possible. Because of the stress factor, it is not advisable to subject a pregnant cat, or a nursing mother and young kittens to travelling.

If there is no room for a litter tray (pan), lay some form of absorbent padding – absorbent kitchen paper, or a baby's nappy (diaper) – on the base. Avoid newsprint, especially if you have a light-coloured cat whose fur might stain. Spread one of the cat's usual sleeping blankets or towels on top, and add a favourite toy.

◆ LEFT
A pedigreed cat is going off to a show. As it is travelling alone with the driver, the carrier will have to be firmly secured on the back seat of the car.

◆ BELOW LEFT
A Seal Point Siamese emerges from its lightproof and draughtproof container.

COMFORT IN TRANSIT
Seasoned cat show travellers suggest that the cat carrier should be placed as far away from the engine as possible, away from engine noise, and from direct blasts of dry air from heaters and fans. Some carriers have a specially designed cover to keep out light and draughts (drafts). Otherwise, on cold days, you can cover the carrier with a blanket or towel. Do make sure there are sufficient gaps for ventilation. In the early days of cat shows, owners would send their prize animals by train in such carefully sealed baskets that on occasions the cats arrived dead from suffocation.

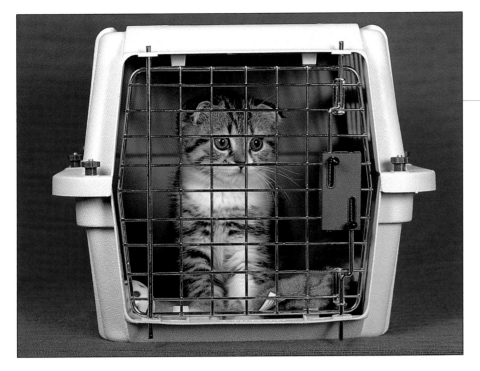

A sturdy carrier suitable for an air journey has a ridge around it to guard against the ventilation holes becoming blocked.

label carrying the owner's name and address, together with instructions for any feeding or watering that might be necessary should be securely attached. If the journey is to be a long one, and the carrier is not big enough for a litter tray (pan), line the base with plenty of absorbent towelling or a disposable nappy (diaper).

Some airlines allow a cat in its carrier to stay with its owner in the passenger section. Usually, though, your cat will be housed with other animals booked on the flight in a special area of the hold which provides an environment with heat, light and air-conditioning, according to IATA regulations.

BOOK AHEAD

Before booking a bus or coach journey, always contact the company you intend to travel with well in advance to check their regulations on the transportation of animals. Companies have different rules and it may not be possible for your cat to travel with you, if at all. In the United States, for instance, the Greyhound bus line does not permit pets. You will almost certainly have to pay a fare for your pet. Few companies consider them as hand baggage.

AIR TRAVEL

Commercial airlines have well-established regulations for the transportation of pets. These conform to International Air Transport Association (IATA) regulations. It is vital to contact the airline offices at least a month in advance of the travel date to ascertain requirements. You may be required to buy a carrier that has to be ordered by mail from a specialist supplier. In any event, the carrier should be of a strong, rigid material, stable and well-ventilated. There needs to be a handle for ease of carrying, and a door that can be locked to guard against anyone opening it. A

◆ LEFT
For short journeys – to the vet, for example – two cats are company for each other. On longer hauls, this would constitute overcrowding.

CHANGING COUNTRIES

It is not only top breeders who export their highly prized pedigreed cats and kittens to countries around the world. Retirement, career changes or even health considerations can prompt cat owners to move from one country to another, and if it is for any significant length of time, the cat goes too!

Arranging exportation first involves contact with the local animal health offices of the relevant government department – the Ministry of Agriculture, Fisheries and Food (MAFF) in the United Kingdom or the Department of Agriculture in the United States. This should be done as soon as possible and will provide essential information. You will need an export licence, and it is advisable to apply for this about four–six weeks in advance. This is due to the fact that

◆ LEFT
A cat in quarantine has a private shelf and plenty of room in which to run around.

◆ BELOW
So who is on holiday? This quarantine cattery is at Oahu, Hawaii.

◆ BELOW
A show cat is not subjected to the strict
quarantine regulations still imposed in Britain,
as long as certain requirements are met.

vaccination against specific diseases is mandatory for a number of importing countries and has to be administered at a specific minimum time before import is allowed. Many countries receiving cats from the United Kingdom will insist upon the rabies vaccine having been administered at least 28 days prior to import. As the United Kingdom has been, to date, free of rabies, the rabies vaccine is only issued to authorized vets who are Local Veterinary Inspectors (LVI) of MAFF. The application must state details of both owner and animal, date, importing country and method of travel. A special order has to be raised for each individual dose and, in most cases, the injection still has to be given a clear 28 days before the animal leaves the country. In some cases, proof of vaccination against rabies (and other diseases, depending on the importing country) will be required before the issue of an export licence.

Paperwork is scrutinized carefully upon entry at immigration. Often, precise details of the departure date and time, the consignee's address, route and method of travel may be required on the import documents as well as on the rabies vaccine application order. The airline will give you precise details of the type of carrier in which the animal is to be sent, and what you should include in it for the journey.

Some countries insist on a period of quarantine to keep rabies out of rabies-free areas. In Britain, although the law is under review, there is still a statutory six months' quarantine before an imported pet cat may be released to its owners. Do carefully consider the effects on the cat of

such a long separation, and the expense involved. A quarantine kennels may want guarantees of a cat's fitness before accepting it, and may also require a male cat to be

◆ ABOVE
When your cat arrives in its new home, it will need a great deal of attention and to be kept indoors for a while.

neutered (altered). A nine-month-old Greek stray raised by an English family severed a nerve in its leg shortly before it was due to move to Britain. As well as the stress of the journey, it would have had to be neutered (altered) and its leg amputated, followed by six months' quarantine and a complete change of climate and environment. Fortunately, the Greek vet offered it a home.

IMPORT OF SHOW CATS

The British regulations have relaxed a little for animals intended for "trade" – which means show cats are included but not ordinary household pets. Such animals can be imported into Britain without undergoing quarantine, provided that stringent pre-entry requirements are met. These include vaccination against rabies, blood-testing to assess immunity, implantation of an identity microchip, and importation from a registered holder on whose premises the cat has either been born or been continuously resident for the previous six months.

Nutrition and Feeding

If you give your cat a well-balanced diet, it will radiate good health. It will be contented, alert and active, with bright eyes, a glossy coat and a moist nose. Regular feeding and a variety of textures and flavours may also contribute to a contented and healthy cat.

◆ FACING PAGE
Dinner is served on a plate, but if the owner were to disappear, this cat would adapt to finding its own food in the wild.

◆ ABOVE
Two can be company when it comes to meal-times, as long as each cat obtains its fair share.

EATING HABITS

The cat is a carnivore which means that its natural diet consists of the prey which it eats. The cat's teeth and whole dietary adaptation are geared towards the consumption and digestion of entire insects, small rodents, birds, amphibians and fish. While cats do eat some plant matter, they have specific requirements for certain nutrients that can only be found in animal tissues. For this reason, meat must form at least part of a cat's diet. For an owner to try to impose a vegetarian diet would be cruel.

Nutrients are the part of the food that provide energy or raw materials from which the cat builds or replaces its tissues. Unless they are provided in the correct quantity and balance, the cat will not be able to maintain a normal, active life. Nutritional requirements vary at different stages of the cat's life cycle, which is why commercial cat foods are now available for kittens, adults and senior cats. The belief that feeding a cat well makes it less likely to bring its prey into the

house, or that keeping the cat hungry will make it become a better mouser, is ill-founded. A cat does not need the incentive of hunger to hunt; the healthier it is, the more successful it will be as a hunter.

◆ LEFT
A leopard with its natural prey. Even a domestic cat will appreciate the occasional raw bone.

◆ BELOW
Abandoned kittens enjoy a balanced diet and security at a cat welfare home.

ROUTINE

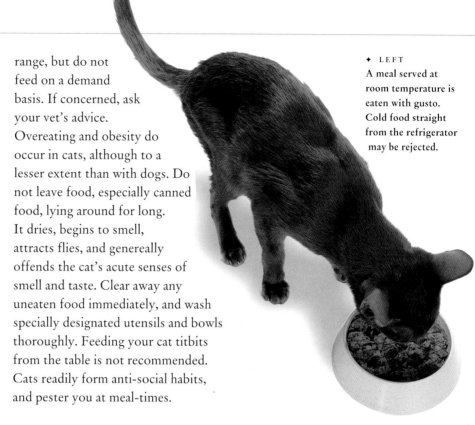

Feed an adult cat once or twice a day. Serve the food in the same place at around the same time each day. A mixture of canned and dry food is a good idea, for variety, and so that the cat uses its jaws and teeth on the dry food. For the correct quantity, follow the manufacturers' recommendations on the can or packet. An adult 4kg (8lb) cat generally needs around 400g (14oz) of canned food per day or about 50g (2oz) of dry food, depending on its lifestyle. Cats with freedom to roam will need more than an indoor cat, and more may be required during cold weather. Avoid giving snacks between meals. If your cat asks persistently for more, check the quantities are within the above range, but do not feed on a demand basis. If concerned, ask your vet's advice.

Overeating and obesity do occur in cats, although to a lesser extent than with dogs. Do not leave food, especially canned food, lying around for long. It dries, begins to smell, attracts flies, and genereally offends the cat's acute senses of smell and taste. Clear away any uneaten food immediately, and wash specially designated utensils and bowls thoroughly. Feeding your cat titbits from the table is not recommended. Cats readily form anti-social habits, and pester you at meal-times.

◆ LEFT
A meal served at room temperature is eaten with gusto. Cold food straight from the refrigerator may be rejected.

◆ ABOVE
A Siamese can persistently ask for more food in a very loud voice. Some indoor/outdoor cats do need more food in cold weather, or simply because they are more active than indoor cats.

◆ RIGHT
A cat takes its meal on a worktop, so that the house dog does not steal its food. Ideally, the area should not be used for human food preparation. A windowsill is more suitable.

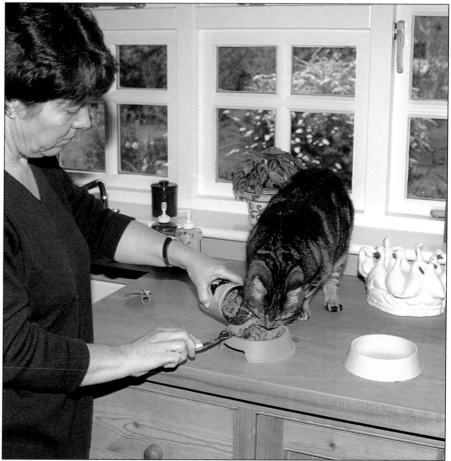

A Balanced Diet

Within its diet the cat requires a balance of proteins, carbohydrates, fats, vitamins, minerals and water. If you give your pet meals at regular times, and offer a variety of fresh and commercial cat foods following the guidelines below, it should get all that it needs without the addition of any dietary supplements such as vitamin pills. Read the labels of commercial cat foods to check the nutritional contents.

PROTEINS FOR STRENGTH

Proteins are made up of amino acids which are the building blocks of the body. They are not only used for growth and repair, but they can be metabolized to provide energy. The amount of protein in a cat's diet depends on its age. As cats become less active with age, they need a less protein-rich diet. In addition, their livers and kidneys have reduced efficiency and are less able to flush out the toxic by-products produced from the body's breakdown of proteins. A kitten, however, because it is growing and building up its muscle mass, needs around 50 per cent of protein in its diet, compared with over 30 per cent

◆ LEFT
Cats enjoy a varied diet and are not averse to raiding the owner's food supplies to achieve it.

◆ BELOW
Natural instinct is the driving force for a cat to hunt, not hunger. Feeding your cat a healthy and adequate diet will not stop it hunting, and could improve hunting performance.

◆ BOTTOM
A pair of Singapura kittens clearly have sufficient animal fats and tissue in their diet to provide them with an abundance of energy.

for a young adult. These levels are around 20 per cent more than those required by a dog of comparable age. The cat's digestive system processes proteins so efficiently that only 5 per cent of total protein absorbed is lost through waste products. Regular ingestion of protein must occur or the cat loses weight and condition. In the wild, feral cats acquire the essential amino acids through a variety of captured animals. Protein-rich foods are meat, fish, eggs, milk and cheese. Today, all nutritional needs are covered in the commercially available, scientifically formulated cat foods.

FATS FOR ENERGY

Fats are the second major source of energy for cats and should form a minimum of 9 per cent of the dry matter of the diet. The cat can digest up to 95 per cent of the fat it consumes; any excess is stored beneath the skin to provide insulation and protection for the internal organs. However, an imbalance between intake and fat used up through normal exercise can lead to an excess of fatty deposits and obesity. Fat is broken down in the body to fatty acids, which are important in the formation and maintenance of cell membranes throughout the body. In addition, fat also provides fat-soluble vitamins to the cat, including vitamins A, D, E and K. Some fatty acids are essential to the cat's diet, and are almost entirely absent from vegetable foods. They come from animal fat and tissue.

CARBOHYDRATES FOR BULK

Carbohydrates are the major energy source for most animals, but the cat can, in fact, survive without them. The

◆ LEFT
Night vision can be helped by vitamin A. This should be provided by a balanced diet that includes some liver, for example.

◆ LEFT
The teeth of the wild cat and its domestic descendants are geared to killing and eating small animals. A vegetarian diet would not be appropriate for your cat.

cat's main natural food sources, birds and mice, are relatively low in carbohydrates, apart from what is found in the stomachs of the prey. However, carbohydrates are a considerably cheaper energy source than protein-rich meat and fish, and are therefore usually incorporated into most commercial cat foods.

Carbohydrates can provide a beneficial boost of readily available energy at times of growth, pregnancy, nursing or stress. They are also a useful source of fibre, which although not digested by the cat, provides bulk in the faeces. A wild cat would obtain fibre from the fur, feathers or stomach contents of its prey, but the domestic cat obtains it from most commercial cat foods in the form of cellulose or plant fibre.

Carbohydrates should not make up more than 40 per cent of the diet.

MINERALS AND VITAMINS
Proteins, fats and carbohydrates are macronutrients, whereas vitamins and minerals are micronutrients – they are required in only small quantities. A cat synthesizes vitamin C for itself, and therefore needs no

extra. Vitamins A, D, E and K work together to refine the bodily functions, and they should all be present in a healthy, balanced diet, together with the vitamins of the B complex. An excess of vitamins can be harmful. Cats fed exclusively on liver,

for example (which they love because of the high fat content), may be getting an overdose of vitamin A which is stored in the liver. This can lead to serious arthritic problems involving the legs and spine, even in young cats.

◆ ABOVE AND ABOVE RIGHT
Commercially available snacks, such as these biscuits and milk-flavoured drops, should be given in ones and twos, as an occasional treat, not in bowlfuls as a main meal.

◆ RIGHT
A determined attempt to reach the treats at the bottom of the jar is likely to end in success. It is wise to keep cat-friendly food in sealed containers in cat-proof cupboards if you do not want your pet to help itself at will.

Minerals need to be available in the correct amounts which, in turn, have to be correct in relation to each other. The daily requirements even of macro minerals (which include phosphorus, calcium, sodium, potassium and magnesium) are measured in milligrams (one thousandth of a gram). Trace or micro minerals are also necessary, but daily requirements are measured in micrograms (a millionth of a gram). A cat that has a regular and balanced diet is unlikely to suffer from mineral deficiency, and supplements should not be necessary.

Calcium and phosphorus, for example, are both present in milk, and are very important for the growing kitten. Kittens fed on an all-meat diet and deprived of adequate supplies of milk will develop serious bone abnormalities because they are receiving too much phosphorus (present in meat protein), and not enough calcium. For many years, Siamese breeders weaned their kittens on to a meat and water diet in the belief that milk caused diarrhoea. As a result, bone problems often occurred.

✦ BELOW
A pedigreed cat not interested in its food could be ill or simply not hungry. It may also be bored with the same meal served up yet again and be yearning for variety.

✦ ABOVE
Greek feral cats fend for themselves on the harbourside, their diet of fish supplemented by scraps thrown by tourists from the tavernas.

✦ ABOVE
A raw meat treat for a kitten exercises its jaws, cleans its teeth, and reminds it of its natural diet. It is a good idea to serve it outside!

FOOD SOURCES
You can supplement your cat's canned or dry commercial food for the sake of variety. It is obviously more time-consuming to prepare special meals, but leftovers and scraps can introduce different tastes and textures with minimal effort and preparation. It is essential, however, to have an idea of the benefits and drawbacks of certain foods, and the danger of an unbalanced diet, such as too much liver and vitamin A. If you want to feed your pet exclusively on home-prepared foods, it is advisable to discuss this with your vet, particularly with regard to types, variety and amounts.

FRESH MEAT
A house cat may traditionally have lived off table scraps and odd bits of meat and fish thrown out for it – which probably provided perfectly good nutritional levels. The feral cat will eat a small rodent in its entirety, including bones, innards and muscle and will benefit from all the nutrients these contain.

If you want to feed your cat on raw meat, this must be supplemented with other foods, such as pasta and vegetables for carbohydrates, minerals

and fibre, that will provide the equivalent nutritional content of the bones and intestines of the naturally caught rodent.

The best meat, irrespective of type, has a valuable protein content of about 20 per cent. It is best served raw or lightly cooked as many of the vitamins can be destroyed, and the proteins denatured in the cooking process. Protein decreases and fat content increases as the cuts of meat become cheaper. Fat is not a problem, as the cat is well able to digest it and convert it into energy.

Poultry can be served, giblets and all, but make sure the bones are removed, as they become brittle with cooking and could be dangerous. Large pork or lamb bones, however, can provide a cat and kittens with hours of gnawing pleasure and also help to develop jaw strength, keep the teeth clean, and reduce the risk of dental problems in old age. Generally, avoid meats with additives and high salt content such as ham, bacon and sausages. Offal, such as liver and heart, is rich in minerals such as iron, but is also rich in vitamin A, too much of which can cause serious arthritis.

FISH

Uncooked fish has a protein level of over 10 per cent, while fish roes have a high protein level of 20–25 per cent. Raw fish should only be a rare treat, however, as it contains an enzyme that destroys some essential B vitamins. This could result in a variety of symptoms affecting the nervous and gastro-intestinal systems and skin. Oily fish, such as herring or sardines, is highly nutritious and is also higher in fat, making it a better choice than

white fish. A weekly meal of oily fish may help a cat to cope with the fur balls that collect in its stomach, as well as providing fat-soluble vitamins.

VEGETABLES

Cats on a diet of commercial cat food do not need vegetables. Sometimes they eat grass, which is considered to be a natural emetic and possibly a source of minerals and vitamins.

Vegetables are often included in commercial or home-prepared foods as a cheap source of protein and fibre.

DAIRY PRODUCTS

Milk has a useful fat and protein content, as well as lactose (milk sugar), all of which can be beneficial during periods of growth, pregnancy, lactation or stress. Cheese and milk also provide useful minerals such as calcium and phosphorus, but are not part of the cat's natural diet, and should be an occasional treat. Too much can cause diarrhoea, particularly in an older cat. Eggs mashed or scrambled are full of protein and vitamin A, but should never be fed raw as they contain an enzyme that can also destroy some essential B vitamins.

PREPARED CAT FOOD

Over the last few decades, there has been a tremendous revolution in feline feeding methods. Today there are commercial foods available that cater for all stages of a cat's life. These are available in dry, semi-moist or canned forms, and, in addition, there are deep-frozen foods which come the closest to fresh meat or fish. If the commercial foods are manufactured by reputable, well-known brand names, you can be sure that the contents displayed on the wrapper are balanced. If they are marketed as complete foods, they are complete, and the only necessary addition is drinking water. No vitamins, minerals, or other supplements are necessary. However, cost does increase with quality, and the most expensive varieties are those that are scientifically researched and geared to the dietary needs of cats in each of the three major stages of development: kitten, active adulthood and old age.

Do check the labels for additives (preferably minimal), ingredients and breakdown of nutrient content. Bear in mind, however, that while the average protein content of a can of

◆ ABOVE
Dry food (10 per cent moisture) can be kept longer when opened and left longer in the bowl than wet food, without becoming tainted.

◆ ABOVE
Semi-moist cat food has a moisture content of 40–50 per cent, and so the cat will require less supplementary water than with a dry-food diet.

◆ ABOVE
Canned food (75–85 per cent water) dries and spoils if not eaten immediately. Supplementary biscuits provide exercise for the jaw.

food may be only 6–12 per cent, this is usually the total content per 100g (3.5oz) of food, rather than being calculated on a dry-weight basis. About 10 per cent protein in canned food is equivalent to over 40 per cent dry weight, and is therefore acceptable.

If your cat is fed an exclusively dry diet, fresh water should always be available and changed at least once a day.

WATER
Water is vital for many functions within the body. A cat can survive for 10–14 days without food, but a total lack of water can result in death within days. The daily intake depends very much upon factors such as the moisture content of the food and the climate or temperature. Cats are not great drinkers, and many will hardly seem to drink at all, as they obtain most of their needs from their food. Fresh meat and canned food are made up of about 75 per cent water, whereas dry food contains only about 10 per cent. Because of the domestic cat's evolution from desert dweller (the African wild cat), the kidneys are extremely efficient at conserving water. However, fresh water should be always available, especially if your cat eats dry or semi-moist food.

◆ LEFT
Meat is meat to these two cats; acceptable food has been found, and it will save a great deal of time and bother for their owner if they have the same thing all the time. Some cats appear to demand variety, but it is not essential for good health.

SPECIAL NEEDS

◆ BELOW
It may take six months or more of carefully controlled dieting to return this obese cat to a normal weight. Weight reduction in cats is more difficult than in humans or dogs.

A great deal of research has gone into specialized diets for specific conditions such as heart disease, digestive disorders, lower urinary tract disease, and obesity. If you think your cat needs a special diet, seek the advice of your vet. Most of the diets are only available on prescription.

THE ELDERLY CAT

In young and adult life, cats need protein for growth, to replace worn-out tissues and also as a significant energy source. As cats grow old, they become less active, vital organs start to deteriorate, and their need for protein is reduced.

If you maintain the cat on the same diet it had when it was young and active, there will be an excess of protein. This throws strain on the kidneys and liver, as the protein has to be broken down and eliminated from the body. If the kidneys are not fully functioning due to age, the body tries to maintain the status quo by increasing thirst, and the cat starts to urinate more. This flushes out some of the toxic products, but at the same time removes some essential vitamins and minerals.

Elderly cats in general require a protein level that is reduced from 40 per cent dry weight to about 30 per cent. There needs to be a corresponding increase in fat levels to ensure that sufficient non-harmful energy is available, but not in quantities that might cause obesity. Carbohydrates (such as starches and sugars) should be avoided, as these are more difficult for the elderly cat to digest and can cause diarrhoea and other problems. Sometimes weight loss is noted in an elderly cat even though appetite has not diminished, or may even have increased. In such circumstances, consult your vet, as this may be due to a condition such as hyperthyroidism, which can be treated.

◆ ABOVE
Perhaps its owner has left stale water in the cat's bowl. In any event, the movement of the drips makes this a far more exciting way to drink.

◆ LEFT
An elderly cat's diet should supply easily assimilated protein in the right quantities to sustain energy but not overload the system.

◆ ABOVE
An active adult cat needs – and can assimilate – a higher level of protein in its diet to fuel its lifestyle than an elderly cat.

MOTHERHOOD

The first sign of a cat's pregnancy will
probably not be a noticeable increase
in abdominal size but a demand for
more food. If the queen is in good
condition at the time of mating, she
should not need extra food until about
the last third of the pregnancy (seven –
nine weeks). By this time the foetuses
will be growing in the womb and space
is at a premium, so the cat needs
frequent small meals, up to four times
daily. The total quantity should only
be increased by about one third. Top-
quality, nourishing food of low bulk is
of special importance at this time.

NURSING

To maintain the amount of milk
needed for her kittens, a nursing
queen will certainly at least double her
normal food intake. Food should be of
high quality and low bulk – in other
words, as much energy and nutrients
packed into as small a volume as
possible. These requirements are most
easily met by some of the special high-
energy diets specially devised for
nursing queens. Alternatively, kitten
food can be used.

THE KITTENS

Kittens suckle from their mother
exclusively for the first three or four
weeks of their lives. As they become
more aware of their surroundings they
may start to nibble at their mother's
food, a sure sign they are ready for

weaning. The queen will happily
continue to nurse her litter to some
extent well into their third month of
life. However, by the time they are
about eight weeks old, the greater part
of the kittens' diet will usually be

provided by the owner. There is a fine
line between allowing the kittens to
gorge themselves, which may cause
digestive problems, and giving them
enough to maintain healthy growth.
The weaning process should be

◆ LEFT
The young, active adult cat often cannot last a whole day before the next meal and will need an extra snack in-between.

◆ BELOW
A Persian kitten matures over four years and frequent, nutritious meals need to be given during this time.

gradual, and the kittens fed little and often, with small quantities of high-protein food well chopped so as to be easily consumable. The easiest method of weaning is to use one of the readily available, well-established kitten foods, either in the dry or canned versions.

During the actual weaning process, canned foods are probably preferable, as the kittens may be attracted by the meaty smell. However, the dry foods are just as nutritious and have proven success. Do plan feeding times carefully so that mother and kittens may eat the extra meals in peace, away from other animals or disturbance in the household.

HOW MUCH, HOW OFTEN?

At about eight weeks old, kittens should be fed little and often. If you are feeding dry kitten food (which can be left out for longer than canned food), you can try providing it on a continuous basis for the kitten to nibble as required. Such a routine should be avoided, however, if your kitten shows a tendency to be overweight. Four or more meals a day for the kittens is normal, and can be gradually reduced to about three meals by the age of three to four months, and two meals at six months.

THE YOUNG ADULT

The feeding regime can gradually be reduced to one main meal as the kitten reaches adulthood at nine to twelve months of age. However, young, active cats will become very hungry if they have to wait 24 hours between meals. Many owners therefore offer a snack in the morning, with the main meal at night. If this is done, it is important to ensure that the main meal is reduced in quantity by the equivalent of the earlier snack, so that too many calories do not lead to weight problems. Most breeds of cat reach their adult size at about a year of age, although some of the longhaired breeds continue to develop until they are about four years old.

If you do have a slow-maturing cat, it is essential to ensure that adequate food of high quality is available throughout the growth period. A routine of two or three meals a day with a dry-weight protein value of over 30 per cent should continue over the growth period in order to maintain peak development.

◆ BELOW
These 12-week-old kittens are likely to be demanding three meals a day.

Grooming

Cats are fastidious animals and devote a large part of their waking hours to grooming themselves. A little extra help from their human friends is required by longhaired and semi-longhaired cats. Even for shorthairs, the grooming process is important. It can be a pleasurable, bonding and rewarding experience for both cat and owner. Extra grooming also contributes to general health, for it stimulates the blood vessels just below the skin and improves muscle tone.

◆ FACING PAGE
A ginger cat uses his paw to clean the parts the tongue cannot reach. The paw stimulates secretions from the glands on the head, which it then transfers to other parts of the body.

◆ ABOVE
A satisfied customer – a Burmese Red – poses for photographs after a grooming session.

THE NATURAL WAY

The cat is well-equipped to groom itself: tongue, teeth, paws and claws are all pressed into service. The cat's tongue has a rough surface which, combined with saliva, helps to remove grit and sticky substances from the fur. Even though cats are very flexible, there are areas they cannot reach directly with the tongue – so the front paws are licked and used rather like a face flannel (washcloth). As the coat dries, the cat nibbles the fur back into place with its small incisor teeth and removes any foreign matter that the washing process failed to dislodge.

The back claws act almost like a wide-toothed comb and remove larger objects from the coat. The front paws stimulate slight oily secretions from glands around the head, and transfer them to other parts of the body during grooming. The cat is preening its coat with its own perfume, which can then be used to mark territory.

◆ ABOVE
A fluffy silver and white kitten shows her remarkable flexibility as she grooms her hind leg. Careful grooming is particularly important with long fur, to remove any matting that could lead to a skin infection.

CHANGING COATS

In the natural state, the cat sheds its coat once a year, usually in spring. However, the process is dependent on light and temperature. In warm, artificially heated and illuminated homes, indoor cats tend to shed throughout the year. It does not happen in one vast shedding of fur, but in discreet areas across the body so that hair loss is hardly noticed – except on the owner's carpets, furnishings and clothes.

When self-grooming at any time of the year, the cat dislodges loose fur, some of which is swallowed. This gradually builds up into a fur ball (hairball) which can eventually solidify into a pellet in the cat's intestine. Most cats automatically bring up a small fur ball every few days or so, but sometimes one can become stuck, causing loss of appetite and a rundown condition. In extreme cases, a vet may need to operate to remove the obstruction. The fur ball problem can strike at any time, although longhaired cats are most at risk. The occasional meal of oily fish may help ease the passage of the ingested hair.

◆ LEFT
A Silver Tabby licks a front paw so that it can then use it rather like a face flannel (washcloth) to wipe its face.

◆ BELOW
The grooming process is completely absorbing for these two kittens. As well as being necessary, grooming is an activity that cats enjoy.

HUMAN AID

A feral cat in good physical condition usually keeps itself reasonably well-groomed. Domestication and selective breeding have resulted in changes to the cat's coat, such as longer hair, that sometimes require more maintenance than the cat is able to provide for itself. Assistance is then needed from the owner. Older cats, too, may lose the motivation and energy to groom themselves and welcome extra help.

You can remove some of the loose dead hairs which accumulate just by stroking a cat. The polishing action gives the coat a beautiful sheen. Some experienced owners claim that the best time to groom a cat is just after washing the dishes, for if your hands are very slightly damp, stroking is even more effective. Thin rubber gloves have a similar effect in removing loose hair.

EQUIPMENT

The grooming equipment you need depends on the type of coat your cat has. You will also gradually discover what works best for your pet. If you have a pedigreed cat, ask the breeder's advice. First-hand experience, especially from a breeder who keeps show cats, can save time and money.

Start regular grooming as a part of a kitten's routine as soon as it comes into your household. An older cat may need some encouragement to submit to the experience, but will probably soon enjoy it immensely, if you are gentle. Choose a quiet time in the cat's observed routine, make sure all you need is accessible and settle the cat on a towel on your lap. It is pointless trying to restrain a cat that just wants to play; scratches are far less likely if the cat is relaxed.

✦ CLOCKWISE FROM BELOW
Narrow/wide-toothed grooming comb, flea comb, ball-tipped brush, slicker tail brush.

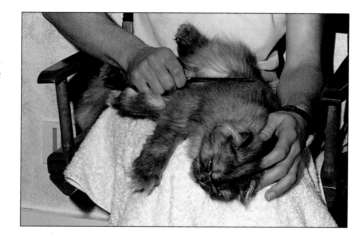

✦ LEFT
A longhaired cat is lying down on a towel specially reserved for its grooming. Having a waste (trash) bin nearby is also a wise move.

✦ BELOW
Finish off a grooming session with a stroke and hear that cat purr. Stroking also removes any stray loose hairs and gives a final polish.

GROOMING A SHORTHAIRED CAT

Supplementing the self-grooming of a shorthaired cat is really only absolutely necessary if you are showing. But an extra groom, say twice weekly, does help keep loose, dead hairs under control and off the furniture. It is also a good opportunity to check for fleas, or the onset of any ear or dental problems. In addition, the activity is pleasurable for both cat and owner. The process is, of course, far simpler than for a longhaired cat. Grooming aids can include a metal

CHECKLIST

♦ towel

♦ rubber-bristled brush

♦ wide-toothed metal comb

♦ natural, soft-bristled brush

♦ flea comb

♦ chamois leather or velvet glove

♦ cotton wool

♦ ear cleaner

♦ eye wipes

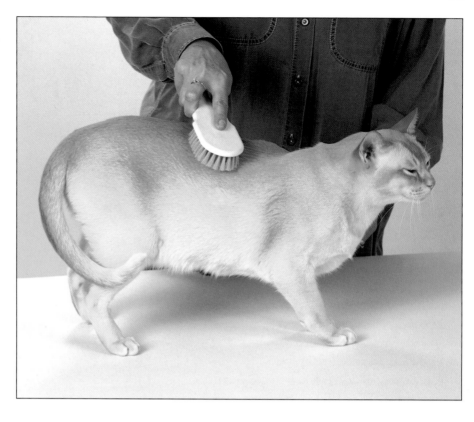

comb with round-tipped teeth, a soft, natural-bristled brush to settle the fur, a brush with stiffer bristles (a rubber brush is essential for Rex cats, as it does not scratch the skin), and a polishing cloth of silk or chamois leather. Start the grooming session by gently stroking the cat to relax it. Use the stiff brush first, brushing very gently along the lie of the fur, to loosen the dead hairs and dirt. Brush the whole body, but be especially gentle in delicate parts around the ears, armpits and groin,

♦ BELOW LEFT AND RIGHT
When grooming is finished, it's time to rest and watch a friend finish off his tail. Cats often groom together if they have the opportunity; it is an important social activity.

♦ ABOVE
A soft-bristled brush settles the fur after any static triggered by the use of a metal comb.

◆ BELOW
A rubber brush is not only gentler on the
shorthair's skin, but the cat seems to relish the
feel of it, too. It removes not only dead hair but
dandruff as well.

and under the belly and tail. Next, use
the metal comb to extract the dead
hairs. It may set up some static in the
coat, causing fur to clump together or
the guardhairs to develop a wispy life
of their own. This will be corrected
with the soft-bristled brush, and a
final polish with the chamois leather,
velvet or silk.

A DRY SHAMPOO

It is rarely necessary to wash a
shorthaired cat unless it is a pale-
coloured exhibition cat, or unless the
cat has become greasy – from sitting
under a car, for example. Some
exhibitors give their shorthairs a bran
bath to remove excess grease, dirt and
dandruff. Warm a good five or six
handfuls of natural bran flakes in the
oven to a comfortable hand-hot
temperature. Rub these over the cat,
avoiding the face and inner ears,
working the hands thoroughly

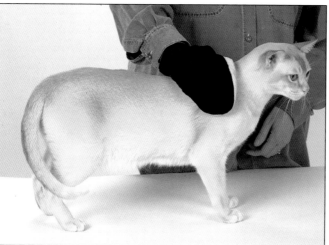

◆ LEFT
A final sheen is
encouraged on a
shorthair's coat by
stroking it with a
chamois leather or
velvet glove. A silk
scarf would do the
job just as well.

through the coat; then simply brush it
all out with a soft brush. A coat that is
predominantly dark will take on a
shine immediately; pastel blues and
creams may take a couple of days
before their texture and shine reach
the peak of perfection.

◆ RIGHT
A contented and very sleek
Red Burmese following a
full grooming session.

GROOMING A LONGHAIRED CAT

Longhaired cats, whether they are Persians or semi-longhairs – the so-called self-grooming breeds such as the Maine Coon Cat or Norwegian Forest Cat – all need considerable grooming help from the owner. This is true whether the animal is purebred or not. Longhaired cats pick up dirt and debris in their coats, and they need help to keep the fur clean and free from tangles. This must be done daily. If not, the hair mats, particularly in the armpits and groin, and can become uncomfortable. A severely matted coat is unyielding and prevents the cat from moving with ease. Any movement results in individual hairs being pulled. The build-up of fur leads to deterioration in the general condition of the coat and a much greater likelihood of hairballs.

Grooming procedures are more elaborate than for the shorthairs. Start with the wide-toothed comb with blunt teeth to ease out tangles and debris. Try the comb on yourself before you try it out on the cat. If it does not feel sharp on your head, it should be fine for the cat. To deal with obstinate knots and tangles, sprinkle them with unscented talcum powder and ease them free with your hands. A sprinkle of talcum powder also helps pick up excess grease and dirt. It should be brushed out thoroughly at the brushing stage. Make partings in the tail, and brush each parted section sideways. Finish with a well-earned stroke in all the right directions.

1 Use the comb gently to ease out any tangles, knots and twigs. Sprinkle with talcum powder once a week. Do the underbelly and legs first.

2 Brush the body fur firmly in sections against the lie of the fur towards the cat's head. Brush thoroughly to remove talcum powder, if you have used it.

3 Use the fine comb for the neck fur. For Persians, the fur should be combed upwards to form a ruff beneath the chin.

CHECKLIST FOR SHAMPOO AND GROOM

- ✦ towels
- ✦ wide-toothed metal comb
- ✦ fine comb
- ✦ natural-bristled brush
- ✦ unscented talcum powder
- ✦ feline or baby shampoo
- ✦ shower attachment
- ✦ hairdryer

✦ RIGHT
A Maine Coon is groomed fit for going on exhibition.

SHAMPOO AND STYLE

Washing a cat is time-consuming, but essential if you are to show your cat. Unless the idea is introduced during kittenhood, a cat may object to being bathed, so it is helpful to have two pairs of human hands.

Make sure the room is warm, free of draughts, and escape-proof. A large, flat-based kitchen sink is ideal. Allow plenty of clear space around the sink, with a stock of dry towels nearby, and one on the draining board. Have all you need at hand before you start.

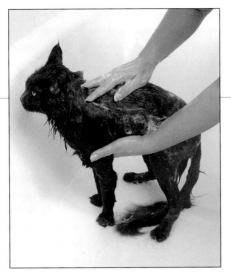

1 Fill the sink with warm water to about 5cm (2in). Talk soothingly to the cat all the time. Using a shower attachment, test the water first, then wet the fur thoroughly. Apply a little shampoo and work into a lather. Make sure no shampoo goes near the cat's eyes, nose or mouth.

2 Rinse thoroughly and repeat the shampooing process. If you are using conditioner, put a drop on the back and work it through the coat with the wide-toothed comb. Rinse thoroughly and then squeeze down the whole body, legs and tail to remove excess moisture.

3 Lift the cat from the sink and wrap it immediately in a towel. Rub gently to absorb most of the water. You may need several towels!

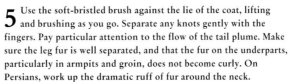

4 Set the hairdryer on low. Do not direct the airstream too close. Lift and comb the fur as you dry (this is easier if the dryer is on a stand), and stop when the fur is still slightly damp and tacky. If your cat objects to a hairdryer, do not persist, but resort to towels, brushes and patience.

5 Use the soft-bristled brush against the lie of the coat, lifting and brushing as you go. Separate any knots gently with the fingers. Pay particular attention to the flow of the tail plume. Make sure the leg fur is well separated, and that the fur on the underparts, particularly in armpits and groin, does not become curly. On Persians, work up the dramatic ruff of fur around the neck.

ATTENTION TO DETAIL

EYES

The discharges that accumulate in the corners of the eyes can be removed carefully with your finger. Short-faced cats are prone to show tear stains beneath the eyes, which can be cleaned with a special preparation available from pet stores or the vet's surgery.

MOUTH AND NOSE

A dark brown or black tarry secretion on the cat's chin indicates an excess production of sebum from the hair follicles, which is used in scent marking. A similar condition, known as stud tail, can occur around the base of the tail. Veterinary treatment is usually necessary. Recurrence may be prevented by cleansing with special anti-bacterial shampoo from your vet.

TEETH AND GUMS

Keeping your cat's teeth clean reduces the risk of gum disease which has escalated with the advent of modern

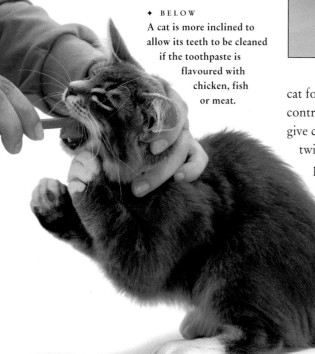

◆ **BELOW**
A cat is more inclined to allow its teeth to be cleaned if the toothpaste is flavoured with chicken, fish or meat.

◆ **LEFT AND BELOW LEFT**
Daily cleansing of the area around the eyes is particularly necessary with Persian cats. This kitten is being introduced to the idea at an early age. A cotton wool bud (swab) dampened with tepid water is used, and the area is gently wiped with absorbent tissue.

cat foods. If tartar can be kept under control, the risk is reduced. Some vets give cats a general check-up once or twice a year, and if necessary, perform a scale and polish under general anaesthetic. The alternative is for the owner to clean the cat's teeth once or twice a week. Special toothbrushes that fit over your finger and cat food-flavoured toothpastes make the job easier, but do not necessarily guarantee

◆ **ABOVE**
The owner cleans tartar from the outside surfaces of the kitten's teeth. The cat's rough tongue will take care of any tartar build-up on the inside surfaces of the teeth.

A shorthair has its ears checked as part of its grooming routine. A slight build-up of wax means a gentle wipe with absorbent tissue.

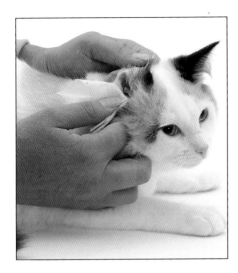

success. Just before feeding time, you could try wrapping a piece of fabric sticking plaster around the index finger. Smear this with a little wet cat food, and gently try to rub against the teeth while holding the head.

EARS

If ears appear soiled on the inside, wipe them out gently with a soft absorbent tissue on your finger, dampened with olive oil, liquid paraffin or ear cleaner from the pet shop. Never clean further than you can see, and do not use cotton wool buds (swabs). An abundance of dark brown, dry waxy material may indicate mites, in which case veterinary treatment is necessary.

CLAWS

Some Siamese cats and their derivatives, such as Balinese, Oriental Shorthairs and Oriental Longhairs, are unable to retract their claws completely and are therefore ill at ease on hard, uncarpeted floors. Elderly cats of any breed may have similar problems. The nails continue to grow and, because older cats take less exercise, are not worn down. Due to stiffness, they are

not fully retracted either. Trimming the nails will help. Outdoor cats should have only their front claws clipped, so that they are not completely disarmed if they meet an enemy, and will be able to climb should escape be necessary.

If claw clipping is necessary, ask the vet to do it, for a mistake could be dangerous. On light-coloured claws, a dark blood vessel can be seen. Cutting

◆ RIGHT
A thorough self-groom for this cat will help keep fleas and parasites at bay, and in warm weather, help it keep cool. The saliva takes the place of sweat in humans, evaporating and cooling the cat.

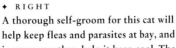

this (called cutting to the quick) causes copious bleeding and pain. Declawing, or onychectomy, is considered an unnecessary mutilation in the United Kingdom. It is widely practised in the United States, and is often carried out at about the same time as sterilization. It is a major operation that removes the cat's main means of self-defence, and should be reserved for indoor cats.

◆ LEFT
A Burmese-cross is having its nails trimmed with a nail clipper custom-made for cats. Clippers designed for human nails may split cats' claws. Only the very edges are trimmed. If you are at all uncertain about your skills, it is wise to ask the vet to do this job.

Behaviour and Intelligence

The average cat is considered to be fairly intelligent, but compared with dogs its repertoire of party tricks appears paltry. Dogs, as pack animals, will obey understood commands in order to seek the approval of, or a reward from, the owner, who is considered to be the dominant pack leader. The cat is a more solitary animal and may well understand what it is supposed to do but choose not to comply.

✦ **FACING PAGE**
A kitten practises looking intelligent in front of a mirror. Cats do not have colour vision to the same extent as humans, but they can recognize mental alertness when they see it.

✦ **ABOVE**
The cat has the body and the build of a hunter – and a temperament and instinct to match.

THE ART OF COMMUNICATION

What a cat is inclined to do and what it can do are quite different. By nature and inclination, for example, cats move gracefully, daintily and sedately, yet their bodies are designed for speed and movement. When establishing a relationship with your cat, bear in mind that it will do what you ask not because it considers you dominant, but because it feels inclined to do so.

A well-balanced cat is used to being handled by its owner, and is alert, independent and inquisitive. If a cat is timid, dependent and constantly seeking attention, it may have suffered misuse or lack of socialization when it was young (6–16 weeks).

LEARNING FROM YOUR CAT

Communication is a two-way process; if you are alert and observant, you will notice subtle nuances in your cat's voice and body language. Listen to your pet in the context of its activity at the time and you may be able to link certain sounds with meanings such as hunger or contentment. Vocalization

♦ RIGHT
A well-balanced cat – confident, alert and relaxed.

and vowel sounds – miaowing – vary from cat to cat. Siamese tend to be very vocal and "talk" to their owners, other cats speak hardly at all. Purring – which can be done breathing in or out and for remarkably long, unbroken periods – is generally an indication of contentment. Kittens start to purr from approximately one week of age; they purr when they are feeding and their mother knows that all is well. It is believed that each kitten has a distinctive and unique

♦ ABOVE
A cat may be comfortably settled on its owner's lap, but its ears remain pricked and alert.

purr so that the queen is able to instantly recognize which of the offspring is communicating.

Fear, anger and dissatisfaction are expressed by spits, hisses and snarls. The pitch of a growl drops when a cat is hunting to become a low hypnotic rumbling. Some cats "chitter" and salivate in anticipation or excitement when they catch sight of something to hunt. Strained, high-intensity yowls are reserved for inter-cat communication, and are especially noticeable in a female on heat.

BODY LANGUAGE

When a cat feels good, its ears are erect and forward-pointing, and its whiskers are relaxed. At rest on a familiar lap, it may purr and "knead" its paws, opening and closing them just as it did against its mother's breast when it was suckling.

If its whiskers bristle forwards, ears turn back, pupils narrow to slits, and fur, particularly along the spine and tail, stands on end, the cat is spoiling for a fight. The fur extension may be accompanied by an arched back so that the cat looks as big and menacing as possible. Wide eyes and flattened whiskers and ears are signs of fear. Whiskers are highly sensitive organs of touch and are sometimes used to make friendly contact with another cat.

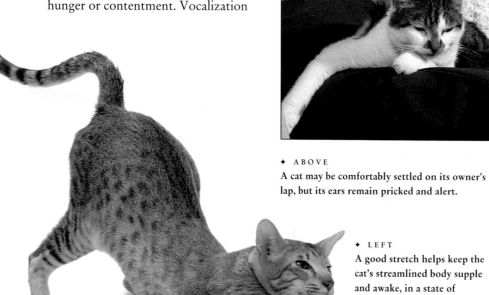

♦ LEFT
A good stretch helps keep the cat's streamlined body supple and awake, in a state of readiness for action.

BASIC INSTINCTS

Cats are nocturnal and may spend up to 16 hours in any one day resting, if not actually asleep. As hunters, they are conserving their energy for the quick bursts of power needed to pursue their targets. Their overwhelming instinct when they go out is to hunt small creatures. This can even be detected in the play of young kittens with toys and leaves. Hearing, sight and smell are geared to the demands of stalking and hunting and these senses are much more acute than they are in humans. Tactile whiskers supplement the other senses, acting as sensors to feel close objects. They may also be used as a friendly whisker-to-whisker gesture with other cats. Cats are sociable and will establish a relationship with other animals or become part of the neighbourhood cat community if they are allowed outside. This community is hierarchical, with the unneutered (unaltered) males and females reigning supreme, and highly territorial.

GENTLE MARKING

Both male and female cats gently assert their territorial rights by rubbing their heads against objects and humans. They leave traces of a scent that is secreted by glands located at various parts of the body, but particularly around the ears, neck and at the back of the head. The scent is also released from between the paw pads when a cat scratches a tree to sharpen its claws.

✦ ABOVE
As this cat rubs its forehead against a chair, a scent is released that proclaims the chair as part of the cat's own territory.

✦ ABOVE
At still only a couple of weeks old, this kitten has not begun to acquire trust or domesticated patterns of behaviour; it is still in its feral state, expressing fear and aggression at intruders.

✦ LEFT
A cat pounces. Its specially adapted eyes, with their wide angle of vision, are able to make the most of limited light, enabling a cat to detect the slightest movement in dim light.

TERRITORIAL RIGHTS

The cat instinctively carves out a social and hunting territory for itself. This behaviour is most marked in the unneutered (unaltered) male, whose main purpose in life is to pass on his genes to future generations. He may extend his territory to cover an area of as much as 10km (7 miles), maintaining his position in the social hierarchy and priority access to any local females by fighting. His life can be violent and short.

An unneutered female can fight as effectively and as viciously as the tom, as she develops and defends her hunting territory. From about four months of age, she periodically attracts all the males in the neighbourhood and regularly becomes pregnant.

DOMESTIC IMPLICATIONS

For the domestic neutered (altered) cat, its own home and garden are the focal points of its territory. An unneutered cat will extend the area

◆ ABOVE
A cat sprays to mark the boundaries of what it considers to be its territory. If the cat – whether male or female – has been neutered, the smell is unlikely to be obvious to humans.

◆ LEFT
Two cats demonstrate their affection for each other by rubbing their foreheads together. Other signs of friendship may include licking each other or brushing whiskers.

and challenge the neighbourhood cats. Kittens that are brought up together usually co-exist happily unless there are too many cats in the household, which could result in some territorial marking. If an adult cat is introduced into a home where there are cats already, care and sometimes expert guidance is needed. Among neutered cats, territorial rights may be resolved by some violent vocals, body language, and the establishment of non-violent dominance. If the cats are unneutered, it is a different story.

SPRAYING

The cat marks the boundaries of its patch with a spray of concentrated, very strong-smelling urine. It will also

♦ OPPOSITE
A male Burmese goes
hunting: it could
roam as far as 10km
(7 miles) in search
of food and female
company if it is
not neutered.

♦ BELOW
Son, aged six months, is keen on keeping close
to his mother. The dominant, unneutered
female, however, is not always this complacent,
and often asserts her independence.

♦ RIGHT
A kitten begins to
explore outside,
ready to take its
place among the
local community and
hierarchy of cats.

do this if it feels threatened or insecure, for example, if strange visitors or animals come into the house. The most common and the most pungent spraying comes from unneutered males, but entire females spray, especially when they are on heat. Neutered cats also spray, but the odour is usually less offensive.

In extreme situations, the marking may involve dropping faeces away from litter trays (pans). This is not simply dirty behaviour, but dysfunctional, and the causes must be established. A cat that constantly re-marks its territory is trying to reassure itself that it is worth something. The wise owner checks with the vet for medical advice. Home treatment of attention and affection may solve the problem. If the behaviour continues, you may be referred to an animal behaviourist.

THE EFFECT OF NEUTERING
Neutering (altering) dramatically reduces a cat's urge to exert territorial rights. Territory becomes confined to

an area around the home (although this will still be robustly defended by a neutered cat of either sex).

In a neutered, or castrated, male, the means of producing the hormones that fuel sex drive – the testes – are removed. Castration takes place ideally from four months of age. It is done under general anaesthetic. No stitches are needed, recovery is complete within 24 hours, and there is no discernible traumatic effect on the cat. Long-term, however, the animal's territorial, sexual and hunting behaviours are modified. A female is

neutered or spayed by the removal of her ovaries and uterus, or womb, so that she cannot become pregnant. She no longer comes on heat or attracts all the local males. The operation is ideally carried out from four to five months of age. Once the cat has recovered from the anaesthetic, she is usually fine. Long-term she may become more friendly and placid. Desexed animals do tend to convert their food more efficiently, and may be less active. If they start to look plump, some attention to diet may be necessary.

♦ RIGHT
Two neutered (altered) Burmese, who have
known each other since kittenhood, are happy
to share their limited territory of house and
garden amicably.

BEHAVIOURAL PROBLEMS

It is sometimes difficult to recognize symptoms of stress in the solitary, individualistic feline. Some breeds are more nervous than others. Highly strung Orientals, for example, can react very badly to strange situations, and even the first visit to a cattery may change the personality. Stolid domestic shorthairs may be equally upset, but are more likely to react aggressively – by hissing, scratching and biting. Cats probably show stress to a greater extent than dogs, but the first signs are sometimes too subtle for us to notice.

SYMPTOMS OF STRESS
When feeling vulnerable, a cat withdraws into itself, and cold aloofness is one of the first clues to its condition. A cat about to go into battle tries to appear as large as possible, but in distress it tries to become mouse-sized. Fur is flattened, tail is curled round and the cat crouches. If the situation continues, the cat starts to shake. Salivation, vomiting and defecation can also be signs of nervousness and tension.

A cat may react actively or passively when it is frightened. Typical, active signs are pupil dilation, arching back, piloerection (the hair stands on end) and hissing. A cat may react to any attempts at reassurance, such as vocal

intonations or body contact, with further aggression.

Passive symptoms of fear are more subtle and harder to detect. The cat may hide or try to appear smaller, placing the ears back and becoming immobile. A timid cat will start at the slightest movement or unexpected noise. This may be because it was abused as a kitten, or

simply because it lacked proper socialization. If you breed, it is important to socialize your kittens to prepare them for everyday household life and noise.

DEALING WITH FEAR
Mild fear may be overcome by the owner. A timid cat needs a safe, quiet place to retreat to, such as a covered bed. Avoid forcing your attentions on the cat – wait for it to approach you. Always move slowly, speak to it softly and evenly and keep strangers or strange situations at bay until it has become more confident.

It is important to identify the cause of a cat's fear so that you can deal with it. This may not always be easy, unless it is obvious – a one-off visit to the

✦ ABOVE
An aggressive cat seeing off an unwanted visitor. Neutering makes a cat more placid.

✦ LEFT
A timid cat crouches or hides when feeling threatened by the slightest noise or an unexpected situation.

vet, for example. There may be an ongoing situation, such as mild teasing behaviour by a child, or persistent noise or confinement. Once the cause is established, it must be removed and the cat's confidence regained.

It may be that you can persuade the cat to overcome its fears. Cats have a highly developed flight response and when faced with any threatening situation, such as being trapped in a carrier or a car, their immediate reaction is to try to get away. You may be able to control this with soothing words or by gradually making the cat realize it needn't be afraid by exposing it little and often to the situation.

After an initial shock reaction, cats often settle down in catteries or veterinary hospitals after about 48 hours. If they are handled, however gently, during that time, they may associate the handling with the initial fear and bridle every time anyone approaches to feed them. Left alone, they usually calm down and soon start to make overtures to the very people that they hated the day before.

DEALING WITH AGGRESSION

If a cat that is normally calm and well-behaved suddenly starts to scratch and bite, it may be ill, bored or frightened, and the underlying cause should be addressed. It is important to train a kitten from the beginning that aggressive behaviour is unacceptable, even in play. A firm no, immediate cessation of play, and a light tap on the nose whenever it bites or scratches should correct this behaviour. Do remember that a cat likes its independence, and if you impose your attentions on it when it does not want them – for example, if it is asleep – it may react instinctively by attacking you.

◆ ABOVE
A kitten in listening mode. It is important to talk encouragingly to your pet when it has behaved well, and never shout at it or hit it. A firm, quiet "no" and a tap on the nose should be sufficient to stop any mischief.

◆ ABOVE
Scratching is fun for the kitten, but does not do the soft furnishings much good. Provision of a scratching post and a little training should solve the problem.

◆ ABOVE
Play with your indoor cat as often as you can to ensure it gets enough exercise and attention, or its boredom could turn to destructive tendencies.

TRAINING AND LEARNED BEHAVIOUR

Switched-on, intelligent cats will soon learn to manipulate doting owners. They can also be trained to produce predictable repeatable behaviour. The degree of training depends very much on the amount of time the owner has to spend with the cat. A kitten's play is, in fact, its instinctive means of acquiring hunting and survival skills.

Although many hunting actions are instinctive, they are also learned from other cats. Solitary, hand-reared kittens do not learn to hunt.

Each kitten is an individual with a unique temperament and balance of skills. In encouraging and extending a kitten's play, you can observe the strengths and weaknesses in its temperament and skills repertoire. Observing and enhancing natural

♦ LEFT
A Bi-colour Ragdoll kitten has retrieved a toy. It may take it back to its owner for it to be thrown again.

traits is the secret behind the methods of successful animal trainers. All cats show skill at balancing and spacial awareness, but some are much better than others. A kitten may pick up a piece of crumpled paper and bring it to its owner to be thrown again. You can encourage repetition of this trick with a tasty titbit and pretty soon you will be boasting about your "retriever" cat!

You can train your cat to conform to certain household standards, using spoken commands which the cat is well able to understand and respond to.

ESTABLISHING COMMUNICATION

The first step in training is to establish communication between cat and human, and a kitten should be given a name as soon as possible. If an adult cat joins the household, it is advisable to retain its existing name even if you dislike it. If you use the cat's name repeatedly when you are attracting its attention, it will soon learn to respond. From there it is easy for the cat to learn certain command words. Repetition of the verbal message, spoken firmly in a low voice, and

♦ LEFT
Each kitten is an individual with its own strengths, weaknesses and special skills. This kitten's speciality seems to be acrobatics.

♦ RIGHT
Kittens and young cats enjoy playing hide-and-seek – as long as they are found quickly, congratulated and cuddled.

◆ LEFT
The intelligent cat helps itself to a treat.

best sofa, say no, gently but firmly, take it to the scratching post, and place its paws on the post. If the cat uses the post, give it some praise and a stroke.

USING THE CAT FLAP
Practice and encouragement is also the key to training a cat to use a cat flap. Make sure the door is at a comfortable

◆ ABOVE
To dissuade a cat from nibbling your houseplants, provide it with its own pot of cat mint. You could also try wiping the leaves of plants you want to protect with a solution of lemon juice and water.

never shouted, is the key. Avoid shouting, for this can traumatize a cat and lead to behavioural problems.

SAVING THE FURNITURE
A cat scratches a tree – or your furniture – to sharpen its claws, to mark its territory, or just for the satisfying feeling. If you want to conserve your furniture, therefore, provide your cat with a scratching post, and, as an extra incentive, rub some catnip into it. Whenever the cat begins to assault the curtains or the

◆ LEFT
A cat enjoying the companionship of its young owner. Although independent, most cats are social animals and prefer to have company.

height for your cat and that the flap swings easily. Place some tempting food on the far side of the door and gently push the cat through. Then open the flap slightly and call the cat back. Repeat a few times and the cat will soon learn to operate the flap itself.

◆ ABOVE
Here's a positive response to an owner's call. From the look of expectancy and the line of the tail, it is probably supper time.

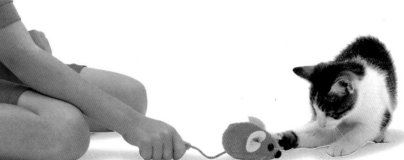

◆ LEFT
Boy and kitten play together. This is important for both – the child learns to be gentle and kind to animals. The kitten does not become lonely or bored and hones its hunting techniques.

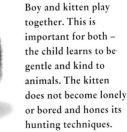

General Care and Everyday Health

A cat is a survivor, and if it is injured, will often keep going regardless, making it difficult to spot if anything is wrong. Getting to know your cat's character, giving it regular checks, and understanding a little about the strengths and weaknesses of its body will help alert you to the first signs of illness or injury. Vigilance and care will keep the vet's bills down, too. If an emergency arises, knowing how to deal with it may save your cat's life and increase its chances of a full recovery.

◆ FACING PAGE AND RIGHT
Two images of cats in prime condition. Bright eyes, alert expressions and a proudly carried tail are all indicators of sound physical and mental health.

HOW TO TELL IF YOUR CAT IS SICK

The cat's coat is a barometer of health. It reflects the quality of its diet and general condition, and should be gleaming and free from dandruff. The healthy cat's eyes are bright and clear with no discharge, redness or blinking. The tissue around them is pale pink in colour rather than red and inflamed. Nose leather is cool and slightly moist from the cat's tear ducts, and licking also keeps the nostrils moist.

Often, it is only by knowing your cat and understanding how it normally behaves, looks and reacts within its usual environment that you can tell if anything is wrong. You are the mirror of your cat's health, so do not be afraid to mention anything abnormal that you have noticed, no matter how small. The vet may only see your cat once a year and does not know its normal character or behaviour. Particular points to look out for are changes in eating or drinking habits.

SIGNS OF A SICK CAT

The first sign that your cat is not well may be a change in its normal behaviour or appearance that may only

✦ ABOVE
A Red Tabby is interested in the life going on around it, as every healthy cat should be.

✦ ABOVE
An alert expression, pricked up ears and a glossy coat suggest that this cat has a balanced diet and a healthy, contented life.

✦ LEFT
A cat playing is in character – if it were suddenly to become uninterested in playing and listless, this would be a sign to the owner of possible ill health.

WHEN TO CALL THE VET

If your cat is displaying any of the following symptoms, call the vet immediately:

- ✦ blood in vomit, urine or faeces
- ✦ excessive thirst
- ✦ swollen and tender abdomen
- ✦ high temperature
- ✦ vomiting and diarrhoea together
- ✦ bleeding from penis or vulva
- ✦ straining when it tries to pass urine
- ✦ shallow, laboured breathing
- ✦ after a road accident

be perceptible to you. If a normally friendly cat shows signs of aggression, or an outgoing animal suddenly becomes withdrawn, timid and shy, look for other signs of illness. Lack of response to being called may be due to fever or temporary deafness caused by ear mite infestation.

COAT

A stary, ungroomed look to the coat with abnormally raised fur is a general indication of ill health.

STOOLS

If you still have cause for concern, check the cat's stools: they should be firm and without extreme or pungent odour. If you have an outdoor cat, confine it if possible and provide a litter tray (pan), so that you can make this check.

Where cats have access to dustbins, diarrhoea may be caused by a stomach upset resulting from eating contaminated food, but could be a sign

UNDERSTANDING YOUR CAT'S ANATOMY

The cat's skeleton provides support and protection for the vulnerable, internal organs. The entire feline skeleton is strong but light, as befits its function as a hunter.

The coat normally comprises a dense, soft undercoat covered by coarser hairs which are known as guardhairs. The density of the fur adds further protection to the skin (epidermis) from which it grows.

Skin consists of many layers of cells. These are constantly reproducing to compensate for the loss caused by sloughing of the cells which die and are shed from the surface as scurf.

TAIL Tail bones are joined by a complex machinery of small muscles and tendons, making the tail capable of a great range of movement. This enhances balancing potential and has also developed as a barometer of the cat's emotional state.

HEAD is that of a typical predator, with a strong skull protecting the brain. It is capable of a wide range of movement due to the very flexible neck.

EYES Deep, large eye sockets facing forward protect the eyes. Binocular vision gives the depth of focus needed by a hunting animal in order to judge distances accurately.

EARS Large, cup-like outer ears collect a vast range of sound. This is helped by tiny muscles which give the ears great flexibility of movement. The inner ear assists with balance.

BACK The back muscles are well developed to allow the cat to carry heavy weights over long distances. The spinal column ranges from the closely positioned bones of the chest to the longer, heavier lumbar vertebrae which support the weight of the body organs.

PELVIS is fused to the vertebrae of the lower back, and these are also linked to the progressively smaller bones of the tail.

TEETH are those of a typical predatory carnivore – canine teeth, or fangs, for killing; incisors for gripping; heavy, sharp molars for chewing and tearing. This process is helped by a very flexible lower jaw arrangement which allows sideways movement so that the tearing process becomes very efficient.

BACK LEGS Movement is restricted to backwards and forwards only. The way in which the knee opposes the position of the elbow at the front, allows for the enormous spring which gives the cat the ability to pounce.

FRONT LEGS are capable of some rotation so that the pads can be presented to the face, for use in the washing process.

PAWS are long so that the cat actually walks on its fingers and toes which are supported by the sensitive fleshy pads. Claws are capable of being retracted.

of something more serious, especially if it is persistent. Constipation, causing the cat to strain, can also be a problem, especially if there is any blood in the stools.

EYES

If the third eyelid – the haw or nictitating (blinking) membrane – is visible, it indicates an infection or that there is a foreign body in the eye. Any signs of redness or inflammation or excessive and persistent, thick, yellowish discharge are cause for concern. If either pupil appears dilated or does not react to bright light, this needs prompt veterinary attention.

EARS

Clear wax in the ears is normal, but a dark brown waxy deposit may indicate ear mites that need veterinary treatment. Look out for seeds, such as grass seeds, too. A seed may lodge in the ear and enter the ear canal, making the cat shake and scratch its ear. The wall of the ear canal and flap (pinna) is

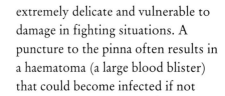

extremely delicate and vulnerable to damage in fighting situations. A puncture to the pinna often results in a haematoma (a large blood blister) that could become infected if not

treated. If the ears are very hot, the cat may be running a temperature, but before rushing to the vet, check this is not due to your cat lying in the sun or next to a radiator!

✦ ABOVE
An owner gently holds back the ear to check that there are no scratches on the pinna (the inner lining of the outer ear). Also check for dark, waxy deposits.

✦ ABOVE
As part of the regular care routine, make a random check in the fur by parting it until you can see the skin.

✦ LEFT
As in humans and other animals, the state of a cat's eyes can indicate problems elsewhere in the body. This cat's eyes are those of a radiantly healthy animal.

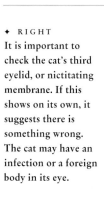

✦ RIGHT
It is important to check the cat's third eyelid, or nictitating membrane. If this shows on its own, it suggests there is something wrong. The cat may have an infection or a foreign body in its eye.

SICKNESS

Light vomiting is very often no cause for alarm. It may be due to the cat having bolted down its food too fast, a reaction to something it has caught and eaten, to grass that it has chewed to clear its system out, or a physiological response to remove hairballs. Persistent vomiting, however, especially if it contains any blood, is important, and is reason enough to check with the vet.

TEMPERATURE

A good indication that the cat has a raised temperature is if the ears feel hot. A rectal thermometer is needed in order to take a precise temperature reading, which should be 38–38.5°C (100.5–101.5°F). Unless you have been taught how to do this properly, it is best left to a professional.

PULSE

Key pulse points in a cat are located under the forearms (armpits) and back legs (groin). The pulse rate may vary between 120 and 170, depending on how active the cat has been recently. The average is 150.

REGULAR CHECK-UPS

The caring and wise owner checks the pet regularly to make sure it is in top condition. Early signs of conditions such as mite infestation or fleas will prevent more serious problems developing later. The check-up can be at a time when you are relaxing with your cat, or if it is one that needs regular grooming, as an integral part of the grooming routine. If a cat does show any signs of ill-health or

✦ ABOVE
Modern cat food does not give a cat's teeth the exercise and cleaning power that would come from hunted food. It is therefore important to check them regularly.

discomfort, you can go through the checking points described on the previous pages. Then, if you do need to take it to the vet, you can give a detailed report on anything unusual you have noticed.

FUR AND BODY

One good reason for grooming your cat regularly, even if it is a shorthair, is that you will be quickly alerted to any lumps, or signs of attack by fleas, ticks, mites or lice. If the grooming process rakes out some grit-like dirt, check further. Comb the cat over moistened absorbent paper. If the grit leaves a red stain, these are the blood-gorged faeces of fleas. If not, the cat has just been rolling in the garden.

Small, raised grey or whitish lumps indicate ticks. These can irritate the cat considerably as the tick's head is buried deep into the skin, leaving only the body visible. They should be removed as soon as possible but great care has to be taken to ensure that the head is removed as, if left behind, an abscess or sore can develop.

EARS, NOSE AND MOUTH

Check that ears are clean and free of dark waxy deposits and seeds. Even minor scratches need to be kept clean to prevent infection. Check for broken or discoloured teeth, swollen gums and bad breath, and make sure there are no lumps (enlarged glands) around the neck.

PAWS

The claws of an indoor cat need to be checked regularly in case they need clipping and to prevent them from ingrowing. Also check for any soreness or wounds on the pads.

CHOOSING A VET

✦ BELOW
If your veterinary practice operates an open-surgery system in which you simply turn up without making an appointment, there may be several other customers there before you.

Do not wait until an emergency arises before you look for a vet. It is wise to have made arrangements before you bring a new animal home. If you found the kitten locally, ask the sanctuary, home or breeder. You may be able to continue with the vet a kitten has already visited for its initial check-ups and inoculations. If the kitten is from a different area, ask friends in the neighbourhood who already own cats, or a local cat club for recommendations (addresses and telephone numbers are available from the Governing Council of the Cat Fancy in the United Kingdom, the Cat Fanciers' Association in the United States and equivalent organizations in most other countries).

WHICH VET?

Selecting the right vet for your pet is just as important as finding the right doctor for your family – but there is one great difference. While doctors only deal with one species – the human one – vets have to cope with a

wide range of different animals, from hamsters to cows. They are unlikely to be specialized in all fields, and not all will be up-to-date with feline ailments. This may be a problem if you live in a rural area, as veterinary practices may be geared to large animals such as cattle and horses. In urban areas, most surgeries are small-animal practices, devoted to the care of cats, dogs and other small domestic pets.

If you have time contact a number of different practices; telephone first if you wish to visit. Ask for a list of fees for consultation, and the cost of routine care items such as inoculations, blood tests, flea and worming products.

QUESTIONS TO ASK

Before you go, consider what you want from the vet. If you have a neutered (altered) cat that rarely goes out, you will probably have to visit the vet only once a year for the booster inoculations, so enquire about policy for routine check-ups. If your plan is to show or breed from your cat, you

✦ ABOVE
If your pet is to have an anaesthetic, the vet may advise taking it in the night before. In this way, the surgery can control food intake and the cat has time to settle down.

✦ LEFT
A cat has its annual check. This is an opportunity for comments on general condition, any necessary booster inoculations and restocking of worming and flea treatments.

✦ RIGHT
A kitten has its first check at about nine weeks. This will coincide with the first inoculations, and with pedigreed animals, will probably take place before they leave the home where they were bred.

will need to think more seriously about locating a vet who is perhaps interested in breeding, and knowledgeable about pedigreed breeds and showing. This is usually easier in a city than in a rural region.

Once you have found a practice that is cat friendly, it is worth going through a mental checklist of what you need to know.

Check opening hours. Is an appointment needed, or does the practice run on an open-surgery basis whereby you turn up unannounced between specified hours? Both can operate well in an efficient practice, but if you are working, you may need a combination of both options for maximum flexibility. You will also need to make sure that there are weekend and occasional evening surgeries.

Check that there are arrangements for emergencies around the clock. If so, will your cat be treated by one of the practice vets or a separate emergency staff? This may be significant if you have a pedigreed

✦ ABOVE RIGHT
A cat eats grass as a natural emetic – it may help to clear the system of obstructions, such as fur balls (hairballs), and provide extra vitamins.

✦ BELOW
An Asian Red Self is a picture of good health.

animal that requires special attention. Also, what is the policy regarding home visits? This may be important if you are intending to breed from your cat, in case you need help at the birth. Is the practice a veterinary hospital or does it specialize in feline medicine and surgery?

If it is a member of a national advisory organization (such as the Feline Advisory Bureau in Britain) it will be well up-to-date with all the latest health care information.

Ask about the attitude towards alternative or complementary treatments, such as homoeopathy, chiropractice and acupuncture. Look for a positive, holistic approach, as the benefits of these treatments, especially for older cats, can be substantial.

STANDARD TREATMENTS

However hardy your cat is, it runs the risk of being struck down by a killer virus infection unless it is inoculated and boosted on a regular basis. If a cat contracts one of the diseases for which preventative vaccines are available, it is very serious, for there is no treatment that can be guaranteed to save it. All a vet can do is to treat the symptoms and minimize suffering, and hope that your pet's natural immunity will fight the illness.

INOCULATIONS

In the first few days of its life, a kitten's resistance is boosted by the antibody-rich colostrum that is the mother's first milk. Although this is replaced by normal milk after the first few days, this also contains some antibodies so, as long as the kittens are feeding, the mother's immunity will pass down to them through the milk. As soon as weaning starts, this natural protection diminishes. From now on, immunity has to be built up actively by the kitten and will no longer be acquired passively from the queen. Active immunity can be built up by exposure to infections or, more safely and securely, by inoculations. Taking your cat to the vet to be inoculated is a vital part of routine care. Inoculations are given at 9–12 weeks; the kitten is then kept in for a week or two to prevent exposure to infection while the aquired immunity from the vaccine becomes effective. Inoculations subsequently need to be boosted every year. Some kittens or adult cats may feel a little under par for a few days after first inoculations or the annual booster, but it is rare for there to be any major problems.

FREEDOM FROM WORRY

Over the past 30 years, there have been enormous steps forward in the prevention and cure of feline ailments. The diseases that used to pose the greatest risk to pedigreed and non-pedigreed felines alike, are no longer a problem if the regular, recommended inoculation programme is followed.

◆ LEFT
Six-week-old kittens may be introduced to new social experiences, but three weeks before their first vaccination, they must not be exposed to other cats in the outside world.

WHICH INOCULATIONS?

Recommendations regarding vaccinations vary in different countries. In the United States, for instance, where, in urban areas, owners are often advised to keep their cats indoors, both cat flu viruses, feline infectious enteritis (feline distemper) and rabies are considered the core inoculations. Those against chlamydia, feline leukaemia virus and feline infectious peritonitis are often considered necessary only for cats likely to be exposed to risk in the outside world. However, bear in mind that your cat could escape and come into contact with one of the diseases you decided not to inoculate against. Take your vet's advice.

THE KILLERS

The most serious infections are: cat flu (viral rhinitis), which encompasses two viruses that affect the cat's upper respiratory tract; feline infectious enteritis; chlamydia; and feline leukaemia virus. Rabies should be added to the list in countries where the disease is known to exist. Although these are not the only viruses to affect the cat, these are the major viral conditions that have wrought havoc in the past among domestic cats.

Effective vaccines against cat flu and feline enteritis have been around for several years. A vaccine to treat the leukaemia virus is a more recent addition. As yet, in the United Kingdom, where rabies does not exist, the vaccine can only be administered by authorised vets to cats that are going to countries where the disease exists.

GENERAL CHECK-UP

The vet will only inoculate your cat if it is in good health, so do not take it if it is below par for any reason. At the same time as the annual booster vaccinations, ask the vet to give your cat a check-up – to look at ears, teeth, gums and general condition. With luck, this will be the only time the vet sees your cat. You can also stock up with treatments for worms and fleas.

WHAT TO DO WHEN

- ✦ 9 weeks: first vaccination
- ✦ 12 weeks: second vaccination
- ✦ 16 weeks: spaying for females
- ✦ 4–6 months: neutering (altering) for males
- ✦ 6 months: start flea treatment
- ✦ monthly (after 6 months): renew flea treatment
- ✦ every 6 months: worm treatment
- ✦ every year: booster vaccinations and check-up

NEUTERING (ALTERING)

◆ BELOW
A recently spayed female shows the shaved area where the incision was made. There is a slight possibility that the fur may grow back a different colour in this area.

Neutering, altering or desexing not only prevents reproduction but also the inconvenience of the female cat coming into heat (oestrus) or calling. In the female cat this is called spaying. In the male the operation, castration, reduces the tendency to spray and also the odour of the male cat's urine.

The operation has the effect of modifying behaviour associated with sexual desire and establishing and marking territory (see the chapter on *Behaviour and Intelligence*). The result is that the desexed cat is usually more stable and affectionate, and bonds more easily with the family. Recent work in Britain and the United States has shown that the operation in either sex can be carried out earlier than was

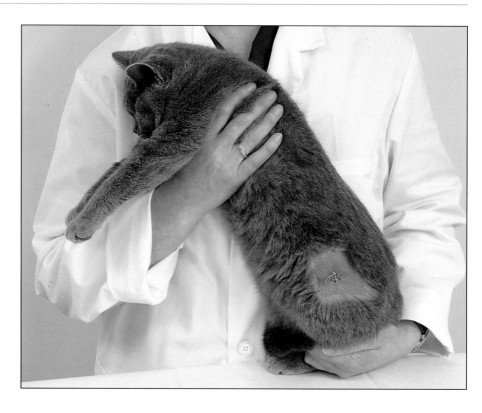

◆ BELOW
Burmillas are generally known for their good nature, but any aggressive tendencies will be further modified by the desexing process.

previously thought with no ill effects. Some rescue organizations now desex kittens before they are homed at eight to twelve weeks, but the majority of vets prefer to carry out the operation when the kitten is older, at four to six months. As both operations are carried out under a general anaesthetic, no food or water can be taken for about 12 hours beforehand. The operation cannot be reversed in either sex.

CASTRATION

The operation involves the removal, under general anaesthetic, of the cat's testes. Tiny incisions are involved and usually no stitches are necessary. Within 24 hours the cat is usually back to normal. Both kittens and adult cats can be castrated. If you consider giving a home to a stray tom, castration will ensure that he settles quickly, is less aggressive, less territorial and less

likely to roam. This also means that he is less likely to pick up infections and be involved in traffic accidents.

SPAYING

Female cats do not miss motherhood, and gain security, as they no longer have the urge to roam when coming into heat or calling, and are no longer targeted by unneutered (unaltered) male cats. Spaying or altering the female cat is more complicated than in the male. The cat's ovaries (where the eggs are produced) and womb (uterus) are removed to prevent her coming into heat. She should not be on heat at the time of the operation. A small area of fur is shaved on the abdomen and an incision made, which has to be stitched afterwards. The spayed female cat is usually back to normal quickly but will appreciate care, warmth and light meals for about a week, until the stitches are taken out.

HOW LONG WILL YOUR CAT LIVE?

◆ BELOW
A Blue Bi-colour Persian father seems to contemplate the continuation of his pedigreed line with one of his kittens.

From about the age of ten to twelve years, a cat may begin to show signs of growing old. This may not be immediately apparent as the slowing down process is very gradual. Internal organs may not work as well as they once did and joints may become that little bit stiffer. Over time the cat seems to restrict its activities, is far less playful and becomes a creature of sedentary habits. Particular health conditions such as diabetes or arthritis require constant supervision and medical intervention.

The oldest cat recorded was a tabby called Puss who was said to have lived for 36 years. The oldest pedigreed cat on record is Sukoo, a Siamese who died in 1989, at the age of 31 years. These are exceptional ages, however. Most cats live for about 14–16 years and a few may reach 20 years. With pedigreed cats there is a very accurate means of determining age, as they are normally registered with an exact date of birth and registration number.

When you first get a 12-week-old kitten, it is very likely that its lifespan will be something between ten and fifteen years. This could mean that the cat will become a companion to your children as well as to yourself. A longer life is not unusual, in which case it may well live to see your grandchildren as well. To borrow from the dog world, a cat is for life, not just for Christmas. This has to be thoroughly understood before a kitten joins the household.

Neutered (altered) cats have a slightly longer lifespan than those which remain unneutered. This is particularly true of male cats. An unneutered (unaltered) tom will fight

◆ BELOW
A Blue Bi-colour Persian father seems to contemplate the continuation of his pedigreed line with one of his kittens.

to defend territory and the resulting injuries and infections may shorten his life. Females lead a much quieter life, and a career spent having kittens, in an environment in which her condition is well-maintained, appears to have little effect on the female's longevity.

Apart from differing nutritional requirements at various stages of its life, a cat's physical responses slow down as it gets older and joints become stiff. This not only has the effect of reducing suppleness and agility, but has implications for the daily care of the cat such as grooming.

◆ RIGHT
The start of a long relationship: this kitten will probably live long enough to be a companion for its young owner throughout her childhood and teenage years.

COPING WITH DEATH

When the end comes, it can be rapid, as though a clockwork motor has run down. Very old cats settle into a routine which reflects their capabilities. It seems important for a cat to maintain its dignity to a degree greater, even, than that of many other animals. This can be extremely difficult when the efficacy of bodily functions is being challenged by old age. A few elderly cats are distressed by the loss of vital sensory equipment through deafness or blindness. Grooming becomes difficult as flexibility is reduced, and incontinence may occur, both of which can upset the naturally fastidious cat.

Your cat may die in its sleep but this does not happen often. If, however, it is suffering from ailments that give it chronic pain or prevent it from responding to its natural instincts, you need seriously to consider how kind it is to keep it alive. A vet can end an animal's life painlessly on the request of its owner. The cat is injected with an overdose of anaesthetic which literally puts it to sleep. Many vets will allow you to be present for your pet's last moments, if you wish. Others can only advise; the

✦ ABOVE
A rather portly middle-aged cat that will have to lose some weight if it is to have a healthy and trouble-free old age.

✦ BELOW
Producing two to three litters a year has left this 10-year-old farm cat with a sagging stomach. It would be kind to have her spayed.

✦ ABOVE
A 10-year-old tabby and white that could well have several more years of contented living as long as a healthy diet is maintained and disease and infection do not strike.

owner must make the decision, except in exceptional circumstances when the vet takes responsibility. Euthanasia can be regarded as a final gift to an animal that has shared your life.

MOURNING

The natural lifespan of a cat is a fraction of human life expectancy, and yet a cat may be a day-to-day companion over a significant section of your life, such as your entire childhood. When your cat dies, you may consider burying it in the garden, in a favoured snoozing spot, for instance. If not, there are pet cemeteries where cremation or burial can be carried out.

There will inevitably be a period of mourning which may, initially at least, feel as intense as it would for a member of your human family. This is quite normal. You have lost a member of the family and a very special one. This is

the little furry body that snuggled up to you when you were feeling ill, depressed or annoyed. You will remember the rumbling purr of greeting and trust, and the times when you could not express your feelings to anyone else but the little cat that listened and soothed you into eventually finding a solution.

◆ RIGHT
Two old friends have aged in different ways. Perhaps the overweight male on the chair should give up his seat for the thin and frail female.

◆ LEFT
An 8-week-old Cream Burmese kitten with a lifetime ahead of it, lives for the moment with its toys.

◆ ABOVE RIGHT
A cat grows old with dignity and favours warm spots such as the top of the stove, but beware of the danger a hot stove may present.

◆ RIGHT
A gravestone and rose commemorate the passing of a much-loved cat.

Injuries and Ailments

Cats traditionally live longer than dogs. Twenty years is not unusual. If you provide a balanced diet, the correct inoculations and regular check-ups, there is no reason why your cat should not live a long and happy life. However, illness or injury can strike at any time, so it is important to keep an eye open for any unusual behaviour in your pet that might indicate all is not well. In most cases of injury or disease, you will need to call the vet, but much can also be done at home in the way of first aid and general nursing.

◆ FACING PAGE
An injured leg is a stressful situation for a while, but the adaptable cat will adjust until the injury has healed.

◆ ABOVE
Although this cat had to have one of its legs amputated, it is able to lead a full and active life.

HOME NURSING

A sick cat should be confined in an area that is warm and free from draughts, quiet and capable of being easily cleaned and disinfected. The first two requirements are relatively easy to fulfil, whereas the third could cause some problems. Many modern homes are carpeted throughout which makes disinfecting difficult. If there is not a separate utility room with a floor that is easily cleaned, you should consider buying a large, plastic travelling carrier which comes apart so that every part can be thoroughly cleaned.

Use a disinfectant agent recommended by your vet – it is most important to avoid any substances containing coal-tar, wood-tar, phenol, cresol and chloroxylenols. These

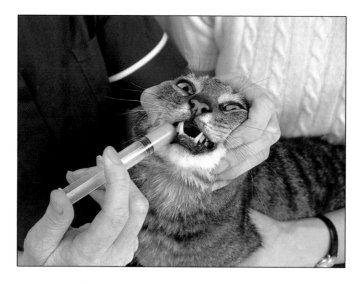

◆ LEFT
Special syringes, available from your veterinary practice and some pet shops, will help you administer medicines.

◆ BELOW
A warm, comfortable bed and plenty of tender loving care are essential when nursing a sick cat.

agents are fine for use with people but can be lethal for cats. If a condition is seriously infectious to other cats, you should set aside some old clothes and shoes to wear when handling the sick cat, and wash thoroughly afterwards. Always dispose of any used bandages or applicators promptly. Thoroughly clean up any vomit or faeces without delay and disinfect the area carefully.

BEDSIDE MANNER

You can help your cat's recovery tremendously with care, love and attention. Spend time talking quietly, maintaining appropriate physical contact without being overwhelming, and ensuring that its bodily needs are catered for. The cat may not be able to do anything for itself and, therefore, feeding, watering, grooming and assisting with toilet procedures become your responsibility. While this is very time-consuming, the bond you have already achieved with your cat will grow even stronger. The veterinary nurses (technicians) will help if you need advice on the various techniques involved with the grooming, feeding and toileting of a sick cat.

ADMINISTERING MEDICINES

Your vet will always give advice and instruction on how much and how often you should administer any medication your cat needs for treatment. Medicinal preparations come in several forms – liquids, pills, capsules, drops and lotions. The secret of administering any of these

successfully and with least disturbance to the animal is to have confidence in your ability to do so. However, some cats will object tooth and claw to having any foreign object forced into their mouths. If this is the case with your cat, you will need to ask someone to assist you and, if necessary, wrap the cat securely in a towel to help immobilize it.

Liquid medicines can be given using a plastic syringe obtainable from your vet or from most pet shops. After use it should be cleaned thoroughly and then stored for future use in a sterilizing agent such as one of those used for baby feeding equipment. Draw up the amount for one dose into the syringe. Holding the cat's head firmly, gently insert the syringe between the lips, at the side of the mouth. Push the plunger gently so that the cat receives the dose slowly and gradually, allowing it time to swallow. This reduces the risk of any liquid going into the lungs, which could cause pneumonia to set in rapidly in the case of a sick cat. Pill poppers which look like elongated syringes are available if you have

difficulty opening your cat's mouth. The pill is placed into the popper and a plunger pushes the pill to the back of the cat's tongue. Direct the instrument towards the palate rather than pressing on the tongue. Hold the cat's mouth closed and stroke its throat until it has swallowed.

DROPPING IN

Most preparations designed to be dropped into the eyes or ears are supplied with a dropper or a dropping nozzle. If not, droppers can be purchased from chemists (drugstores). Always carefully read the directions about how and when to apply the medication, before using.

The membranes of the eyes and ears are very delicate and it is most important for the cat to be held securely. Another pair of hands makes the job much easier.

With eye drops, one drop is usually sufficient. For ear drops, hold the pinna (ear flap) firmly to open the canal, and place two or three drops into the ear, then massage gently. Ear drops are usually oily and overdoing the drops results in a greasy head.

ADMINISTERING TABLETS

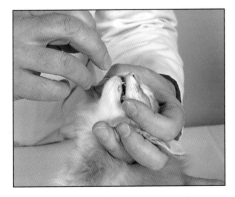

1 Hold the cat's head firmly, with your fingers on either side of the jaw, and gently pull the head back until the jaws open.

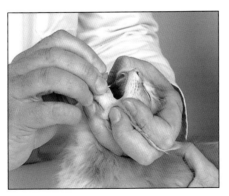

2 Talking quietly and encouragingly to your cat throughout the process, drop the pill or capsule at the back of the cat's tongue.

3 Hold the mouth closed and massage the throat until a swallowing action shows that the pill or capsule has been ingested.

ACCIDENT AND INJURY

Emergency treatment is often required for accidents within the home. Do not assume that a cat or kitten will automatically know its physical limits or be able to tell, for example, which plants are poisonous. It might well be able to fall from any angle and regain its footing, but only within certain heights. A cat falling from a balcony is just as likely to sustain serious damage as any other animal. Cats can be as vulnerable to accidents as children, and you should keep a constant eye on safety in your home.

It is valuable to know what on-the-spot treatment you can give before the cat receives veterinary attention. In extreme situations, this could make the difference between life and death. A cat that is very frightened or in pain may instinctively withdraw, and scratch and bite if handled. If this

✦ LEFT
A cat is so intent on stalking a moving leaf or insect that it may end up on a branch that cannot support its weight and fall.

happens, talk calmly and keep the cat as warm, comfortable and confined as possible until professional help is available. As with any emergency, the first rule is not to panic and the second is to rely on your common sense. However inexperienced, you will learn by careful observation to recognize the real emergency. Prompt first aid is all that is needed, but if you are in the least doubt about the seriousness of any condition, seek professional help immediately. All veterinary practices have to offer a 24-hour emergency service. Phone the surgery number first to check for any special emergency arrangements, or at least to give the surgery advance warning of your imminent arrival.

A cardboard box is a good carrier in an emergency; if an injured cat is placed on a board serving as a stretcher, it could easily fall off. Keep the cat warm by covering with a blanket and call the vet immediately. Try not to panic and handle the cat as gently as possible.

THE FIRST-AID KIT

✦ sterile pads and dressings

✦ bandages: 2.5cm and 5cm (1in and 2in) widths

✦ stretch fabric adhesive strapping

✦ lint padding or cotton wool roll

✦ cotton wool balls (uncoloured)

✦ antiseptic wipes, cream and lotion (as recommended by your vet)

✦ small, blunt-ended scissors

✦ tweezers

✦ nail clippers

✦ non-prescription soothing eye drops

✦ ear cleaner

✦ liquid paraffin

✦ kaolin mixture

✦ antihistamine cream

✦ rectal thermometer

✦ water-based lubricant

✦ eye dropper

✦ 5ml (1 tsp) plastic syringe

✦ sterilizing agent

✦ Elizabethan (medical) collar

✦ surgical gloves

✦ suitable carrier or box

IMMEDIATE ACTION

What should you do in an emergency? If the cat is in a situation where further injury could occur, such as a busy road, move the animal carefully. Depending on the position of the injuries, try to grasp the cat gently by the scruff and support its weight with the other hand. Put it in a suitable box or carrier. If the cat is unconscious, take precautions against choking by clearing any blood or vomit from the mouth and pulling the tongue forward. The head should be below the body level when the cat is lying down so that any fluids can run out.

If there is severe bleeding try to stem it by putting a pressure bandage (like a tight bandage) over the wound. This works well in areas such as the limbs. Otherwise, try applying finger pressure to the wound.

CHOKING

If a cat is fighting for air and gasping for breath, wrap it in a blanket or towel to immobilize it, and try to look in the mouth to see if there is any obstruction. While someone is calling the vet, you could try to dislocate the object by shining a small torch down the gullet and pulling the object out with a pair of tweezers. Take care you are not bitten. If a sharp object has been swallowed the problem should be dealt with by a vet. If the cat swallows a length of string or thread, do not pull it out. Leave it or tie the exposed end to an improvised collar so that it is not lost on the way to the vet.

FOREIGN BODIES

If grit, seeds or other objects become lodged in a cat's eyes or ears, you may be able to use ear or eye drops or olive oil to float them out. Do not use tweezers in these areas. A cotton bud (swab) can sometimes be used gently to remove foreign bodies in the eye.

If potentially dangerous substances such as oil, paint or chemicals are spilt on a cat's coat, wash them off immediately with a dilute solution of mild detergent or soap and water. Patches of fur that are badly soiled should be cut off carefully and the area washed with soap and water.

✦ ABOVE
A cat that roams freely may have a more active and varied life, but it also runs a greater risk of accident and injury than the indoor pet.

✦ BELOW
Although cats can swim – and Turkish Van cats like this one are supposed to have a particular love of water – they will drown if enough water enters the lungs.

RESUSCITATION SITUATIONS

A completely collapsed cat which may appear dead can sometimes be resuscitated if you act swiftly. The condition most frequently occurs with a newly born kitten. It is very simple to assess if there is still a heartbeat by feeling for a pulse in the armpit. If no pulse is found it does not necessarily mean that brain death has occurred and you may still be able to resuscitate the animal by gently massaging the chest between finger and thumb and holding the head down.

HEART ATTACK

There has been a recent increase in the number of cats, especially pedigreed cats, who collapse and die of a condition called cardiomyopathy, of which there are various types. An apparently healthy cat may suddenly keel over and die. This condition is thought to run in families, but the mode of inheritance is unclear and is the subject of much research worldwide. Sometimes, in mild cases, massaging the chest between finger and thumb does help.

ELECTRIC SHOCK

A cat can sustain an electric shock as a result of chewing through electrical flexes and cords. Switch off the electricity immediately to prevent further shock. The vet's advice should be sought as severe burns to the gums and lips can result.

DROWNING

It takes very little liquid to cause drowning. All that is required is enough for the lungs to be filled so that oxygen is unable to enter the bloodstream. Patting the cat's back

HOW TO RESUSCITATE A CAT

There is no point in being squeamish if the cat's life is to be saved. A feline kiss of life is difficult to administer and will require coming into intimate oral contact with either the cat's nostrils or mouth. The instinct to save life is very strong so, for most owners, this aspect of resuscitation will not pose a problem.

1 Clear the airways of any vomit or blood and check that the tongue is pulled forward. Hold the cat's head gently backwards and blow into the nostrils. If the nostrils are restricted in some way, pinch the cat's mouth open with your fingers pressing both cheeks to create a restricted opening, take a deep breath and blow into the mouth. Do not overdo it, as a cat's lungs are very much smaller than a person's.

2 Between each breath, gently massage the chest to allow the air to trickle out, and maintain a rubbing motion on the cat's chest to try to stimulate heartbeat. Keep on with the mouth-to-mouth process until the cat can breath regularly by itself. It may be that this form of resuscitation does not work, in which case heart massage is the last option.

3 Heart massage may damage the cat. A delicate rubbing motion will just not stimulate the heart into beating so, with the cat on its side, preferably supported on a blanket or towel, press downwards firmly on the chest just behind the front leg, about once a second. In some cases, ribs have been broken in elderly animals, but the cat has survived. If this does not work, at least you know that you have done everything possible.

may be all that is needed to expel the water from the lungs, but more often drastic measures have to be employed such as swinging the cat by the hind legs in an attempt to get the liquid out. Then resuscitation can begin (*see box*).

ANIMAL BITES

The cat that roams freely outside is much more likely to come into contact with other animals than the house-bound feline. Fights over territorial rights around the home are likely. The bite of any animal, including other cats, dogs, rodents and snakes, can be dangerous, as many bacteria are carried in the mouth.

It may not be immediately obvious that your cat has been bitten. Usually a cat that has been hurt will find a quiet, secluded spot to lick its wounds, quite literally. This is the cat's own first aid, as its saliva contains a natural antiseptic. You may not discover a

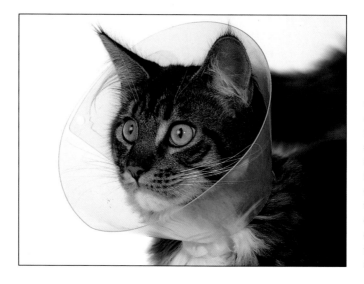

◆ LEFT
An Elizabethan (medical) collar is attached around the neck to prevent a cat from reaching back or down to lick a wound or medical dressing. The cat's owner then has to take on all grooming responsibilities.

IMMOBILIZING A CAT THAT IS FRIGHTENED OR IN PAIN

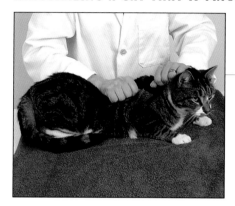

1 Place the towel on a table and the cat on the towel. Place one hand firmly on the cat's neck to control its head. Press the other firmly on the cat's back so that it lies down.

2 Keep one hand firmly on the cat's neck so that the head is under control throughout. With the other hand, bring the towel over the cat's neck, legs and body so that the legs are restrained.

3 Still keeping a firm but gentle hold on the neck, tuck the towel underneath the cat's body. Do not forget to talk to your pet in a calm voice all the time you are doing this.

hidden bite until you actually touch the site of the wound and the cat reacts. Keep the cat warm and comfortable and seek advice. Delay could mean that the cat will develop infection which will make treatment more complicated and therefore more traumatic for the cat. Wounds will need regular cleaning and bathing with a suitable antiseptic.

ABSCESSES

Any untreated puncture wound is liable to become infected and result in an abscess, which is a large, pus-filled swelling. Without treatment, the abscess may eventually burst, with a real risk of septicaemia (blood poisoning) due to toxins from the untreated abscess entering the bloodstream. The original puncture wounds soon heal, so the correct treatment will involve a trip to the vet so that the abscess can be lanced, allowing it to drain properly.

Septicaemia is serious, as it is with people. The onset is rapid and within hours a cat can be running a very high temperature. This may be followed by fits, sickness, a rapid fall of temperature to sub-normal level, collapse and death.

The greatest cause of an abscess is a bite or claw puncture from another cat. Such wounds are invariably sustained during a fight, so the most common abscess sites are around the head and neck, paws, and at the base of the tail.

SNAKE BITES

Many snake bites can be poisonous and may be followed by swelling around the wound, progressive lethargy and hyperventilation which may be accompanied by fits, followed by collapse and coma.

Once the wound site has been identified, try to apply a tourniquet above the punctures as quickly as possible (*see box*). The most likely site of a bite is on the leg, near the paws, in which case the tourniquet should be applied to the upper leg. If the wound is around the face or neck, then there is little that can be done.

When applying a tourniquet to a snake bite, the aim is to prevent the venom entering the bloodstream. However, remember that the application of a tourniquet cuts off the blood supply to the limb. The tourniquet should therefore be slackened every two to three minutes to ensure that the tissues are kept alive, even if this results in releasing a limited amount of the venom into the bloodstream. If this is not done, there is a possibility of such severe tissue damage that the limb would have to be amputated.

TO APPLY A TOURNIQUET

1 Place a loop of soft, narrow fabric, such as a stocking or a tie, around the limb, on the heart side of the wound site

2 Insert a pen, pencil, piece of cutlery or thin, strong stick between the skin and the fabric loop

3 Twist the fabric until it is tight enough to cut off the blood supply below it

4 Loosen the tourniquet for a few moments every two or three minutes and then re-tighten

5 If there is any swelling, apply a cold compress by wrapping a few ice cubes in a cloth, or (an athlete's tip) use a packet of frozen peas

6 Gently wash the affected spot with a recommended antiseptic, diluted to the manufacturer's instruction

7 Any bleeding should stop. If it does not, the tourniquet is not tight enough

8 Try to bandage the wound and take the cat to the vet as soon as possible. The wound may need stitching

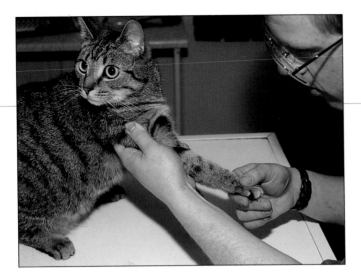

◆ BELOW
If your cat is limping, the first action to take is
to examine the paw for any foreign body, such
as glass or a thorn, which may be lodged there.

◆ LEFT
A vet feels a cat's leg
for any breakages in
the bone or internal
swellings that might
suggest a sprain or
arthritis, to find the
cause of a limp.

STINGS

It is the cat's nature to chase and pounce on insects regardless of any danger. A single wasp sting is not too alarming but remember the wasp is able to sting repeatedly. Although a cat moves fast, a wasp tangled in the cat's fur can sting a number of times before it can be brushed off. In contrast, the bee leaves the sting behind in the cat. The bee sacrifices itself when it stings, and the full quota of bee venom is left behind. Stings can occur in the mouth or throat if the insect is swallowed. This will cause swelling, and breathing and swallowing might be restricted. If external this is unpleasant and painful; internally, it can be dangerous.

The cat may show an alarming allergic reaction to a sting. If the swelling has been caused by a bee sting, the actual sting remnant may be visible. This must be removed if possible, with tweezers. Whether the sting is internal or external, the cat should have veterinary attention without delay.

As a first-aid measure, external stings by bees or wasps may be treated with a commercially available antihistamine cream or lotion. If this is not immediately available, simple home remedies can be used. Bee stings can be treated with alkaline substances such as bicarbonate of soda, whereas wasp stings respond to the application of an acid such as vinegar. The cat should not be allowed to lick at any of these substances.

POISONING

Cats are great wanderers and they may well walk through any range of toxic materials. Transferred to the mouth through washing, such substances can easily cause poisoning, and burning to contact areas. Thorough washing of paws with a mild shampoo followed by thorough rinsing will alleviate some of the pain before the vet is involved. Vomiting, lassitude, apparent blindness, convulsions and collapse are all signs of poisoning. If such symptoms occur, seek veterinary aid immediately.

It is inadvisable to try to find a way of easing the animal's suffering yourself beyond keeping the cat warm and quiet. Take a sample of the substance if you know what it is, or note the name, so that an antidote may be found quickly if available. Your vet will have access to the national poison hotline. In some countries, where stray animals are a

◆ ABOVE
Give a cat a toy to play with in the garden,
and with a bit of luck, this may distract it from
pursuing the local wildlife.

◆ ABOVE
A vital nerve was severed in this cat's foreleg. The
cause was barely visible – a tiny puncture in the
skin, perhaps from a barbed wire fence or an
animal bite. There was no improvement after a
month, and the leg was amputated, but the cat
continued to lead an active outdoor life.

BANDAGING A LEG

1 One person should hold the cat, and the other apply the dressing. Place lint over the injured area and hold it in place with your hand.

2 Use the bandage to bind the lint into position by taking it down over the paw and back up again; then wind it around the leg.

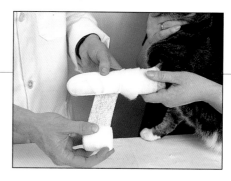

3 Continue winding the bandage firmly (but not so tight that the blood supply is cut off) and evenly around the entire length of the leg.

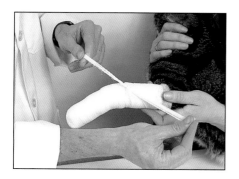

4 Split the end of the bandage leaving two ends long enough to take back around the leg in opposite directions. Tie the two ends together.

5 Tape adhesive bandage over the end of the paw and back up again as before. Wind around the entire length of the leg.

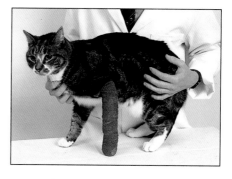

6 Keep the cat indoors for as long as the dressing is on. Change the dressing regularly as advised by the vet, or when it becomes grubby or loose.

nuisance, cats and dogs are sometimes deliberately poisoned by those who consider them pests.

If your cat returns home covered in motor oil, it is important to remove the oil from the coat immediately, as it could poison the cat's digestive system and result in kidney damage. Use a mild household detergent in lots of warm water, and seek veterinary advice if in difficulty.

SCRAPES AND BRUISES

Bruises are much less easy to detect than cuts, though you will suspect their presence if the cat becomes unusually unhappy about your touching the spot where the bruise is rooted. Similar signs are apparent if an abscess is developing on the site. As with human bruises, some come to the surface of the skin reasonably rapidly, whereas deep-seated bruising can take days to work its way out. Seek professional advice if

in doubt. Bruises and contusions respond very well to the application of *Hamamelis virginiana* (witch-hazel). Although such a remedy can be taken orally in very limited doses, it is better to prevent the cat from licking off any application by putting a medical collar around the neck.

STRAINS AND LIMPS

The cat may limp and resort to excessive washing of the injured spot. If you suspect something is amiss, first examine the paw carefully to see if there is a splinter or thorn in it, and remove it with tweezers if possible. Disinfect the area and keep your eye on the cat. Confine the cat indoors, and if there is no improvement, ask the vet to have a look at it.

If the problem is a strain, a cat will not rest of its own accord, and continued physical activity could not only aggravate the strain but also prevent it from healing.

BURNS

Cats attracted by cooking smells may leap on to unguarded cooking areas and even into ovens, and may be scalded by spilled hot liquid. A cat may also receive appalling burns, externally and internally, if it comes into contact with any of the lethal chemicals to be found in the house and garden.

Once the skin is burned, the body institutes its own first-aid regime. Body fluids are rushed to the affected area, and a blister forms protecting the underlying tissue. Do not burst the blister as the fluid in it helps to prevent infection. You can bathe the burn with ice-cold water until all heat has been taken out of the damaged area. Call the vet.

You can also apply a sterile, dry dressing loosely over the burn to keep out infection. Do not apply greasy substances – this would be like putting butter into a hot frying pan.

VIRAL INFECTIONS

Viruses need a host body to provide the energy they need to reproduce. Not all viruses cause disease. In the cat, pathogenic (disease-producing) viruses are responsible for such serious conditions as feline enteritis, cat flu and rabies. Some viruses, such as the one responsible for enteritis, are stable and resilient, surviving for long periods, while others, such as the flu virus, are readily destroyed by common disinfectants. Some viruses produce acute disease very quickly, while others have a long incubation period, like the feline immunodeficiency virus (FIV).

Even though you are able to protect your cat from many serious viral infections by means of vaccination, it is not yet universally common veterinary practice to inoculate against rabies or feline infectious peritonitis. Both vaccines are available worldwide but not necessarily universally licensed. In the United Kingdom, for example, the rabies virus is only used on animals intended for export. If, as is predicted, quarantine regulations are lifted in Britain, vaccination is likely to become mandatory. The viral diseases that are effectively protected against by vaccination include feline enteritis and the flu viruses.

Infections are not necessarily the same as disease. Disease is any impairment of the normal functioning of the animal, and is usually, but not always, caused by infection. For example, cats will become infected with feline coronavirus, but may not show any signs of disease or illness at all. Infections are not always contagious, that is, they need not spread to other animals by contact.

CHLAMYDIA

Chlamydial organisms fall midway between viruses and bacteria (which, unlike viruses, are self-contained cells and do not need a host body) and are responsible for a disease of the upper respiratory tract in the cat, with symptoms very similar to those of cat flu. Minor outbreaks cause one or both eyes to become inflamed and to show an unpleasant discharge. More severe attacks also cause nasal discharge and a subsequent loss of smell and appetite. Chlamydia organisms are susceptible to similar antibiotics to which bacteria are sensitive. A vaccine has been available since 1991, and though the majority of cases are observed in households with pedigreed breeding stock, it is certainly known in the wider cat population.

INFLUENZA (VIRAL RHINITIS)

This is a distressing illness affecting the upper respiratory tract, which is caused by two main viruses, feline calicivirus and feline herpesvirus. Both viruses cause coughing and sneezing. Discharge from the nose and the eyes cause the cat great distress, and a rasping soreness in the throat discourages eating or drinking. Feline calicivirus often causes serious ulceration of nose, mouth and tongue. Feline herpesvirus may cause the nose, windpipe and lungs to become

✦ ABOVE
The acute conjunctivitis and corneal opacity in one of this Blue Tonkinese kitten's eyes are symptoms of chlamydia, a respiratory disease.

◆ RIGHT
A Lilac Cream Burmese-cross kitten has severe conjunctivitis – a symptom of feline flu.

seriously inflamed, resulting in a lot of coughing and sneezing. The cat that is kept warm and comfortable and is encouraged to eat and drink stands the greatest chance of survival. Antibiotics reduce the risk of secondary infections but do not attack the primary viruses. Effective vaccination against cat flu is the best preventative course.

FELINE INFECTIOUS ENTERITIS

This disease, a cat version of the distemper that infects dogs, is also known as feline panleukopaenia and feline parvovirus. The first symptom of this sometimes astonishingly rapid killer virus is usually a very high fever. The virus attacks rapidly dividing cells, particularly in the bowel. Symptoms may include unusually depressed behaviour, loss of appetite, vomiting, and a desire to drink but an inability to do so. Diarrhoea is not always present. Rapid dehydration sets in followed by coma and death. The rapidity of the disease, after its short incubation period, can mean that death occurs two or three days after vomiting starts or even within 24 hours. The disease is highly infectious. Treatment is supportive: keep the cat warm and free from draughts, and administer re-hydration therapy as advised by the vet.

FELINE LEUKAEMIA VIRUS (FeLV)

This virus first came to the notice of breeders of pedigreed cats in the early 1970s. Originally there were fears that it could be a health hazard to humans, particularly children. This is most certainly not the case – the virus cannot be transmitted except to another cat. To begin with, it was thought that particular pedigreed

breeds were more prone to the disease than other cats, but this has not been proven. All cats may be similarly and as rapidly affected when they come into contact with the virus. It was found that a far larger percentage of the normal domestic cat population was affected than expected, and many of these cats lived into old age. This made a nonsense of early veterinary advice that cats with feline leukaemia virus should be euthanased immediately.

Some cats do succumb rapidly to other serious and untreatable infections as the virus wreaks havoc with the cat's immune system, while others are less affected. If one cat is affected within a multi-cat household, it should be removed, as the virus is easily transmitted through saliva or blood. The infected animal could be moved to a single-cat household where it may live out its life without infecting others. Testing for the virus

is through a blood sample. It is possible for a cat to test positive and then, two weeks later, to show a negative result, only having had a passing contact with the virus. For some years, a vaccine countering this disease has been available in the United States, and since 1992, FeLV licences have been available in the United Kingdom.

Most breeders have all their animals, whether elderly, neutered (altered) or young breeding cats, regularly tested to show that they are FeLV-negative. Females are only mated to males which also regularly test negative, so that the kittens are automatically negative too. They can then be protected by vaccination. Many breeders leave this to the new owners. If there are other cats in your home, it should be done immediately. If the kitten is the only pet, inoculation may be left until it is a little older.

◆ RIGHT
Feline infectious peritonitis is carried in the saliva and the faeces. It is essential to disinfect litter trays (pans) regularly. The illness can strike at any age.

FELINE IMMUNODEFICIENCY VIRUS (FIV)

This is a similar virus to the human immunodeficiency virus (HIV) which may lead eventually to acquired immunodeficiency syndrome (AIDS). The feline version cannot be passed on to a human being, and HIV cannot be passed on to a cat.

FIV progressively breaks down the cat's immune system. This leads to the cat becoming increasingly vulnerable to infections. Despite periods of apparently normal health, the cat slowly succumbs to minor illnesses which become untreatable. No vaccination exists at present.

FELINE INFECTIOUS PERITONITIS (FIP)

The virus that causes this disease is found in many cats and normally only occasionally causes a transient diarrhoea. However, in about 10 per cent of infected cats, the virus leaves the intestines, invades the blood

vessels and causes a severe inflammation – which is feline infectious peritonitis. The membrane which lines the abdominal cavity is called the peritoneum, and once the

◆ ABOVE
A cat is spending a night in the vet's pens before surgery in the morning.

blood vessels of this have become infected and inflamed, treatment is extremely difficult, and often unsuccessful. As yet no definitive pattern to the progression of illness has emerged. The disease can be triggered in almost all age groups, even young kittens are susceptible.

Wet FIP is the most common form of the disease. Onset is usually rapid. Just 24 hours after appearing lively, playful, of good appetite and with normal litter-tray (pan) motions, a wet FIP sufferer will be lethargic, will not want to eat very much and will have sickness and diarrhoea. The coat is often staring and dull, but the most dramatic sign is the grossly distended fluid-filled abdomen. There is no cure. Euthanasia is the only option.

Dry FIP is a less common form of the disease and is often difficult to diagnose. The signs are similar to those of other illnesses. Terminally, the cat may have jaundice and show symptoms akin to cat flu, physical disorientation, blindness due to haemorrhages in the eyes and, finally, fits.

The presence of the virus is detected by antibody tests. Cats which show none are designated nil titre count. Over 80 per cent of show cats are seropositive, showing they have had some contact with the disease. Some cat breeders advertise their animals as nil (free) status, but most vets regard a low count as being relatively normal. Many cats, even with a very high titre count may seem normal. It is thought that a stressful situation, such as the introduction of a new cat into the household or a long journey, may tip a cat with a pre-existing viral condition into the full-blown illness.

FIP does not seem to be as infectious as was at first thought. The virus is carried in the cat's saliva and the faeces. Litter trays (pans) should be disinfected regularly and frequently using an agent recommended by your vet. Keeping cats in small, easily managed colonies, observing strict hygiene and, above all, maintaining a stress-free environment should help reduce the possibility of the disease flaring up. The virus is not able to survive very long outside the host and is very susceptible to disinfection agents. There is no vaccination available at present in the United Kingdom although it is available in some European countries.

RABIES

All mammals, including humans, are susceptible to rabies, and the bite of an infected animal is dangerous. Once infected, a cat may show signs of a radical alteration of appetite and voice, with unexpected aggressive

behaviour. An inability to drink gives rabies its other name, hydrophobia – fear of water. Other signs follow – foaming at the mouth, swelling of the skull, jaw paralysis and disorientation.

Treatment is possible but must be started promptly after being bitten by a suspected animal. There is very little hope of any infected mammal surviving once the long incubation period of the disease has passed and symptoms have begun to show. Several countries are rabies-free, including the United Kingdom due to rigorous import regulations. Vaccination is available and standard in countries where rabies exists but, at present, in Britain it is only obtainable for animals that are to be exported.

FELINE SPONGIFORM ENCEPHALOPATHY

This disease is caused by a sub-viral protein that is capable of reproducing itself. It is similar to the bovine form (BSE) that has occurred in the United Kingdom, but not elsewhere. The disease seems to be invariably fatal in cats, and is not diagnosable prior to death. It seems to have been transmitted to cats as a result of eating meat from cattle infected with BSE or sheep with scrapie. The cat develops abnormal behaviour, including failure to groom, and often drools with muscle tremors and an abnormal head posture. However, positive diagnosis is only possible on post-mortem examination.

◆ LEFT
One of the early signs of the feline form of BSE is a disinterest in grooming.

PARASITES

Being aware of the problems and facts about parasites is the first step in prevention. Routine care of any cat or kitten must include checking that the fur and skin are kept free from all parasites.

A parasite is an animal or plant that takes food and protection from a host animal or plant. It survives to the detriment of its host, causing loss of condition, and sometimes death. In some cases, such as ringworm, the parasitic condition of a host cat can be passed on to the humans it lives with.

Preparations to eradicate external parasites such as fleas, ticks, lice, mites and ringworm, as well as internal parasites including worms, are easily available. Ask veterinary advice, follow

◆ ABOVE
A cat is having its regular check for fleas, lice, and ticks. The check-up can be part of a weekly grooming routine.

◆ RIGHT
Excessive scratching may indicate that fleas or lice are present.

instructions carefully, and stick to a strict cleaning regime, and parasites should not be a problem.

FLEAS

The cat with fleas may scratch obsessively, particularly around the neck, and may groom the base of the spine vigorously and spontaneously. It may also worry at the entire length of the spine. Using the tips of the fingers and nails, groom the cat behind the ears, the neck, spine and base of the tail. If this reveals dark, chocolate-brown grit, put these on a damp tissue. If red leaches from them, they are flea droppings, which are largely made up of dried blood.

In severe infestations or where the cat is actually allergic to substances produced by the flea in its bite, patches of scabby skin may be found with the scabs breaking off to reveal sore-looking, slightly weeping patches. This clears up rapidly with the eradication of the fleas.

Fleas move very fast through the fur of the cat and are difficult to catch even if seen. A cat can be attacked by the cat flea, the dog flea and the human flea. They all lay their eggs in the cat's fur; many will drop out and hatch into larvae in cracks in the floorboards, in the weave of fabrics and in carpets. The larvae develop into fleas that immediately feed from any host that may wander by. A flea can live, with periods of feeding and resting, for up to two years, but two to six months is the norm.

Many anti-parasitic preparations, including powders, shampoos and sprays are available from pet stores, supermarkets and veterinary practices. With heavy infestations, both the cat and the environment have to be treated. Long-acting sprays are probably the most effective for the environment. For the cat, one of the easiest and most effective methods is an insecticide that is applied to a small area on the cat's neck. This spot application gives protection to the whole body for a month.

Modern parasiticides are very safe and some are available that can be applied to very young kittens. Your vet will advise on the most appropriate products for young cats.

TICKS

Ticks, like fleas, are blood suckers. However, unlike fleas, they live permanently on the cat. This parasite is normally rural in distribution, but the hedgehog tick is common in urban areas. The tick burrows its head into the host animal's skin, and gorges itself on blood. It can sometimes reach the size of a haricot bean, then drop off to complete its life cycle with no further damage to the cat. However, it could move on to other animals in the home. Removal of a tick requires

precision, to avoid the head parts remaining buried in the skin. The cat itself may be irritated by the tick's burrowing and knock it off, leaving its head behind. This usually sets up chronic infection followed by an abscess or sore which is difficult to heal. A vet can use substances to relax the tick's hold before removing it. A home equivalent is surgical alcohol (or any form of alcoholic spirit). The whole tick is then carefully removed with tweezers or a custom-made tick remover (available from pet stores).

Tick bites can be responsible for a bacterial disease called Lyme disease. This occurs in Britain, but is more widespread in the United States. Symptoms include a reluctance to jump followed by acute and recurring lameness, a raised temperature, lethargy and swollen lymph nodes, particularly around the head and

limbs. Blood tests confirm the cause, and treatment is a four to six week course of antibiotics. Lyme disease should not occur if ticks are prevented. Most flea preparations also prevent tick infestation.

LICE

Fortunately, lice infestation is uncommon on cats, but poor condition and extremes of age make individuals susceptible. There are three types of louse which are known to occur on cats, one blood-sucking, and two which bite. Telltale signs are some scratching, usually not very excessive, combined with dry skin which shows an unusual increase of scurf or dandruff. The lice may be seen quite easily with the naked eye. The eggs, or nits, are laid directly on the lower third of the hair and seem to be glued in place. Anti-flea preparations are effective.

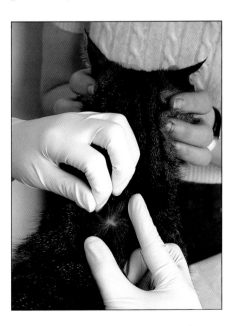 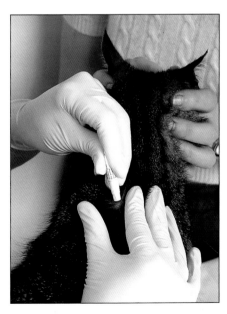

♦ ABOVE, LEFT AND RIGHT
As a preventative measure against fleas and lice, apply an anti-parasite insecticide once a month. Part the fur on the back of the neck and squeeze on the required amount of medication.

MITES

Four groups of mites affect the cat's skin and ears. The harvest mite appears in the autumn (fall). The cat is affected by the larvae which tend to settle in areas where the fur is thin, such as between the toes, on the underbelly, in the groin and around the lips and nose.

The orange larvae are just about visible to the naked eye. They set up irritation which the cat vigorously attacks with teeth and claws, thus creating more irritation. The sores which develop are round, damp and surrounded by scabby skin. Mite infestation is highly contagious and treated with insecticidal preparations.

The ear mite is commonly transmitted from cat to cat. Irritation is sometimes severe; the cat shakes its head, holds the ears almost flat, and scratches furiously. This often leads to secondary infections arising from self-inflicted trauma. Evidence of ear mites is a dark brown tarry substance

in the ears. Because of the ear's delicacy, it is wise to ask your vet to carry out initial treatment. The owner can then cleanse the ear gently.

Cheyletiella mites cause a condition known as "walking dandruff", and are less common. They often seem to cause little irritation to the cat though

there may be more scratching and grooming than usual. Excessive dandruff is the usual sign. The mite normally lives on the wild rabbit and can also affect people (rashes appear on chest, stomach and arms). Treatment is with parasiticides – for both cat and human!

One fortunately rare form of mange is caused by a burrowing mite. It is usually found around the head starting at the base of the ear. There is severe irritation, hair loss and general lack of condition. Blood poisoning can occur in severe cases. Antibiotic treatment is necessary for any secondary infections, while the actual skin damage is treated with the use of parasiticidal preparations.

RINGWORM

Ringworm is caused by a fungus, and can affect humans, especially children. The name comes from the shape of the lesions seen on the skin in humans, which are circular, red, scaly and very itchy. In the cat, particularly the

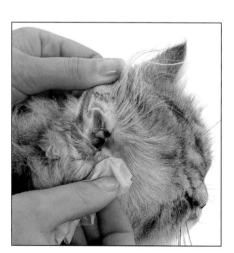

◆ ABOVE
Regular checking and cleaning at grooming time will keep mite infestations at bay.

◆ RIGHT
A vet checks for ear mites as part of the routine examination.

Persian, often all that is seen are tiny pimples and scurf on the skin. (Nevertheless, these cats can still be highly contagious.) At worst, moist, pink sores spread outwards. The fungal parasite lives on the hair and not on the skin, and causes the hair to break off. Ringworm can affect animals that are not in top condition, or that are young, and can be a major problem in longhaired show cats.

Diagnosis is initially by the use of special filtered light (Wood's Light), when about 65 per cent of cases will fluoresce. Laboratory tests are more reliable but take longer. The eradication process is long and tedious. The animals are treated with fungicides, both in the form of baths and external applications, and also tablets. The entire environment, human and animal, has to be carefully cleansed to eradicate all spores. There is no simple answer to the problem. Professional advice on procedure must be taken and, if necessary, the local environmental health department consulted. In the United States and in the United Kingdom, research is aimed at improving diagnostic tests as well as treatments. Considerable headway has been made in the production of a vaccine, but at present only cuts down treatment time.

MAGGOTS

Flies may be attracted to animals by the presence of discharge from wounds, or diarrhoea, and lay their eggs in the fur. Fly strike, as this situation is known, is particularly common in cats in poor condition, such as those in feral colonies. The maggots burrow into the skin and form tunnels which can run for considerable distances. Toxins produced to aid burrowing are absorbed by the cat and cause toxaemia (blood poisoning). If you find maggot infestation on your cat, clean it as thoroughly as possible using soap and water and contact the vet without delay.

BRONCHITIS

Infectious bronchitis is sometimes caused by a parasitic bacterium that lodges in the respiratory tract of animals. The parasite itself does not normally cause disease, but certain strains of the parasite do cause bronchitis. In a dog, this may appear as kennel cough. A cat on the other hand may cough and sneeze, with or without running nose and eyes. Normally, the disease is self-limiting. However, in very young or elderly cats, or those with other debilitating diseases, it can be persistent and troublesome to clear. The organism is sensitive to several antibiotics.

✦ BELOW LEFT
Thinning and bald patches on the hind leg of a Blue Burmese could be signs of ringworm.

✦ BELOW RIGHT
The mark on the head of this Lilac Tonkinese kitten is confirmed as ringworm. The fungal parasites live on the hair, and not on the skin, causing the hair to break.

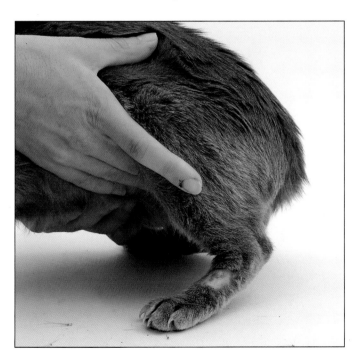

WORMS

The cat is affected by two groups of internal, parasitic worm – roundworms and tapeworms. Effective worm treatments are available, without prescription, from pet stores and supermarkets. However, experience has shown that these may be difficult to administer with total accuracy. Routine worming treatments – and advice – are best obtained from your vet. Worming preparations which give multiple protection to the cat are now available either as tablets or injections. Regular, correctly spaced treatments will keep your cat worm-free. These are often supplied at the same time as the annual booster vaccination, but may need to be given every six months.

ROUNDWORMS

Roundworms include ascarids, hookworms and lungworms. Infestations are difficult to spot unless the attack is severe, in which case, especially with ascarids, a ball of living worms may be voided. If you suspect infestation, you will probably need to take a faecal sample to the vet for accurate identification. Ascarids and hookworms live in the small intestine. They have very similar life cycles but whereas the ascarids are free-floating and feed on food in the process of digestion, the hookworms attach themselves to the lining of the intestine and suck blood. Symptoms are, therefore, slightly different. In a severe ascarid infestation, the cat will have diarrhoea, the coat will be lank, and the cat will generally look uncomfortable. Often the belly is distended ("pot belly").

The main symptom of hookworm infestation is anaemia, which in a cat is most obvious on its nose leather and gums. The gums appear excessively pale, almost white. There is a general

◆ LEFT
A vet checks gum and tongue colour for any undue paleness that could indicate anaemia and possible hookworm infestation.

lack of energy and the cat may become very thin.

The intermediate host of the lungworm is the slug or snail, which could be eaten by a cat. However, it is more likely that they will be eaten first by birds or rodents and the infective larvae reach the cat through eating them. Nevertheless, infestation is quite rare. After a complicated journey through the cat's intestine and lymph nodes, the larvae become adult worms, which eventually enter the lungs via the bloodstream. As a result, respiratory symptoms occur, similar to bronchitis or pneumonia.

TAPEWORMS

Tapeworm diagnosis is relatively easy. Segments of tapeworm containing eggs are shed and attach themselves to the fur around the anus. They look like grains of rice. Tapeworms require intermediate hosts and the flea fulfils this role in relation to the most common tapeworm to affect the cat. Flea control is therefore important. Flea larvae eat the secreted tapeworm segments that contain the eggs. The infective stage of the tapeworm is reached as the adult flea preys on the cat for a blood meal. If the cat catches and swallows the flea, as it may do

while grooming, the process is completed. The infective stage of the second most common tapeworm to affect cats develops in the livers of small rodents. The infected livers and other intestinal parts will almost certainly be consumed by a cat, if it catches one of these animals.

The way to prevent infestation by tapeworms is to eradicate fleas, and discourage your cat from hunting. Both may be impossible targets, but although tapeworms continue to be a problem, their presence does not seem to affect cats much beyond diarrhoea in the case of very heavy infestation.

♦ RIGHT
The abdomen of a cat being palpated; a distended belly may indicate roundworm infestation.

Keep an eye open for roving cats using your
garden as a toileting area. Your animals may be
free of diseases such as toxoplasmosis, but
visitors may not be.

TOXOPLASMOSIS

Toxoplasmosis is caused by
microscopic organisms called coccidia.
The organisms can infect humans,
although symptoms of illness are
rarely felt. If a pregnant woman is
infected, however, the foetus may be
affected, resulting in spontaneous
abortion or brain damage to the baby.
The disease may not even affect the
cat in any recognizable form, although
it may cause a chest infection in
young cats. In older cats there may be
gross loss of condition, digestive
disorders and anaemia. Eye problems
are not uncommon.

The immature egg of the parasite
is passed in the cat's faeces, so that
potential contact with any faecal
matter when changing and cleaning
litter trays (pans) must be countered
by a rigid routine of hygiene. Oocysts
passed by the cat with toxoplasmosis
take at least 24 hours to become
infective, so litter trays (pans) must
be changed as soon as possible after
use and rubber gloves worn.

Small children should be kept away
from litter trays (pans) at all times.
You should also frequently clear away
the faeces of any neighbourhood
cats that visit your garden and use
it as a toileting area.

AREAS AFFECTED

◆ BELOW
A Silver Tabby kitten's runny eyes and nose are probably symptoms of a viral infection.

EYES

Conjunctivitis is relatively common in the cat and can vary from a relatively mild infection often called "gum eye" by cat breeders to more serious conditions such as that caused by the chlamydia organism.

Gum eye is mostly seen in kittens just after their eyes have opened at about seven to ten days, up until the age of about three weeks. The eyes appear to be firmly glued together with a discharge and this may be due to a mild viral infection. Usually, the mother cat will wash the eyes open, but sometimes you will have to help her. To do this, bathe the kitten's eye(s) with a sterile pad soaked in cold water. Always work from the corner of the eye nearest the nose outwards. Should the gum eye persist over a couple of days, seek professional advice.

EARS

A blood blister called a haematoma can occur on the ear flap (pinna) due to excessive shaking and rubbing caused by irritation. Without skilled treatment, a deformed pinna will result in cauliflower ear.

NOSE

Nasal discharges are usually due to viral infections like cat flu and should be treated by the vet. Certain breeds of cat (Persians, in particular) have restricted nostrils, and the flattening, or foreshortening, of the face causes kinking of the tear duct. The cat will probably always have eye and nasal discharges that have to be constantly attended to by the owner. Rarely, a cat may show an asthmatic condition, having become allergic to

one or more of the thousands of substances it encounters each day. Again, your vet should be able to diagnose and may even pinpoint the allergen. Long-term treatment may be necessary.

CHEST AND LUNGS

Inflammation of the fine membrane that covers the lungs and inside of the chest cavity is called pleurisy. Cats may have fluid in their chests for various reasons, ranging from heart failure to injuries. Usually, the fluid is sterile, but it may become infected with certain bacteria, either blood-borne or from a bite or wound. Breathing becomes increasingly difficult, and any sudden exercise results in panting and a wide-eyed, very distressed appearance. The condition needs urgent veterinary attention, and despite chest drains and antibiotic treatment, many cats do not respond, and die of the condition known as pyothorax.

SKIN

Cats can sometimes develop a type of acne, in which blackheads appear on the chin. These are caused by excessive production and secretion of

◆ RIGHT
A young owner tries
to entice her cat to
come out of the
carrier on its annual
trip to the vet.

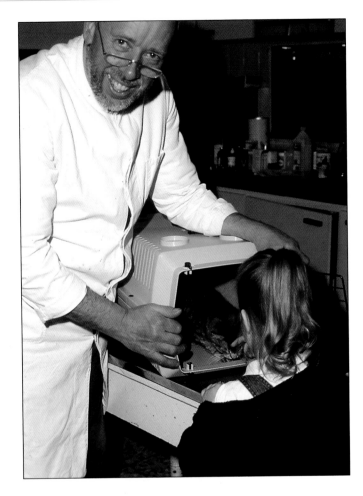

◆ BELOW LEFT
Checking mouth,
gums and teeth is a
vital part of the
annual check-up.

◆ BELOW RIGHT
The vet uses an
ophthalmoscope
to check the
cat's eyes.

sebum, which lubricates the hair. The pores through which the sebum is released may become blocked. When it occurs on the top of the tail it is known as "stud tail". Both conditions should be treated with antibiotics and anti-inflammatory drugs. If your cat has a predisposition for these conditions, keep both areas scrupulously clean to prevent recurrence, and if in any doubt, consult the vet.

Even the best groomed cat can be affected by dandruff. When it strikes, even a shorthaired cat needs to be bathed and a conditioning agent used. If the scurf persists despite your best efforts, there may be something actually wrong with the skin itself.

DIGESTIVE SYSTEM

Constipation and diarrhoea often occur during the life of any otherwise healthy cat. There are

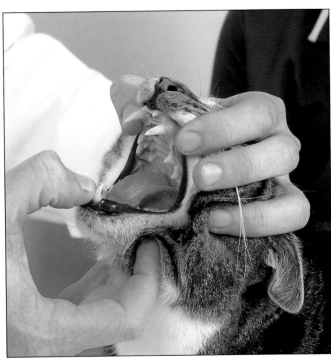

◆ ABOVE
The vet palpates (feels) the cat's abdomen to make sure that it is neither swollen nor tender, and also the glands around the neck and top of the legs to make sure they are not enlarged.

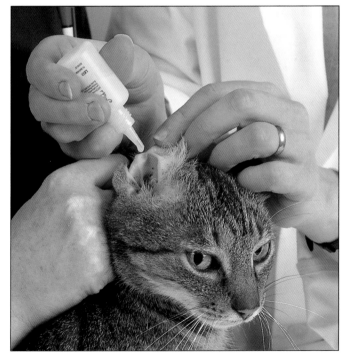

◆ RIGHT
The vet administers ear drops to a cat with a sore ear. The ears are very delicate, so it is always preferable for the vet to check them initially if you think there is a problem.

many reasons why a cat becomes constipated. Fur balls (hairballs) are a usual cause, but sometimes a diet with insufficient bulk or roughage (see the chapter *Nutrition and Feeding*) may be the problem. Introduce some bran or other cereal into the diet, or add a little liquid paraffin to the food. If the condition persists, take the cat to the vet. It may indicate a more serious condition, such as megacolon. If too much liquid paraffin is used, the cat will have diarrhoea.

There are feline preparations on the market, but home-made remedies are often just as effective. These involve a mild diet of bland food which does not upset the system. Try feeding the cat cooked white meat and white fish bulked out with simple boiled rice or pasta. Some cats adore natural yogurt. Another remedy is to sprinkle dehydrated potato granules on the food – it may seem unorthodox, but it works.

With both constipation and diarrhoea, the anal glands, which are situated on either side of the anal opening, may become blocked, infected and swell up. Clearing them out can be done at home, but it is not pleasant and does require some skill, so it is probably better left to a professional.

In addition to being uncomfortable, excessive diarrhoea or straining can cause a condition called anal prolapse. This can easily be recognized – a small section of the bowel protrudes through the anal opening. Do not do anything about this yourself; a vet must immediately put this back into its proper place, possibly with a stitch or two to secure it.

THE BREEDS

CAT BREEDS AND VARIETIES

Cats have lived with humans throughout most of civilization, but it is only in the last hundred years or so that they have been specifically selected and mated to produce distinct breeds. Unlike dogs, which have evolved over thousands of years and have been bred for almost as long for hunting – with correspondingly wide

Chocolate Tabby Persian

differences in size, shape and character – domestic cat breeds cover a much narrower range of size and conformation, coat type and other characteristics.

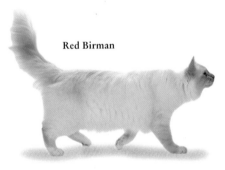

Red Birman

WHAT IS A PEDIGREE?
For a cat to be described as a pedigree simply means that its parents have been known and traced back over several generations, and that a written record has been made of this ancestry. A Persian cat of immaculate Persian ancestry could be mated to an equally purebred Siamese. The resulting kittens would be pedigrees, but they would not be classified as a new Persian/Siamese breed until consistent

and healthy litters had been produced for a number of generations (the number may be three or more, depending on the rules and standards of the registering body). Until breed status is attained, purebred cats can only be shown in an "any other variety" category, if at all.

How the many breeds are classified varies with individual cat fancies, even those in the same country. Some of the cats featured in this book are considered to be different breeds in some countries, but as colour varieties of the same breed in others. Within the Persian or Siamese breeds are established colours or coat patterns

Colourpointed Ragdoll Blue

that may have gained official recognition as breeds in their own right, such as the Black Persian or Seal Point Siamese, while the Silver-shaded Burmilla is simply a colour variety of the Burmilla breed. Some breeds or varieties have identical ancestry but have different names or classifications in Britain, continental Europe and the United States – the British Tabby Point Balinese is equivalent to the American Lynx Point Javanese, while the continental Europeans give the name Javanese to the British Angora! Others, such as the Tiffany/Tiffanie have similar names but are unrelated. Attention has been drawn to such anomalies where appropriate. If it all seems rather confusing, do not worry.

More important is to look through the following pages to see the wonderful range of cats available. We highlight the essential features and characteristics of each breed or variety, so that you can find the one that appeals to you and that is compatible with your own lifestyle and personality.

Lilac Tortie Point Balinese

THE FUR FACTOR
We have divided the cat types into Longhair (Persian), Semi-longhair, and Shorthair groups, although for judging purposes, longhairs and semi-longhairs are often combined. Longhaired cats of Persian type are more demanding as

**Spotted Tabby
Oriental Shorthair**

far as grooming is concerned – their long, soft hair needs to be regularly combed and brushed by the owner. However, all the Persians are placid, dignified animals, very glamorous, and well-suited to a predominantly or wholly indoor life. Most of the shorthaired cats, on the other hand, need little or no help with grooming unless they are going to a show. They tend to be more active and playful by nature than the Persians, and need an owner and lifestyle to match. Semi-longhaired cats cover the middle ground between these two extremes, in that their coats need some attention, but not as much as the longhairs. Their personalities depend on their ancestry. Some are longhaired versions of shorthaired breeds, such as the Somali (a semi-longhaired Abyssinian), which has the energetic and playful characteristics of its Abyssinian parentage. Norwegian Forest and Maine Coon breeds have the cold-weather coats and outdoors personalities of their tough, working domestic ancestors.

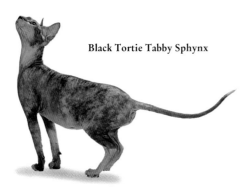

Black Tortie Tabby Sphynx

Within each grouping, the breeds and varieties are listed in order of importance – relating to how long they have been established and how well-known they are. Some, such as the Exotic Shorthair (Exotic) are strategically placed because of their relationship to other breeds – in this case, the Exotic is a shorthair of Persian type and is found at the beginning of the Shorthair section.

GENE POOL BENEFITS

The great advantage of having a pedigreed and recognized breed is that the outcome of a purebred mating is predictable. Although, depending on the make-up of the ancestral gene pool, there may be colour variations within a litter, the type will be consistent. If you decide to breed from your Maine Coon Cat, you will have Maine Coon kittens. The outcome of a domestic non-pedigreed mating is more of a lottery. The individual breeds and varieties are described according to the ideal standards of perfection set by the various cat fancies. Again, these vary from country to country. An American cat fancy, for example, may prefer a tortoiseshell to have well-defined patches of colour, whereas a European equivalent may like the colours to mingle. Such details are important if you wish to show your cat successfully, and to know what the ideal is may help you select a kitten from a litter. However, many a purebred cat falls short of the official view of perfection, but may still have much of the beauty, grace and temperament of its ancestral heritage.

The Longhair Group

The fur of longhair cats can be up to ten times longer than that of a shorthair.
Most pedigreed longhair cats are the various types of Persian. They were probably
the result of mating early types of Angora cats from Ankara in Turkey with the
original Persian cats from what is now Iran. The longhair coat has an underlying
layer of soft hairs topped by longer, coarser guardhairs. Although many longhairs
are fastidious about their grooming, they need extra help from their owner on a
daily basis, even if they are not going to be entered for shows. Another
consideration for potential owners is that longhairs tend to moult all year round,
leaving fur on carpets and furniture. A contented, well-cared-for longhair cat,
however, will bring a glamorous and dignified feline presence into your life.

◆ FACING PAGE
**A Supreme Grand Champion displays
all the glamour and distinctive
features of the classic longhaired
pedigree. Champion Rosjoy Rambo is
a Cream Colourpoint Persian that
won the overall best cat award in
Britain's Supreme Cat Show.**

◆ LEFT
The Tortoiseshell and White
Persian shows off its voluptuous
longhaired coat.

THE PERSIAN CAT

All Persian cats – known officially as Longhair Persian type – have the same basic physical shape and conformation. Their faces are flat with short noses and small ears. Their bodies are broad-chested with sturdy legs and large paws, and they all have a soft, thick fur coat with a distinctive ruff around the neck, and a full, low-slung tail. Persian longhairs come in many different colours and patterns. In some countries, such as the United States, the colour variations are considered as varieties of the same breed, but in Britain, each different colour is listed as a separate breed. Persian cats are among the longest-known pedigreed cats. Longhaired variations of wild species may have spontaneously occurred in colder regions in the heart of Asia, and then gradually become established with subsequent interbreeding. The ancestors of today's Persians were probably stocky, longhaired grey cats brought to Europe from Persia (now Iran) in the 1600s and silken-haired white Angora cats from Turkey (a different type from the modern Angora breed). Today, there are over 60 different colour variations of the Longhair Persian type.

✦ ABOVE
The Red Colourpoint is one of the newer, patterned varieties of Persian cat, but it has the voluptuous fur and cobby body, the short nose and small ears of the type.

BLACK PERSIAN

Black Self Persians are thought to be one of the earliest Persian breeds to have been officially recognized as long ago as the 1600s. Today, however, they are not at all common. The show standard insists on a solid, dense coal-black coat, with no hint of rustiness, shading, markings or white hairs. Kittens often show some grey or rusting, and if this continues beyond six to eight months, it is not considered acceptable. To maintain its lustrous black coat, the cat needs to be kept in cool, dry surroundings free from direct light. A damp atmosphere and bright sunlight seem to fade the black – one breeder retired her show cat so that it could enjoy the sunshine. Like many Persians, the Blacks are affectionate and dignified, although they have a reputation for being more playful than the White Persian.

BREED BOX	
Coat	thick, lustrous; full frill at neck and shoulders
Eyes	copper or deep orange; rims black
Other features	nose leather and paw pads black
Grooming	demanding; thorough, daily
Temperament	placid

✦ ABOVE
A Black kitten shows great promise as a future show cat. Even though a certain amount of rustiness is accepted in kittens, this youngster already has a superb dense black coat.

✦ LEFT
A fully mature Black Persian with a superb coat of solid colour, of the right density and length, and striking, deep copper eyes.

WHITE

The White Persian owes its purity of coat colour to the native Angora cat from Turkey. Although quite distinct from the modern Angora breeds, the native Turkish cats were prized for their silken coats, and the white varieties were the most highly sought-after of all. They provided the incentive to breed a pure white Persian type by crossing Angoras and Persians in the 1800s. A show standard White Self should be dazzling white and free of marks or shading. Kittens may have coloured hairs on top of the head but these should disappear before they

reach the age of nine months. Whites are meticulous self-groomers, but maintaining an immaculate coat is a major challenge for the owner, too. The fur can yellow, especially around the face, legs and tail. However, white grooming powder is available which both cleans and helps guard against staining. The reward for extra effort is a full-flowing, glacial-white coat emphasizing a magical eye colour.

Different varieties of White have been established according to eye colour. Because the original,

BREED BOX

Coat	thick, dense, silky; full frill at neck and shoulders
Eyes	there are three recognized varieties of White Persian:
	Blue-eyed White eyes decidedly blue with deeper shades of blue preferred; rims pink
	Orange-eyed White eyes copper or deep orange; rims pink
	Odd-eyed White one eye blue and one eye orange or deep copper; rims pink
Other features	nose leather and paw pads pink
Grooming	demanding; thorough, daily
Temperament	placid

+ LEFT
This odd-eyed White with well-defined eye colour probably makes a wonderful companion. However, her ears are too large and set too upright on the head for her to make a perfect pedigreed show cat.

+ BELOW
An orange-eyed White with everything a judge is looking for. It has a beautifully groomed, luxuriant coat combined with good type.

+ BELOW
Persian kittens have a woolly coat, without the distinctive ruff around the neck or the fully plumed tail. This one, with its neat ears, cobby body and short face, shows great potential.

blue-eyed variety was prone to deafness (although this is by no means inevitable), it was cross-bred with Blue and Black Persians. The resulting cats were of generally stronger form and build. Some had copper-coloured eyes, others had one orange or copper eye, and one blue eye. The odd-eyed Whites may go deaf in the ear on the blue-eyed side. Whatever the eye colour, both eyes need to be of equal intensity for successful showing.

White Persians are not only glamorous and decorative but happy to be so. Their calm natures make them ideal indoor cats, although they can also be playful.

BLUE

At the end of the 1800s, Blue Persians became extremely popular as pets of the wealthy, and were specially bred to be sold for high prices. They became particular favourites of European royalty. Queen Victoria of England acquired two Blues, Princess Victoria of Schleswig-Holstein was an enthusiastic breeder, and King Edward VII presented medals for the top prize-winners of the day.

One reason for the Blue's popularity may have been because it was thought to be the nearest in colour to the original Persians brought to Europe by traders in the 1600s. The genetic mutation of the breed we know today may well have arisen on the Mediterranean island of Malta – which is why it is sometimes called the Maltese Blue. The blue-grey colouring is a dilution of black. The blue comes from a lavender

◆ LEFT
The Blue was one of the first Persian cats to be established as a breed. In the late 1800s, it became a fashionable asset for the wealthy and aristocratic.

sheen which adds a brightness to the pale coat. This is very much in evidence with the show cat, which is ideally an even, medium to pale blue, with no shading, markings or white

hairs. A dark, slate-grey coat is considered very undesirable. Because of its long, distinguished history of careful breeding, the Persian Blue is often used as the standard Persian type against which other Persian breeds are compared. For this reason, it is sometimes included in breeding programmes to improve the type of other varieties.

The Blue has a reputation for being a very affectionate and gentle cat that enjoys close human companionship.

BREED BOX	
Coat	thick, dense, silky; full frill at neck and shoulders
Eyes	copper or deep orange; rims blue-grey
Other features	nose leather and paw pads blue-grey
Grooming	demanding; thorough, daily
Temperament	placid

◆ LEFT
A Blue with a well-earned aristocratic air. Its evenly coloured coat with a lustrous sheen offsets glorious copper-orange eyes.

CHOCOLATE

There is an element of Siamese in the Chocolate Persian, which may account for a certain sauciness in its nature.

The Chocolate Point Siamese was mated with Blue Persian cats to create part of the formula for the Persian Colourpoint. The Chocolate was an offshoot, and

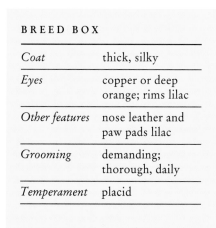

gradually, through generations of breeding, it became a recognized variety in its own right. The ideal show cat has a medium to dark, warm and evenly toned coat with no shading, markings or white hairs. Warmth of tone rather than a deep, dark bitter chocolate is very important. Kittens sometimes show greying, although this often disappears at six to nine months. Eyes should be rich copper-orange with no signs of reversion to pale gold or green.

✦ LEFT
With their Siamese ancestry, the early Chocolates often had shorter fur than most Persians, but this is no longer the case.

✦ ABOVE
The eyes should be copper-orange. There is a tendency for eye colour to revert to pale gold or even tints of green.

BREED BOX

Coat	thick, silky
Eyes	copper or deep orange; rims chocolate brown
Other features	nose leather and paw pads chocolate brown
Grooming	demanding; thorough, daily
Temperament	placid

LILAC

The Lilac Persian, or Lavender Kashmir was, like the Chocolate, an offshoot from the breeding programme for Colourpoint longhairs. It is a dilute form of the Blue with an

✦ RIGHT
A Lilac Persian has a coat colour that is warm and even, with no shading.

BREED BOX

Coat	thick, silky
Eyes	copper or deep orange; rims lilac
Other features	nose leather and paw pads lilac
Grooming	demanding; thorough, daily
Temperament	placid

element of Siamese. This may be the reason why these cats often show an independence of spirit – they are well able to amuse themselves, but quickly bond with their owners.

The perfect pedigree has a thick, silky coat that is warm in tone and even in colour, with no markings or white hairs. Eyes are copper or deep

orange with lilac rims, and the nose leather and paw pads are also lilac. Once the colour Lilac has been produced, Lilac to Lilac matings will only produce Lilac kittens. This applies not only to Persian Lilacs, but to other breeds as well, with the exception of Oriental Shorthair Siamese and British Shorthair breeds.

RED

Only a few decades ago, the Red Persian was one of the rarest of all feline varieties. This was largely because of the need to select parents which had had fine mackerel-striped coats as kittens, combined with long

markings that are characteristic of all Red Persian kittens in certain lights. It is rare for a Red to be free of these markings until the ground colour has intensified with maturity.

BREED BOX

Coat	thick, silky
Eyes	copper or deep orange; rims deep pink
Other features	nose leather and paw pads deep pink
Grooming	demanding; thorough, daily
Temperament	placid with spark

fur and intensity of colour. The fiery red coat is much richer than that of the ordinary ginger tom. For a show cat, it should be even in tone, with no white hairs. Slight shading on the forehead and legs is acceptable. The sex-linked gene which creates the red cannot mask the tabby

◆ RIGHT
It is common for Persians to moult in the summer months, resulting in loss of top coat due to the heat. This lovely example of a Red still shows good type despite being what is known as "out of coat".

CREAM

The Cream Persian is a dilute Red, with probable input from the white Angoras that were cross-bred with Persians in the 1800s. Then, as now, Blue Persians were not only the most popular variety, but the best examples of type, so breeders of other colours used Blue studs in their programmes. Blues are dilutes of Black Persians, and so dilute genes were released into many breeding programmes, eventually resulting in a whole range of dilute colours.

Early Creams had larger ears and longer noses than their modern descendants, and their eyes were almond-shaped. Today's Cream is the result of over a century of very selective breeding that was initially

BREED BOX

Coat	thick, silky
Eyes	copper or deep orange; rims pink
Other features	nose leather and paw pads pink
Grooming	demanding; thorough, daily
Temperament	placid

done in America. The English described these dilute Reds as "spoiled oranges", and did not regard them as an acceptable colour variation until the 1920s. The ideal Cream has no shading, markings or white hairs. The pale to medium cream coat is even in colour with no white undercoat.

◆ RIGHT
A Cream kitten is particularly precious as some breeders think that this variety has smaller litters than other Longhairs.

TORTOISESHELL

The classic Tortoiseshell colouring is a striking blend of black, red and pale red. The exact configuration of colours is very much influenced by the mix of colour genes carried by the female parent. If the female gene has two red XX chromosomes, the offspring will be red. However, if one of the female's chromosomes carries the red gene and one does not, then the offspring will be a mixture of red and another colour or colours – a Tortoiseshell. Because of the complex genetic make-up necessary to create the Tortoiseshell mix of colours, all variations are usually female.

Tortoiseshells, also known as Torties, occur in dilute variations, such as Chocolate Tortie, Blue-Cream and Lilac-Cream. The parentage is reflected in the names.

The object in breeding any Tortoiseshell pedigree is to achieve a perfect balance in the mix of colours. When black and chocolate are intermingled with red, the result can be a brilliant firework display of a coat. Aficionados of these varieties hope that the colours will be well-defined, and better still, that the kittens will

◆ RIGHT
A Black Tortoiseshell shows off its fine cobby build, with solid, squarish body, short, thick legs and large head. Because Tortoiseshells have been cross-bred with a good mixture of other breeds, they tend to show excellent type.

have a dashing blaze of red down the centre of the face. Some kittens show greying in the black fur, which usually grows out after six to nine months.

Tortoiseshells with red in their make-up are said to inherit the allegedly fiery temperament of the Red Persian, though their fans say they are just full of character. They also tend to be particularly attentive mothers. Tortoiseshell queens are mated with Blacks and Reds for the best chance of producing Tortoiseshell kittens in their litter.

The ethereal colour of the dilute Tortoiseshells is said to be complemented by a certain charm and winsomeness of character. According to the British standard, the soft colours should merge into each other like shot silk. In America, distinct bands of colour are preferred.

Eyes of all Tortoiseshells are large, full and deep copper or orange.

◆ ABOVE
This Black Tortoiseshell is differently marked from the one at the top of the page. Tortoiseshells come in several colours, although a mix of red or cream patches on the base coat colour are desirable. No two Tortoiseshells are ever the same.

◆ LEFT
The Blue-Cream is a subtly coloured Tortoiseshell which arose from crossing a Blue Persian with a Cream. The American and English standards differ. The English like the two colours to merge, while the Americans prefer distinctive bands of blue and cream.

BREED BOX	
Coat	thick, silky
Eyes	deep orange or copper
Other features	nose leather and paw pads pink or black, depending on dominant coat colour
Grooming	demanding; thorough, daily
Temperament	placid

BI-COLOUR

In the early days of pedigree breeding, any longhaired cat with a patch of white was regarded with horror. However, there were so few animals without a white spot on the belly or neck, that to fill classes at shows, the Bi-colours were allowed to compete. These solid-coloured cats with white undersides, muzzles, chests, legs and

◆ ABOVE
A Blue Bi-colour is an example of the many variations of the breed. They are available in all the colours accepted for the Self colours such as Red, Cream and Chocolate.

◆ LEFT
A beautifully groomed black and white Bi-colour in full coat shows the distinct white patching that is highly desirable in show cats.

BREED BOX	
Coat	thick, dense, silky; full frill at neck and shoulders
Eyes	deep orange or copper
Grooming	demanding; thorough, daily, especially the white parts
Temperament	placid

feet, were placed along with the Tortoiseshell and Whites, in an "any other variety" category. Eventually, breeders began to consider them seriously as a variety in their own right. The ideal standard is for the white patches to be balanced and even, with a dapper and clearly defined inverted V shape running over the nose.

◆ BELOW
A black Tortie and White displays well-mingled markings, clearly defined white patches, and an exceptionally fine longhaired coat.

TORTOISESHELL AND WHITE

The classic Tortoiseshell's black and red (or its dilute colours) are offset by patches of dazzling white – as long as the cat is well and frequently groomed. In America this variety is called a Calico after printed calico (cotton).

◆ BELOW
Tortie and Whites occur in as many different colour combinations as the Tortoiseshells themselves. This is a dilute colour – Blue Tortie (Blue-Cream) and White.

BREED BOX	
Coat	particularly long and silky; full frill at neck and shoulders; full, bushy tail
Eyes	orange or deep copper
Grooming	demanding; thorough, daily, especially the white parts
Temperament	placid

The English version of this name was Chintz, but this is no longer used. The American standard requires well-defined patches of colour, but in the United Kingdom, any degree of white is acceptable, from some on all four legs, chest and belly, to the van pattern.

TABBY

If Tabby Persians were groomed in the exaggerated bouffant style applied to other varieties, the impact of their rich markings would be diminished. Even though a full coat is still important, the Tabby owner has to take a more laid-back approach to grooming.

The characteristic Tabby markings include triple lines running the length of the spine, a butterfly shape over the shoulders and an oyster (or spiral) on the flanks. Legs and tail should have evenly spaced dark rings, and the underbelly is spotted. Spotted, mackerel and ticked tabby patterns are also shown, apart from in the United Kingdom, where the only recognized variations are blotched (or marbled). Mainstream Tabby colours are Brown, Red and Silver, although other

varieties such as Cream, Lilac and Cameo are being introduced. The Brown Tabby is rich, tawny-sable ground with dense black markings. It was especially favoured by Frances Simpson, the premier breeder of Blue

Persians in the late 1800s. One of her champions became the ancestor of most Brown Tabbies in the world today. Strong types of Tabby from the United States are currently being introduced worldwide.

The Red Tabby, with its rich ginger coat and matching eyes, however, remains the most popular variety. Next in line are the Silvers. They have been subject to dispute over correct eye colour for show cats, especially in the United Kingdom. Elsewhere, a looser interpretation of achievable eye colour has meant that Silver Tabby Persians have now been bred to the very best of type characteristics.

BREED BOX

Coat	thick, silky, often shorter than other longhair varieties
Eyes	*Brown and Red:* orange or copper with no green rim *Silver:* green or hazel
Other features	*Brown:* nose leather brick-red; paw pads black or brown *Red:* nose and paw pads deep pink *Silver:* nose leather brick-red with black outline; paw pads black
Grooming	demanding; thorough, daily; special care brings out markings
Temperament	placid

✦ ABOVE
Tabbies require careful grooming to enhance distinctive markings like those on this Brown Tabby. As well as his characteristic Tabby M on the forehead, his short nose and ears are perfect.

✦ RIGHT
The scintillating fur colour of the Silver Tabby made it a favourite in early cat shows – until it was upstaged by the silvery Chinchilla.

CHINCHILLA

In 1882, a fine-boned, silver Angora-type female cat with no markings was mated with a similarly coloured, non-pedigreed male. Their daughter became the mother of the

first Chinchilla title holder, whose body was exhibited in London's Natural History Museum.

The undercoat of the Chinchilla is pure white. The coat on the back, flanks, head, ears and tail is tipped with black. The tipping should be evenly distributed to give the characteristic silver sparkle. The legs may be slightly shaded with the tipping, but the chin, ear furnishings, stomach and chest must be pure white. Tabby markings or brown or cream tinges are undesirable. There has been great controversy about the required size of a Chinchilla;

the breed is sometimes described as fairy-like, but this is not to do with size – Chinchillas are usually medium-sized and quite solidly built.

◆ ABOVE
The Chinchilla's emerald or bluish-green eyes are outlined in black, creating an eyeliner effect.

BREED BOX

Coat	thick and dense, like swansdown
Eyes	emerald or blue-green; visible skin on eyelids black or dark brown
Other features	nose leather brick-red; paw pads black or dark brown
Grooming	demanding; needs constant attention
Temperament	placid; often livelier than other Persians

GOLDEN

Golden cats may well have occurred as an offshoot of Chinchilla breeding in the 1920s. However, the modern breed became established following an explosion of American imports of Chinchillas into Britain in the 1970s, combined with a New Zealand import from American bloodlines. On the back, flanks, head

and tail the undercoat must be sufficiently tipped with seal brown or black to give a golden appearance. An apricot undercoat deepens to gold, while chin, ear furnishings, stomach and chest are pale apricot. The general tipping effect may be darker than that of the Chinchilla, and tipping on the tail may be heavier than on the body. Legs may be shaded, but the back from paw to heel should be solid seal brown or black. Kittens often show tabby markings or grey at the base of the undercoat.

◆ LEFT
The Golden Persian, originally called the Golden Chinchilla, has the same striking dark rims around the eyes.

BREED BOX

Coat	dense, silky
Eyes	emerald or blue-green; eye rims seal-brown or black
Other features	nose leather brick-red outlined with seal or black; paw pads seal or black
Grooming	very demanding; thorough, needs daily attention
Temperament	placid, but often livelier than other Persians

SHADED SILVER

The Shaded Silver is largely the product of Chinchilla matings to self-coloured longhairs in attempts to improve size and type.

The general effect of a Shaded Silver is of being much darker than the Chinchilla. The undercoat is pure white, with black – never blue – tipping that shades down from the back to the flanks, with lighter tipping on the face and legs. The top side of the tail is also tipped, but the chin, chest, stomach, insides of the legs and underside of the tail are pure white. The tipping extends to a third of the complete hair length. The hair on the foot pad to the joint may be shaded to black and there is no barring on the legs. Lips are outlined in black. No tabby markings or brown or cream

BREED BOX	
Coat	thick, dense, silky
Eyes	emerald or blue-green
Other features	nose leather brick-red outlined with black; paw pads black or seal
Grooming	very demanding; thorough, daily
Temperament	placid, but often livelier than other Persians

◆ ABOVE
The darker tipping of the Shaded Silver compared with the Chinchilla is quite clearly seen. The Shaded Silver is derived from Chinchilla cross matings. In Britain it took a long time for it to be recognized.

tinges are permissible in a show cat. In the United States, breeders mated to the best Persians available (Black or Blue) and then inbred to regain the Chinchilla breed features. Shaded Silvers were the inevitable consequence, and throughout the history of Silver Persians in the United States, both Chinchilla and Shaded Silver kittens have been produced in the same litter.

SMOKE

Smoke Persians are the result of cross-breeding Chinchilla, Blue and Black. The traditional Smoke colours are Black and Blue – but the introduction of the red sex-linked gene, followed by the gene for Chocolate, led to the entire range of longhair colours being represented. Black Smokes were the first to be introduced. Blue Smokes were initially kept as pets rather than show cats, because they were considered to be poor-quality Blue Persians.

All Smokes are cats of striking contrasts. The undercoat should be as white as possible, with the tips shading to the appropriate colour.

The darker points are most defined on the back, head and feet, and the light points on the frill, flanks and ear tufts.

BREED BOX	
Coat	thick, dense, silky; full frill
Eyes	large, round; orange
Grooming	very demanding; thorough, daily
Temperament	placid

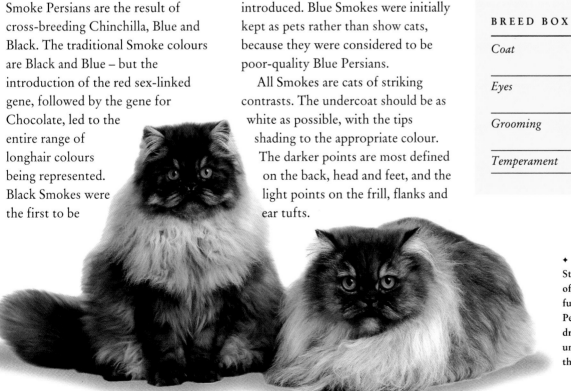

◆ LEFT
Startling orange eyes are offset against the darkest fur colouring of the tipped Persians. The Smoke shows dramatic ash white undercoat contrasting with the full colour.

CAMEO

The Cameo was regarded as a delicious accident for a great many years, but towards the end of the 1950s, the breed was formally registered in the United States. The formula for creating Cameos turned out to be extraordinarily straightforward, with kittens of consistent colouring appearing in the first hybridization.

✦ LEFT
A Persian Red Shell Cameo has fur that is tipped at the very ends to give a shimmering effect.

BREED BOX

Coat	thick, dense, silky; full frill at neck and shoulders
Eyes	large, round; deep orange or copper
Grooming	demanding; thorough, daily
Temperament	placid

Apart from Red and Cream Cameos, there are Blue-Cream and Tortoiseshell variations.

There are two levels of colour tipping to the fur. In the Shell Cameo, colour is restricted to the very tips of the fur to give a soft sheen like mother-of-pearl. The Shaded Cameo has heavier tipping, and normally occurs in the first crosses between a Chinchilla and a Red or Cream cat. In all Cameos, the undercoat should ideally be as white as possible with the tips shading to red or tortoiseshell in the Red series, and shading to cream or blue-cream in the Cream series. The deepest intensity of colour is most defined on the mask, along the spine from the head to the tip of the tail and on legs and feet. The light points occur on the frill, flanks, undersides and ear furnishings.

PEWTER

Breeding from Tortie Cameos produces cats with black rather than red, cream or tortoiseshell tipping. These cats are a relatively recent development and have their place as

BREED BOX

Coat	thick, long; full frill
Eyes	deep orange or copper
Other features	nose leather and paw pads brick-red
Grooming	thorough, daily
Temperament	placid

Pewters. They are very similar in appearance to Shaded Silvers but with orange or copper eye colour. Pewters are recognized in the United Kingdom only with black tipping. The coat is exceptionally long – almost to the point of obscuring the cobby build – with a full neck ruff ending in a frill over the front legs.

✦ ABOVE
Orange-copper eyes distinguish the Pewter from the similar Shaded Silver Persian. This cat's distinguished neck ruff descends satisfyingly deep to finish between the front legs.

COLOURPOINT (HIMALAYAN)

The entire catalogue of Persian longhaired cats until this point has been based on a solid colour cat modified by the introduction of the tabby pattern, sex-linked colour, silver or white patching. The pioneers of Colourpoint breeding fused the Persian type longhair with the Himalayan (which is why this breed is known in America as Himalayan) pattern of the Siamese cat. The result was a cat of Persian type with long hair and the restricted coat pattern of the Siamese. The points (mask, legs, feet and tail) are evenly coloured and there is a good contrast between the points and body colour. Light body shading, if present, should be confined to the shoulders and flanks, and

◆ LEFT
Cream Colourpoint Rosjoy Rambo, Supreme Grand Champion, has the wonderful blue eyes of a Siamese set against the red-gold cream of his fur.

POINT COLOURS

Individual organizations recognize point colours that include the Silver series and Red sex-linked Silver series. In Britain, the point colours are represented by four distinct groupings:
Solid point colours – Seal, Blue, Chocolate, Lilac, Red and Cream
Tortie point colours – Seal Tortie, Blue-Cream, Chocolate Tortie and Lilac-Cream
Tabby point colours – Seal Tabby, Blue Tabby, Chocolate Tabby, Lilac Tabby, Red Tabby, and Cream Tabby
Tortie Tabby point colours – Seal Tortie Tabby, Blue-Cream Tabby, Chocolate Tortie Tabby and Lilac-Cream Tabby
   In the United States, seven varieties are recognized:
Blue Point, Chocolate Point, Seal Point, Flame Point, Lilac Point, Blue-Cream Point, and Tortoiseshell Point

should complement the points. The mask covers the entire face. It should not extend over the head, although the mask of a mature male is more extensive than that of a mature female. Kittens are born white and fluffy, the point colours starting to appear in less than a week.

   Attempts to transfer the Siamese pattern to Persian type were being made before World War II, but the cats were not shown until 1957 in California, and were only officially incorporated into the Persian breed by the Cat Fanciers' Association in 1984. Breeding lines have since expanded to develop the full range of point colours. The Colourpoint Persian has now outstripped the Blue in the longhair popularity stakes.

BREED BOX	
Coat	thick, dense, no trace of woolliness; glossy; full frill over shoulders and continuing between front legs
Eyes	large, round; brilliant blue
Other features	nose and paw pad colour matches the point colour
Grooming	demanding; thorough, daily
Temperament	placid

◆ BELOW
The darkened points of the Siamese are blended with all the characteristics of the Persian Longhair. This cat is a Blue Colourpoint.

The Semi-longhair Group

Many semi-longhair breeds, such as the Norwegian Forest Cat, are of natural ancestral type; others, such as the Ragdoll and the Somali, are relatively new "manufactured" breeds.

In each semi-longhair breed, the coat seems to have a distinct pattern of growth that is like no other. However, in its fullest expression – in the Maine Coon Cat, for example – there are the common features of lynx-like ear tufts, inner ear furnishings and a chest ruff which can reach right down between the front legs. Coats can be rather shorter over the main part of the body but there is a drift of fur on the flanks and "breeches" on the back legs. Paws often show tufts between the toes under the paws, and tails are long and plume-like.

♦ FACING PAGE
Some of the semi-longhair breeds have developed coats that provide protection against hard winters; the Maine Coon Cat is one.

♦ ABOVE
Semi-longhair versions of shorthaired breeds have been developed. This Blue Somali is like an Abyssinian apart from its longer coat.

BIRMAN

◆ LEFT
The pale coat and coloured points on face, legs and tail are similar to those of a Siamese cat. However, this Blue shows the distinctive white paws that are unique to Birmans.

The Birman falls somewhere between the Siamese and the Persian in its character, build and length of fur, yet it is very much a breed of its own. It also has the distinction of being the sacred cat of Burma.

All Birmans have colourpointed features – darker coloration on the ears, face, tail and legs. The original Birman was seal-pointed, but there are now blue, lilac, chocolate, and a wide range of tortoiseshell and tabby points. All are now regarded as different breeds, but share the same blue eyes, dark points, white feet, body shape and general temperament.

The Birman body has some of the mass of the Persian's, with thick-set legs and a broad, rounded head. However, the body and legs are longer than those of a Persian, and the face is pointed rather than flat, with a longish, straight nose and relatively large ears.

The unique and most distinctive feature of the Birman is its paw design. Each forepaw ends in a symmetrically shaped, white glove. The show

BREED BOX	
Coat	long, silky; full ruff around the neck and slightly curled on the stomach
Eyes	almost round but not bold; deep, clear blue
Other features	white mittens on forepaws; longer white "gauntlets" on rear paws
Grooming	relatively easy with regular brushing and combing
Temperament	gentle, individualistic, extremely loyal

◆ BELOW
The mask, tail and legs of Seal Point Birmans take their colour from the rich brown of Burmese soil, according to one legend.

◆ RIGHT
The Seal Point original has now been joined by many differently coloured varieties of the Birman, but all have clear sapphire eyes and a sweet facial expression.

standard is for the white to end in an even line across the paw and not pass beyond the angle of paw and leg. The white areas on the back paws taper up the back of the leg to finish just below the hock, and are known as gauntlets. These white finishing touches are the result of a rare recessive genetic trait, although, rather more romantically, there are various legends that explain

The Red Point Birman has a cream body colour with warm orange points, the trademark white paws, but pink nose and paw pads.

their origins. One version tells of a raid on a Burmese temple in which the high priest was killed. A white temple cat leapt on to the priest's body, and immediately its fur turned gold in the light radiating from the resident goddess. The cat's eyes reflected the sapphire of the goddess's own eyes, while legs and tail took on the rich brown of the Burmese soil. The paws that rested on the dead priest, though, remained white, a symbol of purity.

A more recent story reports that in 1919, a pair of seal-pointed Birmans was given to French explorer August Pavie and Englishman Major Gordon Russell. The male died on the journey back to France, but the female survived and bore a litter. This queen may have represented the beginning of controlled breeding of Birmans in France during the 1920s, when Siamese and bi-colour Persians were introduced into the programme. The breed was officially recognized in 1925. Its character reflects the Persian and Siamese input. It is quieter and less active than the Siamese, but not as docile as the Persian. The queens mature earlier than a Persian – at around seven months – and are generally very attentive mothers.

♦ RIGHT
The Chocolate Tabby Birman, one of the newer colours, shows pale chocolate tabby markings on ears, mask and tail, while the body is light golden beige.

BIRMAN POINT COLOURS

Seal, Blue, Chocolate, Lilac, Red, Cream

Tortoiseshell points in all colours apart from Red and Cream

♦ RIGHT
A Blue Tortie Tabby Point displays a magnificent coat and tail. A Birman's coat needs some extra grooming, but is less demanding than that of a longhair breed, and rarely becomes matted.

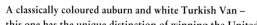

TURKISH VAN

♦ RIGHT
A classically coloured auburn and white Turkish Van – this one has the unique distinction of winning the United Kingdom's Supreme Cat Show two years running.

Ancestors of the Turkish Van come from a rugged region in south-east Turkey, around the country's largest lake, the 3675km² (1419 square mile) Lake Van. This may be why this breed apparently loves water – and is sometimes called the Turkish swimming cat. It is not true that all cats hate water, but these cats will actually seek it out and seem to swim as a form of recreation. Turkey's

domestic cats are predominantly white with auburn markings. Even today, in Istanbul, you will see many street cats of this colouring.

On a visit to the Lake Van region in the 1950s, two English women bought a stocky white female cat with flashes of head colour and a full auburn tail.

♦ ABOVE
The "thumbprint" markings on the head of this auburn and white Van correctly (for the show standard cat) do not extend below the eyeline.

Their Istanbul hotel manager told them of another cat – a male with very similar markings. They took both cats back to Britain, and after four years were successfully breeding consistently patterned kittens. The two women returned to Turkey and bought another male and female to add to the new gene pool. The breed was first officially recognized in Britain in 1969 as the Turkish Cat, the name later being changed to Turkish Van.

Despite its fine coat and white colouring, no link with the Turkish Angora breed has been established. The Van is the more muscular of the two breeds, deep-chested with a long, sturdy body. Its legs are medium in length with neat, tufted, well-rounded feet. The tail is a *pièce de résistance*, a full brush in perfect proportion to the body and, of course, coloured and possibly faintly ringed. The cat has a long, straight nose and prominent, well-feathered ears.

The perfect coat is chalk-white with no trace of yellow, with coloured tail and head markings not extending below the eye line or the base of the ears at the back. There is a white blaze on the forehead and sometimes the occasional thumb-print of colour on the body. All colours are recognized (auburn and cream only in the United Kingdom).

Turkish Vans have reached the height of excellence, including the title of Supreme Exhibit at the United Kingdom's Supreme Cat Show.

BREED BOX

Coat	long, soft, silky; no woolly undercoat
Eyes	large, oval, expressive; light to medium amber, blue or odd-eyed
Other features	enjoys swimming; not prolific (litters of about four kittens)
Grooming	relatively easy; daily brushing and combing
Temperament	affectionate, intelligent; not particularly lively; may be nervous

♦ LEFT
The creamy-white Turkish Van is one of the two colours accepted by the United Kingdom's cat fancy, the other being the classic auburn and white.

TURKISH ANGORA

When the Victorians launched their breeding programmes using longhaired Persians and white cats from Ankara in Turkey, the Persian type became dominant. While the Turkish cat was an essential ingredient in the creation of the longhaired Persian of today, its type did not catch on to the same extent as the Persian. The result was that by the early 1900s, there were no Turkish Angoras on the international show scene and the type was nearly wiped out. However, it has always been highly valued in its land of origin, and a handful of cats was kept at Ankara Zoo. They continued to breed there in relative obscurity until rediscovered by the rest of the world in 1963. A pair was taken to America and a breeding programme started, although it is still not recognized by the main United Kingdom cat fancy. The white version, in particular, is now

✦ ABOVE
The pure white Turkish Angora is probably the closest to the first longhaired cat that was brought to Europe from Ankara, Turkey in the 1500s. This one, however, is a highly bred odd-eyed white with a definitely modern form.

✦ BELOW RIGHT ✦
The Turkish Angora's pert and pretty profile and splendid plume of tail can be appreciated on this Black Tortie Smoke.

BREED BOX	
Coat	fine, silky, medium length; wavy on stomach; no undercoat
Eyes	large, almond shaped; amber, blue, odd-eyed; green for Silver cats
Other features	moults heavily in summer
Grooming	relatively easy; daily brushing and combing
Temperament	affectionate, intelligent, can be playful; enjoys peace and quiet

highly prized in its native Turkey. The Turkish Angora is a graceful, small to medium-sized cat, with a neat and attractively tapered head. To begin with, only the white versions were recognized but now there is a whole range of selfs, bi-colours, tabbies and smokes.

✦ ABOVE
A Calico Turkish Angora shows the alert expression and high-set ears typical of the breed.

◆ LEFT
An example of the Usual – or original colour –
with an undercoat overlaid with rich golden
brown and each hair tipped with black.

SOMALI

The Somali is the semi-longhaired
version of the Abyssinian cat.
Although the Abyssinian is a
shorthaired breed, semi-longhaired
kittens have occasionally appeared in
their litters over several decades. In
the United States it was eventually
realized that a new breed was
appearing spontaneously. The long fur
was the result of a naturally long-
established recessive gene within the
breeding population. It may have been
introduced via ticked tabby cats of
unknown parentage in the breeding
programme. These cats would have
been introduced to sustain the
breeding viability of the early
Abyssinians, for the gene pool was
extremely restricted at the turn of the
century – a state of affairs that lasted
well into the 1920s and 1930s. Any

Ethiopian connections, the breed was
named after the nearby African
country of Somalia.

The coat pattern of the Somali is
quite distinctive: it is ticked – with
three two-colour bands of colour on
each hair. The colour combinations
now bred range from the traditional,

BREED BOX	
Coat	soft, fine, dense; lies flat along the spine
Eyes	almond-shaped, slanting; outlined with a darker surround; amber, hazel or green, the richer and deeper the better
Other features	smiling expression
Grooming	easy if done regularly
Temperament	intelligent, lively, alert, interested; may be shy; freedom-loving (must not be confined indoors)

◆ LEFT
The Sorrel Somali is rather paler than the Usual
as the base apricot is ticked with cinnamon
rather than black.

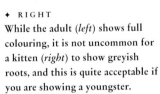

fluffy Abyssinian kittens were initially
regarded as below standard and
banished to pet homes. Then an
American breeder discovered that a
longhaired Abyssinian at a humane
society home had actually been sired
by her own stud cat. The stud was
tried out again to see if a consistent
line of semi-longhairs could be
produced – and the Somalis were
established during the 1960s.
Because of its Abyssinian or

◆ RIGHT
While the adult (left) shows full
colouring, it is not uncommon for
a kitten (right) to show greyish
roots, and this is quite acceptable if
you are showing a youngster.

◆ LEFT
The Blue Somali is attractively marked in a soft blue overlying a pale mushroom undercoat.

◆ LEFT
In recent years, silver variations of the breed have been introduced. This Fawn Silver Somali (silver undercoat ticked with fawn) is quite rare.

SOMALI COLOURS AND PATTERNS

Usual	rich gold-brown, apricot ticked with black
Sorrel	apricot ticked with cinnamon
Chocolate	apricot ticked with dark brown
Blue	mushroom ticked with blue
Lilac	mushroom ticked with lilac
Fawn	mushroom ticked with fawn

Also Red, Cream, six Tortie colours and Silver versions of all these colours

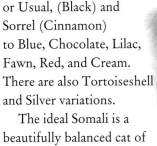

or Usual, (Black) and Sorrel (Cinnamon) to Blue, Chocolate, Lilac, Fawn, Red, and Cream. There are also Tortoiseshell and Silver variations.

The ideal Somali is a beautifully balanced cat of medium build. Its body is firm, lithe and muscular with long legs and a long, bushy tail. It has tufts of fur between its toes. Ears are tufted, too, and are set wide apart, prominent and pricked. The head is slightly pointed and well-contoured.

Although not quite as outgoing as its Abyssinian relations, the Somali is not a cat that is suited to being confined indoors. It is a charming and striking animal, with a bright-eyed, alert and fox-like cheeky demeanour.

◆ ABOVE
The Somali's foreign ancestry is evident in its pointed face and almond-shaped, slanting eyes. Ideally, the eyes are beautifully defined by a dark outline surrounded by a ring of light fur.

◆ BELOW
With its fur lying flat along the back, the coat of the Somali should be distinctly longer around the neck, hindquarters and on the tail – as this Blue Silver shows.

MAINE COON CAT

The Brown Tabby is the traditional Maine Coon Cat pattern. Individuals may take three or four years to reach the size and stature of this one.

The Maine Coon Cat is a fine working cat, as well as one of the longest established breeds. As the first part of its name suggests, it comes from Maine, America's most north-easterly state. This is a land of mountains, forests, lakes and inhospitable winters.

BREED BOX	
Coat	thick, dense, waterproof; has an undercoat
Eyes	full, round with a slightly oblique aperture; all colours (including blue and odd-eyed in white cats)
Other features	big; good climbers; smallish litters (two or three kittens)
Grooming	coat rarely gets matted but regular brushing and combing advised
Temperament	intelligent, calm; freedom-loving (should not be confined indoors)

The Maine Coon Cat is appropriately powerfully built, with an all-weather coat and a reputation for being a wise and skilful hunter.

The second part of its name comes from the long tail and density of fur that have been compared to the similar attributes of the raccoon, an indigenous North American mammal. Like the raccoon, the cat is an exceptional climber. Another theory suggests that the lynx-like tufts on many a Maine Coon's ears are a result of genes inherited from the North American lynx, but this is unlikely. It is more likely that there is a touch of Angora in the breed. Local cats could have bred with Angoras that landed with sailors at the East Coast ports,

or, less plausibly, with the cats sent to America by the French queen Marie Antoinette to escape the French Revolution. (The queen did do this, but it is unlikely that her animals founded a new race of cats.) It may

A Blue Maine Coon Cat shows the ideal head shape and feathered ears typical of the breed. It was once suggested that the ears were inherited from the North American lynx.

A black mantle overlays a paler root colour on the Smoke Maine Coon Cat. The fur is generally shorter over the head and shoulders and lengthens down the back and sides.

simply be that the domestic cats which travelled from Britain to North America with the Pilgrims way back in the 1600s were the true source of Maine Coon Cats, and that the breed's long coat evolved as protection against the severe Maine winters.

The Maine Coon Cat is not only one of the longest established breeds in the world, but also one of the largest. It can weigh 9kg (20lb) and more, compared with an average 2.5–5.5kg (5–12lb) range. Its history rivals that of many more fashionable breeds, and it now has an international following to match. It is the second most popular pedigreed cat in the United States after the Persian. This was not always so.

It was one of the earliest exhibition cats – on show in New York in 1860 and in country shows and fairs in New England. Its early popularity was reversed when there was a craze for

the more exotic Persians and Siamese being imported into the United States in the early 1900s. It was not until the 1950s that Maine Coon Cats slowly began to creep back into favour, and it was accepted at championship level in 1976. Now they are found all over the world with the current top American lines taking the highest honours.

Despite its size, the Maine Coon Cat is a gracious animal, with full cheeks and high cheek-bones, a square muzzle and a firm chin. Its nose is slightly concave in profile. Ears are large, set high and wide apart. The body is long of back, culminating in a very long, bushy tail that tapers at the tip and is carried high and proud. Legs and paws are substantial.

Recently, rexed (curly coated) kittens have been born to apparently purebred Maine Coon Cats in the United Kingdom, indicating that behind some of the pedigrees, a rexed cat has been knowingly or unwittingly introduced. The variation is not approved of by the clubs and associations monitoring the Maine Coon Cat breed. Every attempt is being made to eliminate the gene.

♦ LEFT
Beneath the thick overcoat of the Maine Coon Cat is a solid, muscular body that has all the necessary power for a working cat.

MAINE COON CAT COLOURS AND PATTERNS

Solid	White, Black, Blue, Red, Cream
Tabby and Tortoiseshell	all colours in classic and mackerel patterns, including Silver variations

Also occurs in shaded, smoke, bi-colour, tortoiseshell and white, and van bi-colour. Only one-third white preferred in patched cats

♦ ABOVE
A Tortoiseshell Tabby and White has the required large, oval eyes of the breed, a nose of medium length, and a splendid set of whiskers.

♦ BELOW
A softly coloured Red Silver and White shows paler colouring on chest and paws.

NORWEGIAN FOREST CAT

The Norwegian Forest Cat has been described as the "kissing cousin" of the Maine Coon Cat. The land it comes from certainly has similarities to the forested mountains of Maine. The Norwegian Forest Cat also originated as a natural outdoor working cat, on Scandinavian farms, and its powerful build and skill as a climber and hunter reflect this heritage. Its double-layered coat is heavier during winter, and keeps out both cold and wet. The generous frill and "shirt front" of fur of the neck and chest may be shed during the summer months.

Although it is a big, strong-legged animal, the Norwegian Forest Cat has a certain elegance. Its head is triangular with a long, straight profile, and ears are pointed, open and erect. Like the Maine Coon Cat, it matures slowly and may not reach full stature until four years of age. All colours are allowed except Chocolate, Lilac and

Colourpoint (Himalayan) pattern. The Norwegian Forest Cat is one of the semi-longhaired varieties that have developed as a northern hemisphere speciality. Whether it goes as far back as the Vikings – who describe a "fairy cat" in their legends – is unknown. However, the Vikings travelled not only to the shores of the Mediterranean, and along the rivers

◆ ABOVE
The Norwegian Brown Tabby has the breed's characteristic stance, with a slightly raised rump, and the long, plumed tail raised high.

NORWEGIAN FOREST COLOURS AND PATTERNS

Solid	White, Black, Blue, Red, Cream
Tabby and Tortoiseshell	all colours in classic and mackerel patterns, including Silver variations

Also occurs in shaded, smoke, bi-colour, tortoiseshell and white

◆ LEFT
This Silver Tabby is in full winter coat, with a splendidly well-furnished ruff and "shirt front".

A Black Norwegian Forest Cat demonstrates the breed's typical smooth outer layer of fur that covers a warm, woolly undercoat.

of Asia, but also to the East Coast of North America. It is entirely feasible that the warrior-traders could have found longhaired Asian cats such as the Angora from Turkey, and taken them back to Scandinavia, and even, perhaps, on to America. The Norwegian Forest Cat may therefore quite possibly share the same rootstock as the Maine Coon Cat, its North American equivalent.

By the 1930s the Norwegian Forest Cat was being taken seriously by pedigreed cat lovers in Norway, and it featured at the foundation of Norway's oldest cat club in 1938. However, it only attained full championship status from FIFe, Europe's main feline organization, in 1977, and in the United States in 1993.

◆ LEFT
A Blue Bi-colour displays the distinctively long feathering from the ears, and big, slightly obliquely set eyes. There should be extra points for the splendid whiskers, too!

BREED BOX

Coat	thick; double coat – a woolly undercoat covered by a smooth, water-repellent overcoat; thick ruff
Eyes	large, round; all colours
Grooming	easy; occasional combing
Temperament	alert, active; loves people; freedom-loving (must not be confined indoors); enjoys rock and tree climbing

◆ RIGHT
Norse legends refer to a "fairy cat", and the subtle colours, softness of line and pretty face of this Silver Tortoiseshell Tabby certainly have an ethereal quality.

BALINESE (JAVANESE)

Imagine a Siamese cat with a long, silky, flowing coat and a feathered tail, and you have an idea of the Balinese. It has the same dazzling sapphire eyes and large, erect ears as the Siamese cat – and comes in the same colour variations. However, the Balinese – or Javanese as some colours are called in the United States – tends to be a little less noisy than the Siamese.

Its names are probably inspired by the cat's graceful movement that is reminiscent of an Indonesian dancer. (Further confusion, however, arises because in Europe, the Javanese is the name given to what the British call the Angora!) The ancestry, however, is certainly Siamese. It is likely that in over 100 years of breeding Siamese cats, the recessive gene for long hair crept in and, in the 1940s, longhaired kittens began to appear in purebred Siamese litters. A Californian breeder

◆ ABOVE
Balinese cats are found in all the same point colours as the Siamese. This Blue Point shows how the longer fur of the Balinese can have the effect of making a subtler transition between points and main body colour.

decided to take advantage of this tendency, and in the 1950s developed a fully constituted pedigree breed. The new breed was introduced to the United Kingdom and Europe in the 1970s. Soon, some remarkably beautiful animals were being bred.

The fur of the Balinese is shorter than that of many of the other semi-longhairs, and lies

◆ LEFT
The mask of a Chocolate Point Balinese covers the whole face and merges into the ear colour, as is considered ideal in the breed as a whole.

◆ ABOVE
Look at the dramatic dark stripes, eyeliner and spotted whisker pads of this Chocolate Tabby Point. They will be much admired in a show. This is one of the patterns and colours known as Javanese in the United States.

BREED BOX

Coat	medium length, fine, silky; lies mainly flat along the body; no woolly undercoat
Eyes	almond-shaped, slanted; alert, intelligent expression; clear brilliant blue
Other features	feathered tail
Grooming	relatively easy; regular gentle brushing and combing
Temperament	intelligent, lively, playful, loyal, affectionate but can be aloof

smooth over the body. The cat is consequently easier to maintain. It is of medium build, but long-limbed and lithe, with the distinctly wedge-shaped head and long, straight nose of the Siamese. The mask is complete over the face and linked to the ears by traces of the darker colour (except in kittens). In character, the Balinese is bright and very active but loves its comfort.

✦ **RIGHT**
Bright clear eyes of intense sapphire blue like those of this Chocolate Point are a scintillating feature of the breed.

✦ **LEFT**
Perfectly balanced shading along the spine of this Lilac Point tones in beautifully with a magnolia body colour and the darker points, but ideally there should be no shading at all.

✦ **ABOVE**
Vocal, yes, but the Balinese may not be as loud nor as raucous as its Siamese ancestors.

BALINESE/JAVANESE POINT COLOUR GROUPS

Seal, Blue, Chocolate, Lilac (Frost), Red, Cream

Tabby, Tortoiseshell Tabby

Seal Tortie, Blue Tortie, Chocolate Tortie, Lilac Tortie

ANGORA

This Angora is not to be confused with the Turkish Angora. It is the semi-longhaired variety of the Oriental Shorthair. It has the temperament, body structure and elegance of the Oriental cats, including a tendency towards loud and persistent vocals. They have inherited this from the Siamese element in their breeding programme. The breed was created in Britain from a mating between a Siamese and a Sorrel Abyssinian which carried the longhair gene.

Angoras are lithe and balanced of body with the long legs and almond eyes of their Oriental ancestry, and similarly quick of mind, playful and affectionate. The long, fine coat does not reach its peak until the cat is fully mature. Then its tendency to be wavy and ruffle up at the neck and chin can conceal the fine-boned muscularity of the body beneath, but this is easily felt when you stroke the fur smooth.

The Angora is bred in all standard solid colours, tortoiseshell, tabby, smoke and shaded varieties, but not colourpointed or bi-colour.

✦ ABOVE
The abundance of silken fur on the Cinnamon Angora's underside can conceal the svelte body that lies beneath.

✦ RIGHT
The Oriental lineage of this Chocolate Angora is apparent in its wide-set, almond eyes and wedge-shaped face.

✦ RIGHT
From the large, erect ears along a fine, long nose, this Fawn Angora's head seems to converge in a triangle to a neat, strong chin.

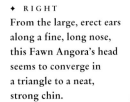

BREED BOX	
Coat	fine, silky, medium length; smooth apart from ruffling at chin, neck and belly; no woolly undercoat
Eyes	large, wide-set, almond-shaped; green, apart from blue- and odd-eyed whites
Other features	tufted ears; long, tapering, plumed tail
Grooming	relatively easy; regular brushing and combing
Temperament	intelligent, lively, inquisitive, active, need company

RAGDOLL

When a Ragdoll is picked up it is supposed to go limp – and that is how it came to be named. There is a far-fetched story that the first Ragdoll kittens are said to have inherited this characteristic, together with an apparent resistance to pain, because their white semi-longhair mother, Josephine, had been injured in a road accident. It is more likely that the Ragdoll's docile nature arises from a happy coincidence of character genes. The breed was created in California in 1963. An early alternative name was Cherubim, while some variations are called Ragamuffins. Although the original breeder claimed non-pedigreed parentage, it is likely that Birman and Burmese genes were present somewhere along the line. However, in the majority of cats the dominant white spotting gene creates the look of the Mitted variety, while the one that produces a similar effect in the Birman is recessive.

The Ragdoll is a cat of powerful build, with big, round paws and a long, bushy tail. Its head is broad and wide-cheeked with a slightly retroussé nose

◆ BELOW
A Seal Colourpointed Ragdoll has distinct, deep brown points.

◆ ABOVE
A Blue Colourpointed gives a good overall impression of the breed's solid, powerful build. Colourpoints have the traditional pattern of complete coloured mask, ears, legs and tail.

and wide eyes of deep sapphire . The three recognized main groupings are: Colourpointed, Mitted and Bi-colour. The Mitted has Colourpointed features contrasting with a pale body, plus white-gloved front feet and rear legs white to the hock or beyond. The Bi-colour is white on the chin, bib, chest and underbody with a triangular blaze over its nose.

BREED BOX	
Coat	dense, silky
Eyes	small, round, slanted; deep blue
Other features	goes limp when picked up
Grooming	easy; daily brushing with soft brush
Temperament	docile, relaxed, easy to handle; needs calm (so suitable to confine indoors)

◆ LEFT
White gloves on the forepaws and longer gauntlets on the rear legs are the distinctive features of the Mitted Ragdoll and bear witness to the probable Birman genes in the breeding programme.

◆ ABOVE
A triangular nose blaze denotes the true look of the Bi-colour Ragdoll. Bib, chest, underbody and front legs are also white.

TIFFANIE

The Tiffanie is a semi-longhaired version of the Asian group of shorthaired cats. It was developed in the United Kingdom during the 1980s and is only just beginning to establish itself as a breed. Burmilla cats featured strongly in the original breeding programme, with occasional injections of Burmese to strengthen the type. The result is that this pretty cat is now found in all the colours and patterns found in the Burmese and Asian breeds. It is a medium-sized cat, although the females tend to be smaller than the males and are particularly dainty. Ears are set wide

BREED BOX	
Coat	fine, silky; pronounced ruff and tail plume
Eyes	slanted; gold to green; green preferred in the Silver variations; gold allowed in self colours
Grooming	relatively easy; regular brushing with soft brush
Temperament	stable, dignified, but inquisitive and sociable

apart, angled slightly forward, and quite large in relation to the head; ear tufts are common. The head, rounded at the top, tapers slightly through butterfly wing-effect cheeks to a firm chin. It is fairly similar in appearance to a breed that was initially developed as the Tiffany in North America. In 1967, a pair of chocolate-coloured, semi-longhaired cats with gold eyes and unknown parentage, produced a litter of six identical kittens and a breeding programme

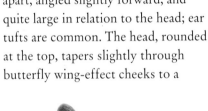

◆ RIGHT
The British Tiffanie, a recent addition to the show circuit, is now found in an enormous range of colours and patterns, as this Brown Smoke version suggests.

TIFFANIE COLOURS AND PATTERNS

Self colours	Black, Blue, Chocolate, Lilac, Red, Caramel, Apricot, Cream
Tabby and Tortoiseshell	Black, Cream, Blue, Chocolate, including Silver versions. The Tabby patterns are less defined on the semi-longhair coat than on the Asian shorthaired equivalent

◆ BELOW
A Brown Shaded Silver Tiffanie shows excellent
shape, with a perfectly straight back from shoulder to
hindquarters, and a soft, feathery tail.

began. However, no Burmese were
included in the programme, nor were
ever produced in any subsequent litter.
The colour and pattern range of the
breed was increased during the 1980s,
and it is becoming more common.
The name has been registered as
Chantilly/Tiffany to avoid confusion
with the British Tiffanie.

CYMRIC

The Cymric is the longhaired version
of the Manx cat. A clear standard of
points has been prepared in the United
States. The variety is not recognized in
the United Kingdom.

The Cymric (which means of, or
from, Wales) was inevitable as far as
genetic inheritance is concerned, even
though the longhair gene is recessive
to the shorthair gene. It was necessary
to introduce tailed outcrosses into
Manx breeding programmes to
strengthen the type. This widened the
gene pool and so increased the
possibility of the recessive longhair
gene finding a match and producing a
longhaired version of the Manx cat.

The first recorded Cymric appeared
in Canada in the 1960s and the variety
gained impetus from that point,
mainly in North America. As with
the Manx, there is the "true" rumpy
version with a hollow in place of a
tail, the stumpy – with a stub of a tail,
and the occasional long-tailed version.
The rumpy's lack of tail is caused
by a mutant gene similar to the one
that causes spina bifida in humans,
and kittens born to cats with this
condition may be stillborn.

◆ RIGHT
A Blue Cymric –
the stumpy
version with a
short stub of a
tail – shows the
chunky bodyline
of the Manx
breed beneath
its heavy fur.

BREED BOX	
Coat	silky with hard guardhairs; not cottony, uneven in length
Eyes	large and round; colour in keeping with coat colour
Other features	may have no tail, a stump or a nearly full tail
Grooming	easy with daily brushing
Temperament	affectionate, intelligent, extremely loyal; likes to be with its owner

The Shorthair Group

Most cats, whether pedigrees or non-pedigrees, are shorthaired like their wild ancestors. Short hair is not only more practical for a wild hunting cat, but also for the domestic animal and its owner. Domestic shorthairs tend to be much more independent and agile than the longhairs, and their body shape can be appreciated. They also need little or no grooming and any wounds can be easily seen and tended. Shorthaired pedigreed cats have been bred into perfect examples of their type from indigenous domestic cats. They fall into two main groups – the sturdy, round-faced American, British and European shorthairs and the long-limbed, lean-featured cats of Asia.

◆ FACING PAGE
A European Tabby Shorthair is an example of a breed developed from indigenous feral cats. It probably has a long and impressive pedigree.

◆ LEFT
The Oriental Spotted Tabby is a long-limbed, lean-featured shorthair of Oriental origin.

EXOTIC SHORTHAIR

The aim in breeding the Exotic Shorthair (known simply as the Exotic in the United States) was to produce a Persian cat without the long hair to reduce the grooming commitment. These shorthaired cats are judged in the Longhair Persian-type section, which can cause some confusion for newcomers to the showing scene.

In facial make-up and expression, body shape and even character, the Exotic Shorthair has all the characteristics of the Persian breeds, and is even available in the same colours and variations. It is a medium-sized cat with a short body, short, thick legs and large paws. The head is round, with a short nose and small, wide-set, round-tipped ears. Breeders

◆ ABOVE
Brilliant orbs of gold-copper are startling against the solid density of the Black Exotic Shorthair. The nose leather and paw pads are black.

BREED BOX

Coat	medium, slightly longer than other shorthairs, but not long enough to flow; dense, plush, soft, full of life; not flat or close-lying
Eyes	large, round, bright; colour reflects coat colour
Other features	small, blunt ears, set wide apart and leaning slightly forward
Grooming	easy; thorough, daily brushing and combing
Temperament	gentle, affectionate, good-natured, inquisitive, playful

◆ ABOVE
Eyes complement the rich red of the Red Tabby's coat. Brilliance of eye colour is an important distinction for this breed in general.

◆ BELOW
A Silver Tabby shows off her eyes lined in black like a Chinchilla. Her shorter coat, however, appears more darkly tipped and the pattern more obvious than that of the longhaired Shaded Silver.

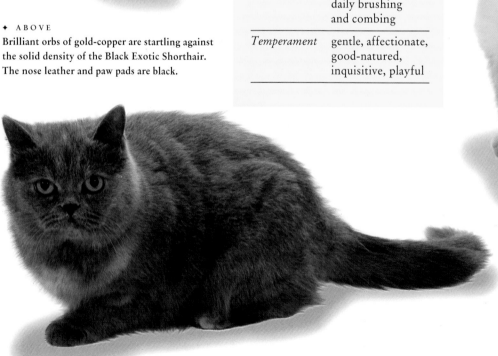

◆ LEFT
The coat of a Blue-Cream Exotic shows definite, but scattered areas of cream among the subtle shades of soft blue-grey.

◆ BELOW
A Tortoiseshell Colourpointed Exotic demonstrates the distinctive Persian body conformation with the large, round head, full body and shortish tail and legs.

of British Shorthairs maintained a policy for a long time of outcrossing to Persian cats every fourth generation or so. They wanted to encourage massiveness of bone and intensity of eye colour in the existing breed, rather than create a new one. Persian type was not, in fact, very distant from the British Shorthair and was therefore likely to improve it.

American breeders, however, did not have a large gene pool of British Shorthairs. They therefore used the Burmese (which was the one really round-headed cat they did have), and later the American Shorthair. The way in which the American cat fancy had developed the Burmese from its introduction in the early 1930s had ensured that its head shape and eye shape were closer than any other breed to Persian Longhair type. This meant it was only a matter of a few generations of kittens before the Exotic Shorthair was successfully developed in the 1960s. Since 1968, Burmese and British Shorthairs have

not been allowed in Exotic breeding programmes in the United States.

It soon became popular, and is now bred in the full range of self colours, bi-colours, tabbies and tortoiseshells, and shaded, tipped and colourpointed varieties. Judging standards are very stringent, with an emphasis on brilliance of eye colour. Any hint of slanted eye shape from the Burmese contribution to its lineage, or a fleck of rogue colour in the iris is frowned

upon. The Exotic Shorthair has the placidity and dignity of the Persian, yet has a playful and affectionate side. It is patient with children, and is contented to be an indoor cat.

Despite being shorthaired, the coat is longer than other shorthaired breeds and requires more attention. It benefits from daily grooming. Try brushing or combing from tail to head, against the pile of the fur to encourage the fur to stand up, brush-like, from the body.

◆ RIGHT
A Tortoiseshell and White Exotic has the required rich tones of red set among the dense black base colour. The red blaze on the face is a bonus.

◆ ABOVE
Persian facial features combine with the blue eyes of colourpointed varieties in this Tortoiseshell Colourpointed Exotic. The colourpointed range is fully represented in the breed.

THE BRITISH SHORTHAIR

The national cat of the British Isles, the British Shorthair, is the result of selective breeding of the best examples of native street cats. It probably stems originally from the first domestic cats that arrived in Britain with the Roman legions in the first century AD. As a pedigreed variety, the British Shorthair (or the English Cat) was recognized from the very start. The early breeders of British shorthaired cats, were, for some reason, usually male and from the north of England. Now

the British Shorthair is the third largest group of registered pedigreed cats in the United Kingdom and popular throughout the world.

It is bred in all the major colour and pattern groups, although to a lesser extent than the American Shorthair, and includes a Siamese pattern. All British Shorthairs have a compact, well-balanced and powerful body. The chest is full and broad; legs are short and strong with large, rounded paws; the tail is thick at the base and rounded at the tip. Of the

British, European and American Shorthairs, the British has the most rounded head. The ears are small and set wide apart, the cheeks are round, the chin firm, and the nose short and broad.

Like its non-pedigreed ancestors and contemporaries, the British Shorthair is a streetwise, muscular cat whose characteristic placidity enables it to adapt happily to life indoors. Its intelligent yet phlegmatic nature makes it a solid and dependable feline companion.

BRITISH BLACK

All the essential characteristics of the British Shorthair type are often seen at their peak in the Black. This is because it was one of the earliest British Shorthair breeds to be selectively bred from the very best of British street

cats in the 1800s. It was also one of the first to be shown at the first national cat show in 1871 at Crystal Palace, London.

The top-rate pedigreed Black should have a dense black coat from hair root to tip, with no hint of browning, stray white hairs, patches or tabby markings. This provides a striking backdrop for the large, round, deep copper eyes with absolutely no green.

Blacks are often used in breeding programmes to improve the type of other Shorthair breeds, particularly Tortoiseshell and Tortie and White.

BREED BOX

Coat	short, thick, fine
Eyes	round; copper, no green
Other features	round-tipped ears; short nose; big round paws; nose leather and paw pads black
Grooming	easy; regular combing
Temperament	companionable, independent, freedom-loving

◆ LEFT
The densely coloured, short fur of the British Black Shorthair is inherited from ancestors reputed to be the familiars of witches, and the butt of superstition and legend during the Dark Ages and medieval times.

BRITISH WHITE

Pure white condensed into the stocky build of the British Shorthair is the epitome of feline luxury and perfection. British White Shorthairs are universally admired, highly valued, and quite rare, although they have been bred since the 1800s.

There are three varieties with different eye colours. Blue-eyed Whites may rarely be prone to deafness. In trying to breed out this defect by crossing with orange-eyed cats, an odd-eyed variety with one eye of each colour was created. Unfortunately, these cats sometimes suffer deafness in the ear on the blue-eyed side. Orange-eyed varieties are therefore the most commonly seen.

BREED BOX	
Coat	short, thick, fine
Eyes	round; clear blue, orange to copper, or one of each
Other features	round-tipped ears; short nose; big round paws; nose leather and paw pads pink
Grooming	easy; regular combing
Temperament	companionable, independent, freedom-loving

◆ ABOVE
A British White Shorthair with a pristine coat is hard to breed and therefore not very common. A pure white non-pedigree might look very like a pedigreed shorthair, but it is more likely to have green eyes rather than copper, blue, or one of each colour.

BRITISH CREAM

The occasional occurrence of a cream-coloured kitten in tortoiseshell litters towards the end of the 1800s provided the motivation to try to produce a Cream pedigree. Some tortoiseshell parentage is necessary to produce the required rich shade of buttermilk, which made it difficult to produce consistently pale coats with no redness or obvious tabby markings.

The result was that the breed was not officially recognized until the 1920s and not fully established until the 1950s. Sometimes tabby markings become more pronounced in very hot or very cold weather. The ideal is cream-haired to the roots – with no patches of white.

BREED BOX	
Coat	short, thick, fine
Eyes	round; deep gold to orange and copper
Other features	round-tipped ears; short nose; big round paws; nose leather and paw pads pink
Grooming	easy; regular combing
Temperament	companionable, independent, freedom-loving

◆ LEFT
British Cream Grand Champion, Miletree Owain Glyndwr, has only the faintest shadow of darker markings, and a gloriously soft-toned coat colour.

BRITISH BLUE

The Blue is the most popular of British Shorthair breeds. Kittens often display tabby markings, but these usually disappear after six to eight months. Because the breed is long established, from the earliest programmes in the 1800s, Blues tend to be good examples of the Shorthair type: broad, muscular and good-natured. Occasional injections of black

♦ ABOVE
A round-cheeked British Blue's hazy blue-grey coat contrasts with big orange eyes.

shorthairs and blue longhairs into breeding programmes have preserved the distinctive slate-blue coat.

BREED BOX	
Coat	short, thick, fine
Eyes	round; copper, orange or deep gold
Other features	round-tipped ears; short nose; big round paws; nose leather and paw pads blue-grey
Grooming	easy; regular combing
Temperament	companionable, independent, freedom-loving

BRITISH CHOCOLATE

The warm, dark-chocolate coloration comes from the introduction of the chocolate gene from longhaired colourpoints into the British Shorthair breeding programme. The coat can be any shade of rich chocolate but it should be evenly toned, without any white, shading or marking.

♦ RIGHT
Despite the British Shorthair's reputation for being stolid and reliable, this Chocolate shows the lively intelligence for which the breeds are also known.

BREED BOX	
Coat	short, thick, fine
Eyes	round; deep gold, orange to copper
Other features	round-tipped ears; short nose; big round paws; nose leather and paw pads brown or pink
Grooming	easy; regular combing
Temperament	companionable, independent, freedom-loving

BRITISH LILAC

♦ BELOW
The stocky, muscular build that distinguishes the British Shorthair from its European and American counterparts can be clearly seen in this Lilac.

The Lilac, a soft-toned blue-grey with a pinkish sheen to it, is a recently introduced, dilute form of the Chocolate. The gene responsible for the dilution produces hairs in which the pigmentation is collected together in clumps, and microscopic areas of hair have no pigment at all. The dilute colour therefore has less depth and intensity than a pure solid colour. Lilac parents only produce kittens of the same colour, unless they carry cinnamon, so once established, Lilacs are easy to keep on producing.

BREED BOX	
Coat	short, thick, fine
Eyes	round; rich gold to orange or copper
Other features	round-tipped ears; short nose; big round paws; nose leather and paw pads pale grey
Grooming	easy; regular combing
Temperament	companionable, independent, freedom-loving

BRITISH BI-COLOUR

♦ BELOW LEFT
The mask over the ears and three-quarters of the face that is such an important feature in the show Bi-colour, suits the rounded features of the British Shorthair very well.

There are many bi-coloured cats on the streets of Britain, but the pedigree version must have well-balanced, symmetrical and clearly defined bands of solid colour and white. The coloured areas can be black, blue, red, cream, chocolate or lilac and in the perfect pedigree, contain no flecks of other colours or any tabby markings. It is also important for the show cat to have the white area covering the nose and lower part of the face, neck and shoulders, chest and forepaws – but over no more than half of the total body area.

BREED BOX

Coat	short, thick, fine
Eyes	round; gold to orange and copper
Other features	round-tipped ears; short nose; big round paws; nose leather and paw pads pink
Grooming	easy; regular combing
Temperament	companionable, independent, freedom-loving

BRITISH TORTIE AND WHITE

This variation of the Bi-colour has tortoiseshell in place of the solid colour areas. In America, these are Calico cats, called after the popular printed cotton fabric. The tortoiseshell element can be bright black and red or dilute colours. As with the solid colour and white, the white areas should extend over no more than half of the body. Tortie and Whites are quite difficult to breed to the preferred symmetry for successful showing.

♦ ABOVE RIGHT
British Shorthairs also come in tortoiseshell without white in mingled shades of red and black, as shown, or the dilute blue-cream shades.

♦ LEFT
The Tortie and White Shorthair comes in delightful dilute versions such as this softly dappled Blue Tortie and White.

BREED BOX

Coat	short, thick, fine
Eyes	round; orange to copper
Other features	round-tipped ears; short nose; big round paws; nose leather and paw pads pink and/or black
Grooming	easy; regular combing
Temperament	companionable, independent, freedom-loving

BRITISH TABBY

The tabby gene is a forceful one, passed on from the wild species from which the European domestic cat has evolved, and familiar in many a non-pedigree. The tabby markings of a show cat, however, must conform to very exact standards, and most importantly of all, be balanced on both sides of the body. There are three main patterns: the classic tabby, the more markedly striped mackerel, and the spotted. Both have a trio of dark lines running along the spine and distinctive, evenly spaced rings around the neck, tail and legs. The classic, however, has dark spirals of colour on its flanks, a winged shape over the shoulders, and a spotted belly.

Tabby colours range from the thick-cut marmalade variety of red on red, the Brown (the Brown Classic is also described as marbled or blotched) and Silver, to the softer dilutes of Blue and Cream.

✦ RIGHT
An alert side profile shows the superb mix of colours in a Tortie Silver Tabby, and the shortish but active tail characteristic of the shorthair.

✦ BELOW
The black-on-silver colouring of the Silver Spotted Tabby shows up the tabby markings to dramatic effect, especially the evenly spaced rings on tail and legs.

✦ RIGHT
A Tortie Tabby British Shorthair combines the rich colouring of the tortoiseshell with the distinctive stripes of the tabby.

✦ ABOVE
Note the well-defined facial markings of this Classic Red Tabby – the lines running down from the corners of the eyes, and the M shape on the brows.

BREED BOX

Coat	short, thick, fine
Eyes	round
Classic Tabby: gold, orange to copper
Silver: green to hazel
Other features	round-tipped ears; short nose; big round paws; nose leather and paw pads brick-red (and/or black for the Silver Tabby)
Grooming	easy; regular combing
Temperament	companionable, independent, freedom-loving

BRITISH COLOURPOINTED

Careful outcrossing of British Shorthairs to Colourpoint Persians resulted in the recent development of the British Shorthair Colourpointed. A certain over-indulgence of hair took a bit of ironing out through breeding programmes, but today's British Shorthair Colourpointed has all the right characteristics of type, with a short, dapper fur coat and sturdy build. The cats come in the same versions of colourpointed as the Siamese, including seal, chocolate, lilac, red and cream. The most recent colours to be accepted are cinnamon and fawn points. All versions have big, round, saucer-like blue eyes, set against the colourpointed mask. The colourpointed features – mask, ears, paws and tail – should be clearly defined in good examples of the breed, and any shading in the body colour should tone in with the point colour.

BREED BOX

Coat	short, thick, fine
Eyes	round; blue
Other features	round-tipped ears; short nose; big round paws; nose leather and paw pads to tone in with point colour
Grooming	easy; regular combing
Temperament	companionable, independent, freedom-loving

♦ ABOVE LEFT
Classic British build combines with delicate Siamese markings on a British Shorthair Lilac Colourpointed.

BRITISH SHORTHAIR COLOURS AND PATTERNS

Self colours:
White (blue-eyed, orange-eyed, odd-eyed), Black, Chocolate, Lilac, Blue, Cream, Red, Cinnamon and Fawn

Tabby:
Silver, Blue Silver, Chocolate Silver, Lilac Silver, Red Silver, Cream Silver, Black Tortie Silver, Blue-Cream Silver, Chocolate Tortie Silver, Lilac-Cream Silver, Brown, Chocolate, Lilac, Blue, Red, Cream, Brown Tortie, Blue-Cream, Chocolate Tortie and Lilac-Cream
Patterns – classic, mackerel or spotted

Tortoiseshell:
Black Tortie, Chocolate Tortie, Blue-Cream Tortie and Lilac Tortie

Patched:
Black Tortie and White, Blue Tortie and White, Chocolate Tortie and White, Lilac Tortie and White, Black and White, Blue and White, Chocolate and White, Lilac and White, Red and White, Cream and White

Smoke:
All self colours (other than white, cinnamon and fawn) and all the tortoiseshell colours

Tipped:
Sparkling white coat with the very tips of the fur dusted with the self and tortoiseshell colours. The Golden Tipped, the non-silver version, has black tipping

Colourpointed:
Colour restricted to the points which can be in all self, tabby, silver tabby, tortoiseshell and smoke colours. Cats have blue eyes

♦ RIGHT
A line-up of British Shorthair kitten breeds. From left to right, Tortie, Blue, Black, and Cream Spotted. Potential owners must remember that while they retain the sweet nature of the breed, mature Shorthairs are big, heavy cats.

BRITISH TIPPED

Like the Longhaired Persian Chinchilla, the British Tipped Shorthairs have a faint dusting of another colour right at the tips of their predominantly white fur, and at the point of their tails. They also share the classic Chinchilla characteristic of nose and eyes fetchingly outlined in black. The tipping (or chinchillation) – which can be black, blue, red, cream, chocolate, lilac or tortoiseshell colours – is such a mere suggestion that it gives a sense of iridescence when the cat moves. The effect may be concentrated in one or two areas to give a ghost of a patch on the flanks or

◆ RIGHT
Sparkling white dusted with black gives an ethereal shimmer to the coat of this British Black-Tipped Shorthair.

back, or rings on the legs. An outstanding feature of the Black and Golden-tipped British Shorthairs is their brilliant green eye colour. The Golden-tipped, unlike the other British Tipped, has a rich golden-apricot undercoat with black tipping. The tipped colorations developed as a result of complex interbreeding of cats with Silver genes, that determined the undercoat colour, with Blues and Smokes. The non-agouti version of the tipped effect produces the British Smoke, which appears to be a self or plain-coloured cat until the hair is pushed back to see the startling silver undercoat. British Smokes are also bred in the same wide colour range.

◆ RIGHT
The Golden-tipped British Shorthair is in fact gold with black tipping. This kitten has the well-defined eyes that are characteristic of tipped varieties.

BREED BOX

Coat	short, thick, fine
Eyes	round; copper to gold; green in Black, Golden-tipped
Grooming	light combing
Temperament	companionable, freedom-loving

THE AMERICAN SHORTHAIR

The American Shorthair should, like the British Shorthair, proudly show its ancestry as a working cat in its power-packed body. In fact, it is very similar in appearance to the British version, although rather more lithe with a less rounded face and slightly larger body.

The American Shorthair is the refined, pedigreed version of the domestic cat of America that probably first came over with the pioneering band of Puritans (the Pilgrims) from England in the 1600s. In fact, it was known as the Domestic Shorthair until 1985. It was well suited to the tough life of the men and women who were pushing back the frontiers of a new country – hardy, lithe and an excellent rodent exterminator. As in Europe, its worth as a hunter went hand in hand with an attitude of suspicion and even alarm from the human pioneers.

By the 1700s, however, cats had become established in human family life, and were even included in family portraits. They were also officially accounted for by the United States Post Office. The British artist, author and cat show organizer Harrison Weir recorded in 1889 that the post office cat's job was to protect the mail bags from being eaten by rats and mice. When kittens were born, the postmaster could apply for an increased food ration for them.

Nevertheless, the first Domestic Shorthair (other than Siamese) to be registered as a pedigree cat in the United States was an imported British Shorthair, a Red Tabby. Her owner cross-mated her with a fine American cat, and registered the first Shorthair to be bred in America, a

✦ ABOVE
An American Tabby Shorthair shows all the essential lithe muscularity of the breed, well proportioned with neat, well-rounded feet.

Smoke called Buster Brown, in 1904. It took another 60 years for the breed to become an established pedigree in its own right. The most important feature for a show-standard American Shorthair is its strength and muscularity of body. Any sign of weakness in build would penalize it.

The American Cat Fanciers' Association recognizes most of the various solid, shaded, silver, smoke, tabby, parti-colour, bi-colour and van groupings. However, they are resistant to lilac and chocolate self colours and colourpointeds.

BREED BOX	
Coat	short, dense, even and firm in texture
Eyes	large, round, wide-set and slightly slanted; brilliant gold, green; white varieties blue-, gold- or odd-eyed
Other features	equable nature and sturdy build
Grooming	easy; regular combing
Temperament	bold, intelligent, inquisitive, active

AMERICAN BLACK SOLID

The perfect example of an American Black Shorthair should have no markings of any colour on its dense black fur, or any sign of rusting. This may mean a limited amount of time in the sunshine for show cats. Nose and paw pads are also black.

AMERICAN WHITE SOLID

The eyes of the solid white cat may be clear gold, deep blue or even odd-eyed as long as the intensity of each colour is equal. The body should be well-knit and powerful with a full, muscular chest. The variety needs to be pure white with no markings at all.

◆ ABOVE
The sweet expression of this American White Shorthair reflects the amiable and affectionate nature of the breed as a whole.

AMERICAN CREAM

◆ LEFT
The buttermilk coat of the Cream Shorthair will become thicker in winter months, as with the breed in general.

The nose leather and paw pads of an American Cream Shorthair are pink, while the fur is ideally an even buff colour with no markings. Judges tend to prefer light shades. The breed should have sturdy legs.

AMERICAN BI-COLOUR

The Black and White Bi-colour should have a V-shaped blaze on its forehead and upright medium-sized ears, with well-defined patches of black, red, blue or cream on white.

◆ RIGHT
The American Bi-colour's tail is as it should be: thick at the root, rounded at the tip, and medium in length.

AMERICAN CALICO

This is the classic Calico Cat of America, its pretty coat colour named after a popular printed cotton fabric. This cat shows the preferred predominance of white on the underparts. There are also dilute versions of the colour combination available, in which the white feet, legs, undersides, chest and muzzle are combined with even, unbroken patches of blue and cream.

✦ LEFT
The Calico Cat is also found in a dilute blue and cream version.

✦ BELOW
The coloured patches on an American Tortoiseshell should be scattered over its body.

AMERICAN TORTOISESHELL

An American Tortoiseshell Shorthair typically has a black coat patched with unbroken areas of red and cream. A show-standard cat is required to have well-defined patches distributed over its body. There are various shaded and tipped and tortoiseshell varieties, too, as well as dilute versions. Eyes may be green or bright gold.

AMERICAN SHADED SILVER

The American Shaded Silver, like the lighter-shaded Chinchilla, ideally has the same level of toning on its face and legs. A distinctive feature of the Shaded and Chinchilla varieties of Shorthair is the black outlining around the eyes and nose.

✦ RIGHT
This Shaded Silver has the rounded head of the breed with well-developed cheeks, and a gently dipping nose.

EUROPEAN SHORTHAIR

The smart version of the feral cat of Europe is a little more streamlined than its British and American counterparts. It is probably the closest of the national shorthairs to the wild species. A clear distinction has been made between British and European Shorthairs since 1982.

The European Shorthair is more elegant than the British, with an emphasis on lithe muscularity rather than round cobbiness. In general shape, it is more like the American Shorthair, though it may be rather larger. It is strong, broad-chested and quite deep in the flank, with fairly long, well-boned legs and rounded paws. The tail is in proportion to the

✦ ABOVE
The leaner features and longer nose of the European Shorthair compared with its British and American equivalents can be seen in this handsome Tabby.

BREED BOX	
Coat	dense; crisp texture
Eyes	slanted, gentle expression; all colours
Other features	territorial, combative towards other cats; prolific breeders
Grooming	easy; regular brushing
Temperament	affectionate, brave, lively, independent; freedom-loving (must not be confined indoors)

body and rounded at the tip, and largish ears are set erect and fairly wide apart.

Unlike the American and British Shorthairs, the European is allowed what is known as open registration in FIFe (the European cat fancy) shows. This means that as long as it conforms to certain standards and characteristic features, and has been assessed and passed by senior judges in Novice classes, any cat may be registered as a foundation pedigree and compete for show titles. Many a worthy European Grand Champion has had its origins in the farmyard! The result of this is that the European Shorthair is particularly adaptable, independent and bright. It also has a remarkably efficient immune system.

✦ LEFT
A pair of European Silver Tabbies display the well-defined "necklaces" and well-spaced leg rings that are characteristic of a good mackerel tabby pattern.

EUROPEAN SHORTHAIR COLOURS AND PATTERNS

Self colours: White (blue-, green- or odd-eyed), Black, Blue, Red, Cream

Tabby: Black, Blue, Red, Cream, Tortie and Blue Tortie
Patterns – classic, mackerel, spotted

Tortoiseshell: Black Tortie, Blue Tortie, Red Tortie

Smoke: Black, Blue, Red, Cream, Tortie and Blue Tortie

Bi-colour, Van, Harlequin: solid colour (Black, Blue, Red, Cream, Tortie, Blue Tortie) plus white

Patched: Black Tortie and White, Blue Tortie and White, Black and White, Blue and White, Red and White, Cream and White

◆ ABOVE
A relatively relaxed attitude to breeding programmes means that there is enormous variety of colour and temperament with the European Shorthair pedigree.

CHARTREUX

The Chartreux is often confused with the British Blue Shorthair, which it closely resembles. There are similarities in robustness, a large, full body, and legs that are shortish in relation to the body. Otherwise, the Chartreux is well-proportioned with large, muscular shoulders, and is rather lighter than its British counterpart,

◆ INSET LEFT
A young Chartreux shows off the sweet expression for which the breed is known.

◆ LEFT
The lighter weight of the Chartreux, as compared with the chunkier British Blue Shorthair, is evident in this cat.

BREED BOX

Coat	dense, soft, plush
Eyes	large, round, expressive; pale gold to copper
Other features	large, muscular shoulders; short, strong neck; sweet smiling expression
Grooming	easy; regular brushing
Temperament	calm, affectionate, intelligent

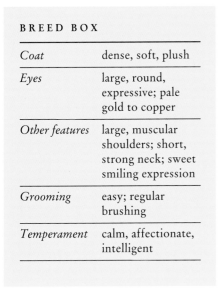

especially in America. Its head is large and broad but not as round as that of the British Shorthair, although the cheeks of adult males are well developed. The nose is short and straight with a slight break, and the muzzle is narrow in relation to the head but not pointed. The Chartreux comes in any shade of blue with silver highlights. It is thought to have been bred in the Middle Ages at the Monastery of La Grande Chartreuse (which was also responsible for the liqueur of the same name). Another version of its origins suggests that the Carthusian order of monks had nothing at all to do with the cat, but that its coat was reminiscent in texture to the fine, wool cloth known as *pile de Chartreux*.

ORIENTAL SHORTHAIR

The ancestors of the Oriental
Shorthairs are, like the Siamese, from
Thailand. They are, in fact, just like
Siamese cats but with all-over coat
colour and pattern rather than the
Siamese colourpoints on face, ears, tail
and legs. The eyes of the Orientals are
usually green rather than the blue of
the Siamese, although in the solid
White, they may be blue or orange
(though the British standard rejects
the orange-eyed). Virtually all colour
and pattern variations are represented,
except, of course, the colourpoints,
making this one of the most diverse of
all cat breeds and groups.

In the United Kingdom and
Europe, the self colours were originally
known as Foreign Shorthairs but the
other varieties have always been

◆ ABOVE
A Red Oriental can show the tabby markings
that come with its red genes, but preferably no
white hairs at all. You can see this cat's Siamese
heritage in its large ears and long, straight nose.

◆ ABOVE
The coat of the Havana is a gloriously warm
brown. It is a purely Oriental cat, unlike the
Havana Brown of the United States.

◆ RIGHT
A wedge-shaped face,
both in profile and
from the front, is
characteristic.
This Black also
shows the long
legs and neat oval
paws so typical of
the breed.

known as Orientals. Each different
colour was given a separate breed
category to enable the cats to be
entered at shows, as they were
excluded from the Siamese classes. In
the United States in the 1970s, all the
variations were grouped together in
the one category of Oriental
Shorthairs, and this broad term is
now universal. However, the
British cat fancy still classifies
the different colours and
patterns as distinct breeds.
There are four fundamental
sub-divisions: solid colours,
shaded, smokes and tabbies.
The Oriental Shorthair type
was developed during the 1960s
by mating Siamese with indigenous
cats such as the British, European
and American Shorthairs. They
have since only been outcrossed to
Siamese, so have a very similar
temperament. They enjoy human
company generally, and do not like
being left alone for too long. In
many ways, their response to

ORIENTAL COLOURS AND PATTERNS

Foreign White:
White with blue eyes (United
Kingdom), or orange or blue eyes
(United States)

Self colours:
Chocolate (Havana), Lilac, Black,
Blue, Red, Cream, Apricot,
Cinnamon, Caramel, Fawn

Tortoiseshell:
as self colours

Oriental Smoke:
any colour with a near-white
undercoat

Oriental Shaded:
shaded or tipped with any colour
with or without silver

Oriental Tabbies:
spotted, classic or mackerel pattern
in all colours with or without silver

BREED BOX

Coat	short, soft, fine, lying flat along the body
Eyes	almond-shaped, slanted; green with no flecks (except Foreign White – brilliant blue)
Other features	loud voice as in Siamese, large ears, big personality
Grooming	easy; can be "polished" with a soft glove
Temperament	intelligent, lively, inquisitive, active, need company

✦ ABOVE
Apart from a wide range of self colours, the Oriental Shorthair comes in every shade and pattern of tabby. This Chocolate Classic Tabby may have a Siamese and a good quality, but non-pedigreed, Tabby in its distant ancestry.

✦ BELOW
This black-on-silver Spotted Tabby was once known in the United Kingdom as the Egyptian Mau. Now it is classified as an Oriental Shorthair, and the Mau is quite a different breed.

humans is dog-like – they may run to greet their owners on their return home, and need to be played with. Their athletic physique has also led to canine comparisons – their length of body and the way they move is like the feline version of a whippet, complete with whip-like tail.

✦ ABOVE
A Spotted Tabby demonstrates that the back legs of the Oriental Shorthair are longer than its forelegs, and that the general body line suggests slender strength.

SIAMESE

The distinctive masked features, dark paws and tail of the Seal Point Siamese cat were described in a 15th-century manuscript of cat poems discovered in Siam (modern Thailand) – which suggests that the cats were already deeply established in the national consciousness. The Seal Point became the Royal Cat of Siam. It could only be obtained from the royal palace in Bangkok by special favour of the King. When members of the royal family died, the cats were thought to aid transmigration of their souls. A cat was placed in the tomb with the deceased. Evidence of its escape through holes in the ceiling of the chamber confirmed that the soul had successfully travelled to the afterlife.

The first breeding pair of Siamese reached Britain in 1884. The required standards then – for what are known as Traditional Siamese (also known as Apple Heads, Opals or Thai Siamese) – called for much stockier cats, rounder in the head than later lines. Their ears were quite small, and their coats as dense and plushy as moleskin. The cats also had a pronounced squint and a kink in the end of their tails, typical of the genetic inheritance of cats throughout south-east Asia, and which are considered defects in the modern pedigree. The Traditional Siamese is still popular among those people who seek a cat less extreme in type than those approved of today by show judges.

The modern Siamese is long-bodied and long-limbed with dainty oval paws. Face on, its head from the tip of the large, triangular ears to the muzzle is a pronounced wedge shape.

SEAL POINT

The original Siamese cat, as described in a 15th-century Thai manuscript, was clearly already well-known at that time. The coat is fawn and the points darken to almost black on the nose and ears. The strong contrast in colour between the points and the pale, even cream of the main area of the coat is important. The dark brown seal points should be restricted to a triangle on the face, the ears, legs and tail. Nose and paw pads are matching dark brown.

◆ ABOVE
Illustrations of a cat with dark points like this modern Seal Point Siamese have been found in a centuries-old manuscript from Thailand.

◆ LEFT
A Seal Point shows off the perfectly balanced lines of the pedigree Siamese, with long neck, long legs and long body following through to the tip of the tail.

CHOCOLATE POINT

Some Seal Points were naturally lighter than others. This characteristic was eventually developed into the Chocolate Point. The brown extremities are a milk-chocolate brown rather than the rich plain chocolate of the Seal Point. The body colour is ivory.

✦ RIGHT
An alert and enquiring mind is suggested by the attitude of this American Chocolate Point.

BREED BOX (ALL VARIATIONS)	
Coat	very short, fine, glossy and close-lying
Eyes	almond-shaped, slanted; alert, intelligent expression; clear brilliant blue
Other features	loud voice, large ears, big personality
Grooming	easy; must be done regularly
Temperament	intelligent, lively, playful, loyal, affectionate but can be aloof

BLUE POINT

The essence of the Blue Point is a main body colour of icy white with mere hints of the pale bluish-brown of the points. The Blue was one of the early variations of the breed to gain acceptance. It is a dilute form of the Seal.

✦ LEFT
The long, straight Roman nose and startling blue eye colour of the breed are finely demonstrated by this Blue Point.

LILAC (FROST) POINT

As its alternative American name suggests, a main body colour with just a hint of off-white moves into the frosted blue-grey of the points. There is a touch of lavender in the point colour, meeting its match in complementary lavender-pink nose and paw pads. This is the dilute form of the Chocolate.

✦ RIGHT
A Lilac Point is carrying on a conversation even while it is being photographed. Siamese are the most vocal and extrovert of cats.

RED POINT

The introduction of the sex-linked orange gene contributed to the Red Point. The points should be reddish-gold with pink nose leather and paw pads, all set off against an ivory coat.

◆ RIGHT
In a Red Point Siamese, the deeper and more intense the eye colour the better – it makes a dramatic contrast against the red-gold points.

SIAMESE COLOUR GROUPS

United Kingdom:
Seal, Blue, Chocolate, Lilac, Red, Cream, Cinnamon, Fawn, Caramel and Apricot with their Tabby and Tortie combinations

United States:
Only Seal, Blue, Chocolate and Lilac are recognized. All other colour combinations are available but are grouped in the category of Colourpointed Shorthairs

In some Federations and Associations worldwide, the Siamese is also recognized with Silver-based points, e.g. the Seal Smoke Point

CREAM POINT

Cream on cream brings an extremely subtle tonal difference. The slightly richer buttermilk points are barely discernible against an ivory coat. Nose and paw pads are pink. The Cream Point is a dilute version of the Red.

◆ BELOW
The fur of a Cream Point Siamese shows dense cream points and the palest of cream bodies, against which the eyes are a deep sapphire blue.

TABBY POINT (LYNX POINT)

There are now many variations of Tabby-pointed Siamese. In the United States only the traditional Seal, Blue, Chocolate and Lilac pointed varieties are recognized, so the Tabby joins all other variations under the category of Colourpointed Shorthairs.

In the United Kingdom, Tabby and Tortoiseshell variations are accepted, even in the new colours such as Fawn, Cinnamon and Caramel.

◆ ABOVE RIGHT
This is a Chocolate Tabby Point, showing clearly defined rings on the tail, and a lovely pale, creamy main body colour to contrast with the points.

PATCHED ORIENTALS

Yet another group linked with the Siamese are the Patched Orientals. These are in essence white Siamese cats with distinct patches of colour or tortoiseshell. Such bi-colour and tortoiseshell and white combinations were previously seen before only in Persians and British Shorthairs. Siamese were mated to patched Cornish Rex cats. Constant back-crossing to Siamese and appropriate Orientals slowly eliminated the Cornish Rex type and increased the amount of white, so that the required balance of white to colour was achieved. These are not recognized by the British cat fancy or by many overseas organizations.

TORTIE POINT

In the United States, the Tortie Point Siamese is bracketed under the more general Colourpointed classification. In the United Kingdom, there are very specific standards. The main requirement is that, as with any of the Siamese, the points are in contrast to the body colour. They should be randomly mottled with various shades of red and cream on whatever the base colour might be. There are Tortie Points in the newer colours, such as Cinnamon, as well as the traditional Seal, Blue and Chocolate.

◆ RIGHT
A lactating Chocolate Tortie Point queen has all the essential Siamese type characteristics, including a tendency to thrash its tail when bored with the photo session!

SNOWSHOE

Rounded, snow-white paws are a most distinct feature of this cat. The Snowshoe is also a unique combination of the Himalayan, or Siamese point pattern, with white spotting. It was

◆ LEFT
The ideal standard recommended for the Snowshoe includes an inverted V between the eyes, which this Blue Point does not quite achieve.

BREED BOX	
Coat	medium short, glossy, close-lying
Eyes	large, almond-shaped; bright, sparkling blue
Other features	white paws
Grooming	easy; regular, gentle brushing
Temperament	Siamese bounce with American Shorthair placidity

the occasional tendency of Siamese cats to have white feet (which was long perceived as a fault) that inspired the Snowshoe's American breeder into action in the 1960s. The Snowshoe inherited its white spotting, and its bulk, from the American Shorthair. However, the long body, point colour, and bounce in its personality come from its Oriental background.

It is a well-balanced and very muscular cat, and when the white is symmetrically marked against the dark points, can be most striking.

The front feet are ideally white only as far as the ankles, while there is a longer gauntlet to the hock on the back legs. The Snowshoe, sometimes known as Silver Laces, is recognized in Seal Point and Blue Point colours.

SEYCHELLOIS

The Seychellois is another example of an attempt to create a new, oriental-type breed. It is a cross between a Tortie and White Persian and Siamese. The long coat of the Persian has not been entirely lost and the variety is recognized (as "unrecognized colour") by the British Cat Association in both

◆ RIGHT
A chocolate and white Seychellois shows its Siamese origins in the distinctive point colours.

BREED BOX	
Coat	very short, fine, glossy; also semi-longhair variety
Eyes	blue
Grooming	easy

coat lengths. It is fundamentally a cat of slender oriental build and features, with a white coat splashed with various colours. There are three variations,

according to the proportion of white in relation to coloured areas: Septième (Seventh), Huitième (Eighth) and Neuvième (Ninth). All have blue eyes.

ABYSSINIAN

Today's pedigree Abyssinian looks like the sacred cats that are depicted in ancient Egyptian tomb paintings. The name comes from the country to the south-east of Egypt that is known as Ethiopia today. The modern Abyssinian is essentially a ticked tabby cat, with tabby markings reduced to a minimum by many years of selective breeding. Some theories suggest that the cat was introduced to the West by

♦ RIGHT
The Fawn Abyssinian is one of the newer colours that has been developed in the United Kingdom.

British soldiers returning from the region in the 1860s. Another claims the breed has its origins in the small African wild cat *Felis libyca*, an example of which was found in Abyssinia and presented to a Dutch natural history museum between 1833 and 1882. The breed was, in any event, established enough to be exhibited at the early cat shows of the 1800s.

Hybridization with domestic cats displaying the ticked tabby pattern gradually diluted the exotic blood. A typical ticked tabby has prominent tabby markings on the head, chest, legs and tail, but in the modern Abyssinian, these have been diluted by breeding ticked tabby to ticked tabby. Residual tabby markings may occur around the eyes, as a dark line along the spine to the tip of the tail, or as faint broken necklets and leg bars. The Abyssinian is a medium-sized, lithe and muscular cat with an arching, elegant neck. Large, cupped ears are set wide apart. The Wild Abyssinian attempts to recreate

BREED BOX	
Coat	short, close-lying, fine but not soft; distinctly ticked, resulting in at least four bands of colour – the roots of the fur are the colour of the base hair, and the final band is ticking colour
Eyes	wide set, large, expressive, slanting, almond shaped; amber, hazel or green
Grooming	easy
Temperament	intelligent, inquisitive, very energetic, playful, loyal; freedom-loving and enjoy hunting

the look of the early Abyssinian cat when it first came to Europe, but is not yet a recognized breed with any reputable organization. It retains the reduced ticked tabby pattern but has a slightly larger conformation than the usual varieties.

USUAL (RUDDY)

The original, or Usual, Abyssinian equates to the brown tabby coat colours. The rich golden brown base colour is ticked with black. The nose leather is brick red and the paw pads are black. In America the colour is known as Ruddy, and is one of the four colours recognized there. The others are Red (the British Sorrel), Blue, and Fawn.

♦ RIGHT
The Usual (Ruddy) Abyssinian coat is sable-like with short fur. All Abyssinian coats share the ticked characteristic, in which each hair is banded with two or three colours. In this case, reddish-brown is topped with darker brown and/or black.

SORREL (RED)

The Sorrel Abyssinian, which was the second colour to be recognized in the modern era, was originally known – and is still known in America – as the Red because of the warm, gingery colour of its coat. The bright apricot base coat is ticked with dark brown. Nose leather and paw pads are pink.

ABYSSINIAN COLOURS AND PATTERNS

Usual (Ruddy), Blue, Sorrel (Red), Fawn, Chocolate, Lilac, Red, Cream	
Silver	in all above colour variations
Tortoiseshell	Usual, Blue, Fawn, Chocolate and Lilac, and Silver versions of these

✦ RIGHT
The handsome, muscular physique of the Sorrel is typical of the breed. Abyssinians are lithe enough, but slightly bulkier than Oriental Shorthairs, and their heads are more rounded.

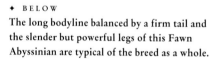

FAWN

The Fawn Abyssinian is a fairly recent addition to the plain colour range. It has a pale-oatmeal base coat powdered with darker, warm brown ticking. The fur pales to cream at the tips of tail and ears, on the toe tufts and at the back of the paws. Nose leather and paw pads are pink.

✦ BELOW
The long bodyline balanced by a firm tail and the slender but powerful legs of this Fawn Abyssinian are typical of the breed as a whole.

BLUE

Blue Abyssinian kittens occasionally occur in the litters of Usual-coloured parents. This is due to two recessive genes of the type that trigger the dilution pairing up and therefore being able to "come out" or be expressed. The undercoat is pinkish-beige ticked with slate grey. Nose leather and paw pads are dark pink to mauve-blue.

LILAC

The undercoat of the Lilac variety is pinkish-cream ticked with a slightly deeper hue of soft pinkish-grey. The nose leather and paw pads are mauve-pink, and eyes, as with all Abyssinians, range from amber to hazel or green.

◆ RIGHT
A Lilac kitten has a distinct break in the line of its nose, and has the expressive eyes and pricked ears desirable of the breed.

SILVER

The Silver Abyssinian is recognized as an official breed in the United Kingdom and Europe, but not in the United States. The colour variations are Sorrel, Blue, Chocolate, Lilac, Fawn, Red and Cream. All have pinkish to mauve nose leather and paw pads, apart from the Usual, which has a brick-red nose and black paw pads. All variations have a silver base coat ticked with the appropriate colour.

◆ RIGHT
One way of judging whether this Silver's tail is long enough for the required pedigree standard is to estimate whether it would reach the cat's shoulders if laid along the back.

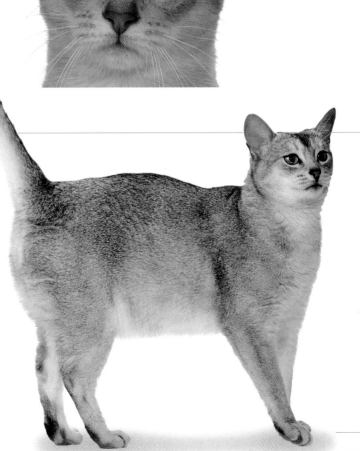

RUSSIAN BLUE

◆ LEFT
A Russian Blue gives an impression of making a complaint, but in fact its voice is so quiet that it is sometimes not even obvious when the queens are calling.

As befits a cat that is said to originate from the fringe of the Arctic Circle (and have a possible Norwegian connection, too), the most distinctive feature of today's Russian Blue is its double overcoat.

From the very start of the cat fancy, two types of Blue cat came into competition with each other at shows all over the world. The domestic British Shorthair was one; the other was known as the Blue Foreign. The names suggest a distinct difference in type between the two varieties.

Blue cats were reputed to have reached the West via merchant ships travelling from the port of Archangel in northern Russia, and became known as Archangel cats. Another import was a blue tabby from Norway. There were probably several other blues from other parts of the world that may have

◆ ABOVE
The Russian Blue has pronounced whisker pads, wide-set, pointed ears and a face more rounded than that of other foreign shorthairs. These combine to give the cat a gentle expression that reflects its nature.

◆ RIGHT
Top-quality coat texture is the single most important point that judges look for in a Russian Blue. It should be dense beneath and fine and short on top.

helped the true blue breeding programme. The type is also known as the Maltese Blue and the Spanish Blue. By the late 1800s, there were enough Blues bred to be shown at the early cat shows. Unlike the cats of today, though, these early Blues had orange eyes.

Later breeding programmes included the Korat and British Blue Shorthairs. Just before and after World War II, a bid to save the Blue from extinction led to the inclusion of a Blue Point Siamese in one breeding programme, and until fairly recently the occasional Siamese pattern was subsequently found in litters of

Russian Blues. Siamese characteristics are now regarded as unacceptable in the breed.

Imports of Blues were brought in from Scandinavia, and many good Russians went to the United States where the standard colour is a little lighter than that required in Europe.

There must be no hint of white or tabby markings on the perfect Russian Blue, but there is a silver sheen to its coat, as the slate-blue hairs often have transparent tips. A medium-sized cat, it combines sturdiness with grace. A gentle expression reflects its reputation as a quiet-spoken, affectionate animal.

An English breeder of Russian Blues maintained that the Russian type referred to a particular shape rather than the colour. Using a white, double-coated female found near the London docks, she began to develop Russian cats in other colours. The project appears to have died out in Britain, but there is a thriving colony of coloured cats in the Netherlands.

BREED BOX	
Coat	plush, heavy, double; brush-like from the body
Eyes	almond-shaped; green
Other features	silver sheen to coat as hairs often have transparent tips
Grooming	easy; gentle, regular brushing so as not to damage the double coat texture
Temperament	quiet, gentle, affectionate

KORAT

In Thailand, a wedding gift of a pair of Korats brings good fortune and happiness. There is no doubt that the Korat has been known for several hundred years. It is one of the distinctive Thai cats (alongside the Siamese and Burmese) described and illustrated in the 16th-century (or earlier) *Cat-Book of Poems* manuscript

◆ ABOVE
The Korat's heart-shaped face is typical; so is the luminous green of its eyes, and the way in which they are round and prominent when open, but appear slanted when closed.

◆ LEFT
A distinctive feature of the Korat is its coat. It shows a subtle silvery tipping.

in the national library in Bangkok. A verse on the Korat reads:

The hairs are smooth with roots like clouds and tips like silver. The eyes shine like dewdrops on a lotus leaf.

It is not surprising that the Korats captured the attention of American soldiers serving in Thailand, and the first was imported into the United States in 1959 (they reached Britain in 1972). The breed attained championship status in America in 1966. The Korat Cat Fanciers' Association was founded in 1965 with the declaration: "The Korat is silver-blue from birth to death. It can exist in no other colour. If any other colour should occur it would automatically cease to be a Korat." Nevertheless, it

appeared that the original imports were not as pure as originally thought, and that a recessive dilute gene might result in the occasional lilac, blue point or lilac point kitten. These have been named as the Thai Lilac and Thai Pointed variations.

The Korat is a medium-sized, lithe and muscular cat, and the females are daintier than the males. The most distinguishing features are the large green eyes set in a heart-shaped face and the silvery sheen of the coat.

BREED BOX

Coat	short to medium length; thick, silky; no undercoat
Eyes	round, large, luminous, prominent; green – colour changes during the course of the cat's early years
Other features	quietly vocal
Grooming	easy; regular brushing and combing
Temperament	loving, very playful

◆ RIGHT
The Thai Lilac reflects recessive genetic traits found in the Blue Korat.

BURMESE

Brown, stocky, smooth-haired cats very like the modern pedigreed Burmese are illustrated in a 16th-century (or earlier) Thai manuscript called the *Cat-Book of Poems*. They are described in the manuscript as *supalak* (copper) cats. Early in the 1900s, a small brown cat was taken from Burma to England and described as a Chocolate Siamese. However, it was not approved of in competition with the Seal Point Siamese, and nothing became of it as a breed.

The foundation of today's Burmese line was eventually laid in the early 1930s. A small brown female of Burmese origin, but probably a hybrid similar to today's Tonkinese, was mated with a Seal Point Siamese in San Francisco. Some of the resulting offspring were dark brown and formed the beginnings of the official pedigree Burmese. The breed was registered by the American Cat Fanciers' Federation in 1936, and in the late 1940s gained rapid acceptance in the United Kingdom. Despite having a genetic pattern almost identical to the Siamese, the Burmese is quieter-voiced, and much more compact of build. Its nose is distinctly different too, having an obvious bend, or break, in its line. The breed is particularly known for having a delightful personality, being sunny of temperament and obviously intelligent. The cats have well-proportioned legs, with the back legs slightly shorter than the front, and neat, oval paws. The tail is straight and of medium length, tapering to a rounded tip.

BREED BOX

Coat	short, fine, glossy, satiny, close-lying
Eyes	wide-set, large, round; yellow to gold
Grooming	little extra grooming is necessary
Temperament	intelligent, active, inquisitive, adaptable, friendly

BROWN (SABLE)

The Brown Burmese is the Usual or original colour, and should be warm and rich in tone with matching brown nose leather and paw pads. (The Chocolate, or Champagne, which was introduced later, is more of a milk-chocolate colour.) Some kittens have faint markings but these usually disappear as they mature. As with all the solid colours of Burmese, the fur lightens in shade on the underparts. Similarly, darker areas may be evident on the ears, mask and tail, like ghosts of the seal points of a Siamese.

♦ RIGHT
The top line of the Burmese's eye slants towards the nose, while the lower line is distinctly rounded, giving the breed its unique expression.

♦ RIGHT
A Brown Burmese shows the breed's tendency to rotundity – unlike its compatriots, the lithe Siamese.

BLUE

The first Blue Burmese was sired in the United Kingdom by an imported American cat. It was the Burmese equivalent of its genetic cousin, the Blue Point Siamese. The ideal tone is soft, silvery slate-blue, with the silver effect more pronounced on ears, cheeks and paws. Nose leather is dark grey and paw pads are a lighter, pinkish-grey.

◆ RIGHT AND LEFT
The density of a Blue Burmese's fur accentuates strong shoulders and a broad, rounded chest. The Burmese is quite a heavy cat for its size!

LILAC (PLATINUM) AND CHOCOLATE

Lilac – or Platinum as it is called in the United States – is a dilute version of the Chocolate (Champagne) Burmese. It became established in the early 1970s. It is a wonderfully soft shade of pinkish dove-grey, and nose leather and paw pads are lavender-pink in keeping.

◆ LEFT
The typical Burmese head is distinctly round, with a short nose and a firm chin, and round-tipped ears spaced well apart. This Lilac shows excellent type.

◆ RIGHT
A Chocolate (Champagne) Burmese shows the typical milky brown colouring that is quite distinct from the richer colouring of the Brown (Sable).

RED

The ideal Red has golden eyes and a tangerine-cream colour to its fur, rather than red. Although tabby markings are almost inevitable on the face because of the orange gene which reveals the tabby pattern, the rest of the coat should be consistent in tone. Any hint of rings on the legs would be considered a fault by show judges. Nose leather and paw pads are pink.

♦ RIGHT
You can see the marked kink in the nose of this Red Burmese. This is known as a nose break and is a feature of the breed in general.

BURMESE COLOURS AND PATTERNS

Solid colours	Brown (Sable), Blue, Chocolate (Champagne), Lilac (Platinum), Red, Cream
Tortoiseshell	Brown, Blue, Chocolate, Lilac

Note that while these varieties are those that are available, not all are recognized as Burmese by every national cat registering body. In the United States, colours outside Sable, Blue, Champagne and Platinum are grouped by the CFA as Foreign Burmese. Other associations call them Malayan.

CREAM

The Cream Burmese was first developed in the United Kingdom in the late 1960s and early 1970s. It is part of the group of colours that arise from the sex-linked orange gene. A Cream Burmese is the dilute version of the Red. If the eyes of a Cream Burmese are deep gold rather than yellow, that is a bonus for the show cat. Otherwise, the ideal coat colour is for an even shade of rich cream moving to slightly darker shades on the ears, face, paws and tail. Paw pads and nose leather are pink.

♦ LEFT
Basic cream is mingled with pinkish dove grey in the Lilac Tortie. There are also Brown, Blue and Chocolate Torties.

♦ RIGHT
Powderings of colour over mask, paws, tail and legs on the Cream Burmese are like ghostly versions of the points on a Siamese.

THE ASIAN GROUP

The Asian Group of cats are Burmese in type, but not in colour, coat pattern or (in the case of the Tiffanie) length of fur. It is a similar relationship to the one between the Siamese and the similar type, but differently coloured and patterned, Oriental Shorthairs, Balinese and Angora. The Asian Group embraces the Asian Self, including the Bombay, the Burmilla and the tabby varieties. The semi-longhaired version of the Asian is the Tiffanie, described in the Semi-longhair section. As with the Burmese, the female Asians are markedly smaller and daintier than the males, but the body type is generally medium-sized, straight-backed and rounded of chest. Legs are medium length with oval paws, and the hind legs are a little longer than the forelegs. The Asian cats carry their medium to long tails high and proud, and the glossiness of their short, close-lying coats is an accurate reflection of their good health.

BREED BOX	
Coat	short, dense, soft and glossy; slightly longer than Burmese
Eyes	yellow to green, green preferred in Silvers, gold allowed in Selfs
Other features	outlined eyes, nose and lips
Grooming	little extra grooming needed
Temperament	stable, dignified inquisitive, sociable

BURMILLA

The Burmilla is the longest established and most popular of the Asian Group of cats, and often the starting point for breeding other varieties. It was the originator of the Asian Group of cats in the United Kingdom, derived from a Lilac Burmese queen and a Chinchilla Silver Persian in 1981. The result was a shorthaired Burmese lookalike with the stunning tipping and outlined features of the Chinchilla. The Burmilla is the shaded or tipped representative of the Asian Group. The shaded varieties are more heavily tipped and obviously coloured than the tipped varieties. The undercoat on both variations is the palest possible silver or golden, but tipped at the very ends with one of the standard or Burmese colours. Nose leather and paw pads are brick-red (terracotta), and dark

◆ LEFT
A Brown-shaded Silver Burmilla expresses the typical inquisitive nature of its type.

◆ RIGHT
On the forehead of the Burmilla there should be an M-shaped mark – as on this Blue Shaded. Other painted face features may be streaks from the outer edges of the eyes and on the cheeks.

◆ ABOVE
The Lilac Tortie Burmilla has a white base coat shaded with a mingling of frosted pink-grey, and dark and light cream. Nose leather and paw pads are complementary lavender or pink; eyes are either amber or green.

BURMILLA COLOURS AND PATTERNS

Standard	gold base coat
Silver	white base coat; colours less intense

May be shaded or tipped with Black, Blue, Chocolate, Lilac, Red, Caramel, Apricot, Cream, Black Tortoiseshell, Blue Tortoiseshell, Chocolate Tortoiseshell, Lilac Tortoiseshell, Caramel Tortoiseshell, plus the Burmese versions of these colours

pigmentation around the eyes, nose and lips should be obvious. One of the cat's particularly appealing features is the outlining of nose and eyes in the same colour as the darker tip. The Burmilla consolidates many of the best points of its parents. It is open and sociable like the Burmese but less demanding and noisy; it is stable and dignified like its Persian forebears, but is rather more adventurous and inquisitive.

◆ ABOVE LEFT
A Black Shaded Silver Burmilla is closest in colour to its Chinchilla Silver heritage and has Chinchilla-like kohl-ringed eyes.

◆ BELOW
Subtle gradations of tone are a delightful feature of the Asian Smoke. This is a Brown, with darker points on tail and face, due to a Burmese gene.

ASIAN SMOKE

The Asian Smoke is, as its name suggests, the smoke variety of the Asian Group. Each hair is silver, while the tip is coloured. Mere suggestions of tabby markings may appear like watered silk on the body, while the head has what are sometimes known as clown marks – frown lines on the forehead and spectacled eyes.

ASIAN SMOKE COLOURS AND PATTERNS

Black, Blue, Chocolate, Lilac, Red, Caramel, Apricot, Cream, Black Tortoiseshell, Blue Tortoiseshell, Chocolate Tortoiseshell, Lilac Tortoiseshell, Caramel Tortoiseshell, plus the Burmese versions of all these colours, all with a silvery-white undercoat

BOMBAY

Because there is an Indian black leopard as sleek and black of coat as this particular domestic cat breed, the Bombay cat is named after an Indian city. The cat's most outstanding features are its gleaming black fur and its large, brilliant golden eyes.

The Bombay was created in the United States in the 1950s in an attempt to breed a pure black Burmese. A Sable (Brown) Burmese was crossed with a Black American Shorthair, and the Bombay was accepted as a championship variety in 1976. An American couple, fittingly named Opium and Bagheera, were exported to France in 1989 to found the European line, and so the type is similar on both sides of the Atlantic.

Not so in the United Kingdom, where Black British Shorthairs were mated with Burmese (although one was later combined with an American Bombay) and ultimately became part of the Asian Group breeding programme. The Bombay is judged in the United Kingdom along the same lines as other Asian self colours. The Bombay on both

✦ ABOVE
With a solid, jet-black coat and deep amber eyes, the Bombay earned the nickname "the patent leathered kid with the new penny eyes" in America, its country of origin.

BREED BOX	
Coat	short, very close-lying and shiny
Eyes	large; gold, yellow to green (United Kingdom); gold to copper (United States)
Other features	patent leather glossiness of coat
Grooming	little extra grooming is necessary
Temperament	sedate, affectionate, needs attention

sides of the Atlantic has a distinct Burmese temperament, is known to purr a great deal, and is a strong and healthy breed. It is a medium-sized cat with a round head that seems large for its body. It has a short snub nose, firm chin and large ears rounded at the tips. Everything about it is black, from the fur that must be jet-black to the tips, to the nose and paw pads.

✦ LEFT
Although the black Bombay is the best known self-coloured Asian, there are many other colours. This Blue had black parents somewhere along the line, each of whom carried a recessive gene that resulted in its dilute colour.

✦ ABOVE
The Bombay is a polished, all-black Burmese type.

OTHER ASIANS

Once the Chinchilla/Lilac Burmese combination had launched the Asian Group, it became evident that an enormous number of variations could occur. Parents were introduced into breeding programmes that carried the sex-linked red gene to produce red, cream, apricot and tortoiseshell Asians. The tabby genes were included for ticked, classic, mackerel and spotted patterns. Colours allowed are Black (Brown), Blue, Chocolate, Lilac, Red, Cream, Caramel and Apricot, all with Silver and their appropriate tortoiseshell combinations, plus the Burmese versions of these colours.

◆ LEFT
The Asian Black Ticked Tabby is more heavily ticked than the Burmilla equivalent. The darkest fur is along the line of the spine, shading to a much paler colour on the underparts and legs.

BREED BOX

Coat	fine, glossy, silky
Eyes	wide-set, large, round; colour ranges from yellow to green; self colours may be golden
Grooming	little extra grooming is necessary
Temperament	easygoing, playful, gentle

ASIAN GROUP COLOURS AND PATTERNS

Self colours	Black (Bombay), Blue, Chocolate, Lilac, Red, Cream, Caramel, Apricot
Tortoiseshell	Black, Blue, Chocolate, Lilac, Caramel
Tabby	classic, spotted, mackerel and ticked patterns in all the above colours and the Burmese versions of these colours, in both Standard and Silver tabby.

◆ ABOVE
Although it has a fine M on its forehead, this is not a tabby, but a Red Self Asian. It is similar to the Red Burmese, but of a considerably deeper, richer and more solid hue.

◆ BELOW
The Caramel Ticked Tabby is one of the rarer dilute colours seen in the Asian Group. This youngster has an excellent M mark on its forehead which will win it a few points.

◆ LEFT
The dominant Tortie colour is black, which this Asian shows very well. The colours can be mingled or in blotches as long as the hairs are coloured to the roots.

BENGAL

The Bengal was developed in an attempt to combine the look of the wild Asian Leopard Cat with the temperament of the domesticated cat. Because this involved crossing domestic cats with the wild cats indigenous to south-east Asia, the breeding programmes have met with some controversy. To gain acceptance, it needs to establish that wild tendencies have been bred out, and that the new breed has the ability to reproduce a consistent type. The first Bengal litters born of wild/domestic parents (known as the F1 generation) tended to produce non-fertile males and only partially fertile females, and in some cases

◆ LEFT
A young Bengal shows off the muscular and athletic body it has inherited from its wild relations, and the spotted tummy so desirable in breeding standards.

the temperament has been unstable. Most associations, therefore, do not allow these early generations to be shown, and they are often not suitable as pets.

Although the modern breed was pioneered in the desert state of Arizona in the United States during the 1960s, it is not registered as a championship breed by all American cat associations. Most of the American varieties are shades of brown. The Bengal is on its way to gaining provisional status in the United Kingdom, where spotted and marbled variations are being bred. There has been a huge increase in Bengal breeding

lines throughout the world, possibly because of the high prices commanded by the kittens.

The concept of hybrids between small wild cat species and domestic varieties is not new. There is a record of a prototype Bengal at the London Zoo sometime before 1889, and at a Dutch cattery during the 1960s.

The modern breed is very striking: it is long, sleek and muscular with beautifully patterned fur. Its coat is its unique feature, quite unlike any other domestic breed, being more akin to the feel of a wild cat's pelt. Smallish, forward-pointing ears extend straight up from the sides of the broadly wedge-shaped head.

◆ ABOVE
This Leopard Spotted youngster is beginning to show the desirable patterns that will be clearly outlined in maturity, but at present are slightly masked by the woolly kitten coat.

◆ ABOVE
The Snow Spotted Bengal is a paler version of the spotted variety. The pale background colour is the result of the recessive Siamese gene, and is complemented by clear blue eyes.

BREED BOX

Coat	short to medium, very dense; and unusually soft to the touch
Eyes	oval, large, not bold
Grooming	regular stroking; some brushing
Temperament	active, playful, loves water

◆ LEFT
A Marbled Bengal displays the dramatic coat pattern and long, prowling bodyline.

TONKINESE

For those who regard the modern Siamese as rather rat-like in its sleekness, and the American Burmese as too Persian and heavyweight, the Tonkinese is, perhaps, a compromise. The breed is also seen as having the points of the Siamese but with a more softly contoured body and a less assertive nature.

The Tonk is the product of mating Siamese and Burmese in America during the 1950s and the following two decades, although the type had occurred spontaneously for a long time. Such mixed parentage means no all-Tonk litters. The offspring from a Tonkinese coupling is likely to be two Tonks, one Siamese, and one Burmese. The Tonkinese cat type displays the mingled characteristics of the two breeds – of medium build, it has a gently wedge-shaped head rounded at the top, though slightly longer than

that of the Siamese. Like the Burmese, there is an angle on its shortish nose, but it is not as pronounced. Tonkinese legs are slim but muscular, and its body is a perfect balance between the length of the Siamese and the

◆ ABOVE
Originally the result of a cross mating between Burmese and Siamese, the Tonkinese should not show too much of an inclination towards either of these foundation breeds, but be a happy medium of the two, like this Lilac.

◆ LEFT
A Blue Tonkinese has the required light aquamarine eyes. Siamese blue or Burmese chartreuse are considered faults.

BREED BOX	
Coat	short, close-lying, fine, soft, silky with a lustrous sheen
Eyes	almond-shaped, slightly slanted; aquamarine
Grooming	easy; regular, gentle brushing
Temperament	equable, lively, inquisitive, relaxed, very friendly

◆ LEFT
The mixture of brown, red and cream in a Brown Tortie Tonkinese needs to be well mingled and should darken at the points to meet the exacting standards set for the breed.

TONKINESE COLOURS AND PATTERNS

Solid colours	Brown, Blue, Chocolate, Lilac, Red, Cream, Caramel, Apricot
Tortoiseshell	Brown, Blue, Chocolate, Lilac, Caramel
Tabby	Brown, Blue, Chocolate, Lilac, Red, Cream, Caramel, Apricot
Tortie Tabby	Brown, Blue, Chocolate, Lilac, Caramel

In the United States the breed is recognized in Natural Mink, Champagne Mink, Blue Mink, Platinum Mink and Honey Mink

tendency to stoutness of the Burmese. Ears are large with rounded tips. The coat pattern shades to a darker tone on the legs, ears, mask and tail. Coat colour too, is a compromise – paler than Burmese but darker than Siamese. The cat has a calm temperament but with a streak of mischief and the welcome addition of hybrid vigour.

It is very important for the point colour to be definitely darker than the main body colour on mask, ears, legs and tail, but without any sharp colour changes such as those seen in the Siamese. Underparts should be lighter than the upper body, which in turn should show gradation of tone rather than sudden changes.

The eye colour of the Tonkinese is neither the startling amber nor chartreuse green found in the Burmese, nor the deep sapphire of the Siamese. It can range from aquamarine blue to greenish-blue or bluish-green. It may take some time for eye colour to settle. Tonkinese generally mature slowly, reaching their final colouring and peak size at about two years of age.

◆ BELOW
This Blue Tabby is a typical example of the Siamese ancestry being too obvious in its extended limbs and slim line. It may not win show prizes, but is nevertheless a beautiful animal.

◆ LEFT
A Blue Tabby Tonkinese has the preferred spectacle-like rings around its eyes and spotted whisker pads. However, the M shape on his forehead could be more distinct.

EGYPTIAN MAU

On ancient Egyptian manuscripts and murals, a cat is depicted that looks very much like the modern breed of Egyptian Mau. The breeder wanted to replicate the cats of the Pharaohs, and founded the breeding line from a native Egyptian breed that seemed to have evolved spontaneously in the Cairo region. The first Egyptian Mau (the name is ancient Egyptian for a sacred domestic cat) kitten was shown in Rome in the 1950s. Its owner emigrated with her cats to America, where the breed was granted recognition by the Cat Fanciers' Association in 1977. It is now available in Silver (charcoal markings on silver), Bronze, and Smoke (black markings on charcoal/silver underlay) varieties. The Bronze, with dark brown to black markings on a warm bronze undercoat, is closest in appearance to the cat depicted on Egyptian murals. Europe did not recognize the breed

◆ LEFT
Spotted cats very similar to this were illustrated in ancient Egyptian manuscripts and murals. The M-shaped mark on its brow is said to echo the pattern on the back of the scarab beetle, which was sacred to the Egyptians.

until 1992. A spotted cat bred from Siamese lines in England during the 1960s was originally called Egyptian Mau, but later became established as the Oriental Spotted Tabby.

The Egyptian Mau is a medium-sized, muscular cat, pleasing to the eye, easy to groom, and with an extrovert personality. It tends to bond with just one or two people, and is not averse to learning a trick or two, or to walking on a lead. Its head is slightly oriental in shape, with large, alert ears, although its muzzle is well rounded. The conformation is generally graceful, with hind legs slightly longer than the front legs, and a well-balanced tail.

BREED BOX

Coat	medium length, dense, lustrous, silky
Eyes	large, alert, almond-shaped, slightly slanted; light green
Other features	spotted coat
Grooming	easy; regular gentle brushing to remove dead hairs
Temperament	affectionate, lively; may be aloof

◆ LEFT
The well-defined spots are the most important features of the Mau. This Bronze is probably the closest in colour to its Egyptian forebears.

SINGAPURA

◆ LEFT
The Singapura is one of the few breeds that is only available in one colour, a warm ivory overlaid with sepia-brown ticking. This one shows characteristic darker shading along the length of its spine.

During the early 1970s, an experienced and influential American cat breeder found a colony of unusual looking cats in Singapore. How they had come to be in a feral state is not known, although there is ample evidence that the cat that came to be known as the Singapura had existed for a long time. Because of the feral state in which they were found, the cats were known as drain or river cats. At one time, they were culled by the Singaporean authorities. Now the Malay government has adopted the animal as the country's national cat, and renamed it *Kucinta*, which means love cat.

The Singapura is on the small side, but stocky and muscular. Its head is round, its ears are large, wide-based

and pointed at the top; its eyes are huge. The neck is thick and short, the muzzle broad, and the nose blunt. The nose and eyes are further accentuated by dark eye-liner outlines.

The characteristic Singapura coat is that of a ticked tabby with some markings on the back of the legs, but not on the front. Its usual colour is called sepia agouti, which is dark brown ticking on an old-ivory ground.

The Singapura quickly took a very firm hold on European affections, and is on its way to becoming an established championship breed.

◆ LEFT
Owl-like eyes are a particular feature of the Singapura, orbs of gold and green fetchingly outlined in black.

◆ BELOW
Small but perfectly formed could be an apt description of the Singapura, but the cats are well-muscled and feel much heavier than they look.

BREED BOX

Coat	fine, short, close-lying
Eyes	large, rounded almond-shaped; brilliant colour
Other features	huge eyes on small frame
Grooming	very easy; regular brushing
Temperament	affectionate, good-natured, gentle, playful

OCICAT

The Ocicat is one of the glorious accidents in the cat fancy. A breeder from the state of Michigan in the United States set out to create a Ticked Point Siamese. She mated a Siamese with an Abyssinian. One of the offspring was mated back to another Siamese male, and a tabby Point Siamese duly appeared. However, one kitten was ivory-coated with clear golden spots. This was the very first Ocicat, its name inspired by the wild ocelot, because of the similarity in coat colour and pattern. Many breeders used the same breeding

♦ LEFT
This Chocolate Silver Ocicat shows all the finer points required of the breed, including hindquarters that are rather higher than the front.

♦ BELOW
At birth, the Ocicat kitten may have a very indistinct pattern. The spots develop as the cat matures, and this 15-week-old kitten is looking promising.

BREED BOX

Coat	short, thick, smooth and satiny with lustrous sheen
Eyes	large, slanted, almond-shaped; all colours except blue
Other features	spotted coat
Grooming	easy; regular brushing
Temperament	affectionate, active

♦ ABOVE
There should be a clear M mark on the forehead of Ocicats, but this is less obvious in the dilute colours such as this Lilac.

formula successfully. Recognition was granted in the United States in the 1960s, although championship status was not achieved until 1987. Preliminary recognition in the United Kingdom did not come until 1998. Ocicats are now available in Brown, Blue,

Chocolate, Lilac, Cinnamon, and Fawn, as well as the Silver-based versions of these colours. A few authorities also recognize Red, Cream and Tortoiseshell. It is a long-bodied, well-muscled animal, with medium-length legs and a long, tapered tail. It has a round head with a prominent muzzle and large, pointed ears.

♦ ABOVE
The spotting on the coat of the Ocicat should be well defined – faint or blurred spots are a serious fault, even on the less contrasted colours of the Lilac and other dilute forms.

♦ BELOW
A Chocolate Ocicat displays an intelligent and friendly disposition – a blend of character and temperament inherited from the breed's original Abyssinian and Siamese parentage.

JAPANESE BOBTAIL

There are representations of the Japanese Bobtail on ancient prints and manuscripts dating back some 2,000 years. On the Gotojuki temple in Tokyo, built during the Edo period (1615–1867), is a famous portrayal of a beckoning Bobtail.

Legend has it that a cat in Japan was warming itself in front of a fire when it accidentally set its tail alight. It ran through the city and spread the fire through the fragile wooden houses, which were burnt to ashes. The Emperor of Japan decreed all cats should be punished and ordered their tails to be chopped off. There is a similar story surrounding the origin of Manx cats.

What actually caused this particular gene mutation is a mystery. Unlike the Manx, the mating of two Japanese Bobtails will produce only more Japanese Bobtails.

An American who lived in Japan after World War II returned to the United States with 38 Bobtails to found a breeding line. Provisional

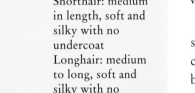

◆ ABOVE
A Red and White Japanese Bobtail shows that, unlike the tailless true Manx, the breed has a very short tail that curls around its rump.

status was granted in 1971, and championship status in 1976. Japanese breeders began to develop a long-coated variation in 1954, although the type had unofficially been around for centuries, particularly in the northern regions of Japan. They were represented in ancient Japanese paintings, but had been ignored by the pedigree cat aficionados. They were recognized in 1991 by The International Cat Association.

The Japanese Bobtail is a medium-sized cat with clean lines and bone structure. It is well muscled but straight and slender rather than massive in build. The set of the eyes combined with high cheek-bones, lends a distinctive cast to the face, especially in profile, which is quite different from other oriental breeds. Its short tail should resemble a rabbit tail, with the hair fanning out to create a pompon appearance which effectively camouflages the underlying bone structure.

The cats are now available in most colours and patterns. In Japan, they are thought of as bringing good fortune to a household, especially the van-patterned Tortie and White, known as the mi-ke (three colours).

BREED BOX

Coat	Shorthair: medium in length, soft and silky with no undercoat Longhair: medium to long, soft and silky with no undercoat; frontal ruff desirable
Eyes	large, oval; colour reflects coat colour
Other features	short, moveable tail
Grooming	easy; regular combing
Temperament	affectionate, intelligent, inquisitive, needs attention

◆ RIGHT
While the Japanese Bobtail is accepted in many colours, it is the Tortie and White, which the Japanese call mi-ke (three colour) that is especially prized.

MANX

A colony of cats became stranded on an island off the west coast of mainland Britain and eventually formed a distinct type. One myth suggests that the tailless Manx cat originated from a mating between a rabbit and a cat; another that the cat was the last to leave Noah's Ark and had its tail chopped in the door. The reality is that the Isle of Man cat community was forced by its confinement into concentrated interbreeding. A mutant gene that led to a spinal malformation spread throughout the community and became the norm. The spine was literally curtailed, ending (in what is described as a true or rumpy Manx) in a hollow where a tail should have been. Cats with brief stumps of tails were also born, and these are called stumpies, stubbies or risers. The gene that causes this condition is related to

BREED BOX

Coat	double, well-padded
Eyes	large, round; colour in keeping with coat colour
Other features	lack of tail
Grooming	easy; regular brushing
Temperament	calm, intelligent, active, loyal; likes to be with its owner

◆ ABOVE
A residual tail is just visible on the Black Manx, which means that he cannot qualify as a true Manx on the show circuit. He will, however, be valuable for breeding purposes.

◆ ABOVE
The strong features typical of the Manx are evident on this Red Spotted Tabby. His cheeks are full, ears are prominent and his nose is broad, straight and of medium length.

◆ LEFT
A true, or rumpy, Manx has a hollow where its tail should be. This Tortoiseshell Tabby and White shows the stocky build typical of the breed. The chest is broad, and the back short. The rump is higher than the shoulder.

◆ LEFT
Manx cats have now been bred in all standard colours and patterns except colourpointed (Himalayan). This is a Blue-Cream rumpy, showing the required absolute lack of tail; it should be completely rounded with no definite rise of bone or cartilage.

◆ ABOVE
Note the front legs of this Manx Bi-colour. They are slightly shorter than the long, muscular hind legs which result in a characteristic rabbit-like, loping gait.

the one that causes spina bifida in humans. If male and female rumpies are mated, some of the foetuses may not develop to full term. Breeders therefore introduce part- or fully-tailed varieties into their breeding programmes. For show purposes, however, it is the taillessness of the rumpy that is accepted as the standard for the breed. It is accepted in all the standard colours and patterns except colourpointed, although Lilac and Chocolate are not recognized by some associations.

MANX CAT VARIETIES

Rumpy shows a hollow where the tail should emerge. This is the Manx cat exhibited at cat shows

Rumpy Riser has few fused vertebrae at the end of the spine. These can be seen and definitely felt, which disqualifies the cat from being shown as a Manx. It is, however, used for breeding

Stumpy has a very short tail that can be moved. The vertebrae are not necessarily fused. This is the form which gives rise to some of the bobtailed cats

Longy has an almost normal length tail. Often these cats are indistinguishable from the normal domestic feline

Cymric is a rare semi-longhair variety, which is described in the Semi-longhair section of this book

◆ BELOW
The occasional tailed Manx is born of Manx parents. He or she will win no prizes for Manx type perfection, but with the typical bulkiness of the type and a freedom from the spinal defects, is an extremely valuable asset to any Manx breeding programme.

REX CATS

The distinguishing feature of all Rex cats is their waved coat pattern. Rex fur grows at a much slower rate than the fur on most cats, and is the way it is because it is less developed. Most cats, both longhairs and shorthairs, have three levels of hair – a fine down undercoat, a layer of bristly awn hairs, and outer guardhairs. On Rex cats (with the exception of the Selkirk Rex) the outer guardhairs are usually non-existent, and the awn hairs are much shorter than usual, resulting in a fine, downy coat that tends to wave or curl. Even the whiskers of a Rex are shorter than is usual.

Another characteristic shared by most Rex cats is their athleticism. They have compact, muscular bodies, and are notably active and agile. Nevertheless, they are ready to bond strongly with their owners and are more likely than many cats to take to going for walks on a lead. The name rex is taken from a curly-coated rabbit of the same name. A geneticist compared the fur of the Cornish Rex cat and the Rex rabbit and found the genetic make-up of each to be similar.

The various Rex breeds are all quite distinct, and were discovered and developed quite independently of each other. They were all, however, due to spontaneously occurring mutant genes. They were named after the regions in which they were discovered.

German Rex cats (which have slighter denser fur) were first bred specifically in East Berlin just after World War II. Ohio and Oregon Rex cats, which were discovered in the states of the same names, do not appear to have survived as breeding lines.

✦ TOP AND ABOVE
Compare the facial characteristics of the Devon Rex (*top*) and Cornish Rex (*above*). The Cornish breed has a longer face, while the Devon Rex has prominent cheekbones and very large ears.

✦ BELOW
The Cornish Rex, with its crisply waved coat, is now available in all colours and patterns, from self colours, to this White and Black Smoke, and all the various colourpoints.

CORNISH REX

The first recorded Cornish Rex kitten was born in 1950 in Cornwall, England, to a plain-coated tortoiseshell and white female. The kitten was a cream classic tabby with white chest and white belly. Its fur was closely waved. It was mated with its mother, and the resulting litter contained two curly-coated kittens. Because of the close interbreeding of the early Cornish Rexes, the gene pool was restricted and the kittens became weaker. Most of the kittens had to be put down, but one survivor, the son of one of the original kittens, was mated to his daughter before she was exported to the United States. Her lineage was strengthened by outcrossed matings with other breeds, and then back-crossed to rex cats to recreate the recessive curly coat. The breed was officially recognized in 1967.

The Cornish Rex has an elongated wedge of a head that curves gently at the forehead. The muzzle is rounded, the chin strong and the profile straight. The ears are startlingly large. The body is hard and muscular, with the legs long and straight, and the tail fine and tapering. The Cornish Rex comes in all colours, patterns and colour combinations.

BREED BOX	
Coat	short, plushy, silky; no guardhairs; waves, curls or ripples particularly on back and tail
Eyes	medium, oval
Other features	big ears
Grooming	gentle brushing, using fingers to set waves
Temperament	intelligent, thoughtful, active

DEVON REX

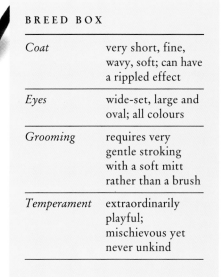

The Devon Rex is affectionately described as having a pixie-like expression – which reflects its mischievous character.

In 1960, another curly-coated cat was discovered in Devon, England, the neighbouring county to the home of the Cornish Rex. A curly-coated feral male had mated with a stray, straight-haired female, and the litter included one curly-coated male. As the curly hair gene is recessive and needs to find a matching one to emerge, the female must have had a compatible gene pool. However, the gene which caused the coat was quite different from that of the Cornish Rex – mating the two breeds resulted in only straight-coated offspring.

The Devon Rex coat is generally less dense than that of the Cornish Rex and, without careful breeding, very sparse coats can result. Physically, the Devon Rex is quite different from the Cornish. It shares the muscular build, slim legs and long, whip-like tail, but it is broad chested, and has a flat forehead, prominent cheek-bones and a crinkled brow. All coat colours, patterns and colour combinations are allowed.

BREED BOX	
Coat	very short, fine, wavy, soft; can have a rippled effect
Eyes	wide-set, large and oval; all colours
Grooming	requires very gentle stroking with a soft mitt rather than a brush
Temperament	extraordinarily playful; mischievous yet never unkind

SELKIRK REX

A curly-coated tortoiseshell and white kitten was born in a humane society in Wyoming in the United States in 1987. It was mated to top-quality Persian breeding lines and the offspring crossed back to the distinctive curly-coated line. The resulting Selkirk Rex embraces both long- and shorthaired cats. The Selkirk Rex Breed Club has stipulated that no outcrosses should be made to other Rex breeds, so that the line retains a strong identity. Only one Selkirk Rex parent is necessary for some rexed kittens to be produced.

The Selkirk Rex has denser fur than other Rex breeds, including guardhairs. Build is stocky and rectangular, but with a rounded head and wide cheeks. The breed was accepted for registration by the American Cat Fanciers' Association in 1992 but is not recognized in the United Kingdom.

BREED BOX	
Coat	lambswool texture, with curled guard- and awn hairs; thick and dense
Eyes	round, full, wide-set; all colours
Grooming	gentle and regular with a wide-toothed comb
Temperament	calm, affectionate, playful

Persian cats introduced into the breeding line mean that the Selkirk Rex has a full body of fur, unlike the other Rex breeds. There are shorthair varieties, such as this Black Smoke (*above*), and longhairs like the Silver Chocolate Lynx Point (*right*).

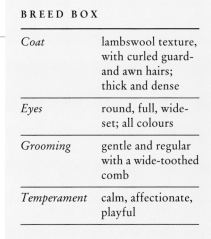

AMERICAN CURL

Early in the 1980s, a stray kitten with strange, backwardly reflexed ears, was discovered in California. Two curly-eared kittens were born to this stray, one shorthaired, the other longhaired. The breed – for this birth heralded the start of the American Curl's rise to fame and fortune – has therefore always had the two coat options. The two kittens were shown at a local show, and the response was electric. It is very rare for the big cat associations to take up a new breed so rapidly, but that is precisely what happened. The American Curl was granted recognition by The International Cat

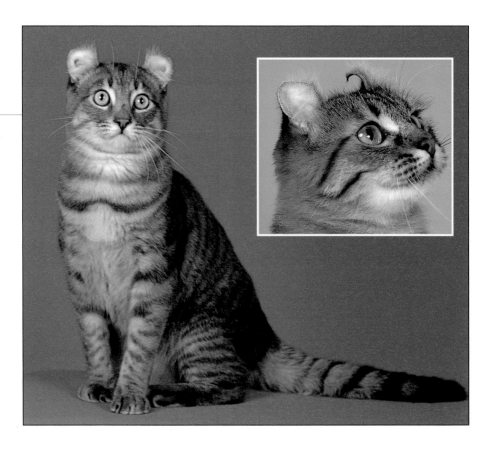

◆ ABOVE
A Blue Mackerel Tabby demonstrates the well-balanced conformation of the American Curl – to match the breed's evenness of temperament.

◆ INSET ABOVE
The extraordinary shape of the American Curl's ear can be fully appreciated in this Brown Mackerel Tabby.

◆ LEFT
A strikingly marked Brown Mac Tabby pricks up its distinctive ears. Ideally, they should curve back in a smooth arc of at least 90 degrees but not more than 180 degrees, and have rounded and flexible tips.

BREED BOX	
Coat	long or short; both are silky, lying flat without plushiness
Eyes	large, walnut-shaped; all colours
Other features	ears curled back
Grooming	relatively easy; regular brushing; check ears
Temperament	eager to please; needs attention

◆ BELOW
Because the breeding line was founded on a pair of kittens which were both curly-eared but had different coat lengths, there are longhaired American Curls, too, as this Red Classic Tabby shows.

◆ RIGHT
Not only do American Curls come in two coat lengths, but there is now a wide choice of colours and patterns. This magnificent cat is a Brown Mac Tabby and White longhair.

Association in 1985, followed by the Cat Fanciers' Association in 1986. It is a winsomely charming cat with ears that curve backwards as though windswept, or the cat is listening very carefully to something just behind it.

The ears should be wide at the base and open. Otherwise, the breed is medium-sized, well-balanced and well-muscled. The legs are medium length with round paws, and the tail is flexible and tapering, equal to body length. The American Curl comes in all colours, patterns and colour combinations.

No other anomalies or physical defects have occurred in the breed, and successful outcrossing to other breeds is continuing to ensure that a strong, healthy type is maintained. However, as yet, the breed is not recognized in the United Kingdom, being rejected on the same grounds as the Scottish Fold.

SCOTTISH FOLD

One day in 1961, a Scottish farmer spotted a little white cat with strangely folded ears. A year later, this cat produced other folded-ear kittens. A British Blue Shorthair was introduced into what had become the foundations

BREED BOX	
Coat	short, dense, plush
Eyes	wide-set, large, round
Other features	ears folded forward
Grooming	relatively easy; regular brushing; check ears
Temperament	a self-assured cat and, because of its British Shorthair and Persian antecedents, generally placid, independent yet very loving

◆ LEFT
Although its country of origin is Scotland, the Scottish Fold is relatively unknown in the United Kingdom, although popular in the United States. Its downward folding ears emphasize the roundness of its head.

of the Scottish Fold. However, it was discovered that the gene that caused the folded ears was dominant, and could also cause skeletal problems in some cats. The Governing Council of the Cat Fancy in the United Kingdom, among others, has resisted recognition of the breed because of the risk of a kitten being born with skeletal abnormalities. This may occur even if a Fold is mated with another, proven breed. The Scottish Fold, found in a wide range of coats and patterns, is a medium-sized cat, which may be short- or longhaired. It has a round head held on a short neck and its nose is short with a gentle curve. Despite short legs, the cat is not inactive.

AMERICAN WIREHAIR

◆ BELOW
Apart from its curly coat and whiskers, the American Wirehair is very much like its compatriot, the American Shorthair.

The coat of the American Wirehair – which, as its name suggests, is its most distinguishing feature – is by no means fully rexed, but it is far more crimped, crinkled and bouncy than that of most cats. The origins of the breed go back to a barn in Upper New York State in 1966. A red and white curly-coated male occurred as a spontaneous mutation in an American Shorthair litter. By 1969, a pure-breeding colony had been established, and the breed was given official recognition by the Cat

BREED BOX	
Coat	springy, tight, medium in length; individual hairs are crimped, hooked or bent
Eyes	wide-set, large, round; all colours
Grooming	minimal with an occasional soft brushing
Temperament	very positive and inquisitive; they never seem to stop purring

Fanciers' Association in 1978. The breed remains more or less exclusively in the United States, but there was a class for American Wirehairs at a Brussels show in 1996.

It is a medium to large cat with a round head, prominent cheek-bones and a well-developed muzzle. It comes in all colours and patterns except the colourpointed (Himalayan) series.

SPHYNX

Hairless cats were supposedly bred by the Aztec people of Central America hundreds of years ago. The last pair of cats of this Mexican breed was presented to an American couple by Pueblo Indians in Albuquerque, New Mexico in 1903. Unfortunately, the male was savaged to death by a pack of dogs and so the breed did not survive. The modern Sphynx breeding programme began in 1966 in Toronto,

◆ ABOVE
The face of a Black Tortie Tabby shows the high cheek-bones, well-defined whisker pads, and backward-slanting, lemon-shaped eyes of the breed.

◆ LEFT
A Black and White Bi-colour Sphynx demonstrates the breed's long, slender neck, very large ears and very short whiskers. The breed is sometimes referred to as the ET of the cat world.

BREED BOX

Coat	a fine body suede
Eyes	large, slightly slanted
Other features	wrinkled skin at key points, few or no whiskers; big ears, whip-like tail
Grooming	fairly easy; more sponging and wiping than combing and brushing
Temperament	intelligent, very lively and playful

♦ LEFT
It is acceptable for a Sphynx to have wrinkled folds of skin around its neck and legs, but it should be smooth elsewhere, like this Brown Tabby.

Canada, when an ordinary shorthaired, black and white domestic cat bore a hairless male kitten. An expert breeder bought mother and son and developed the breed from there.

The Sphynx is not exactly hairless; its skin is covered with a soft, warm down which feels like the furred skin of a peach. There may be visible fur on the brow, around the toes and at the tip of the tail. Otherwise, it is a well-built, sturdy cat with a head slightly longer than it is wide, set on a long, slender neck. The large wide-open ears are tall and the outer edge is in line with the wedge of the face. Cheek-bones are prominent, and in profile there is a distinct break at the bridge of the nose. It has long, slim legs with elegant yet rounded paws – the toes are long, like little fingers – and a long, finely tapered tail.

The skin needs regular and careful cleaning, as the cat perspires and a greasy detritus can build up if neglected, which then has to be scraped or sponged away. The cat is also prone to skin allergies and to developing lumps. However, humans who are normally allergic to cats may find they can tolerate the furless Sphynx.

The breed has been refused recognition by some registering associations on the grounds that its genetic constitution is a malformation. However, it does have official recognition from The International Cat Association as well as independent clubs in Europe, and there is a flourishing group of Sphynx breeders in Belgium and the Netherlands.

♦ ABOVE
This little chap is a Harlequin Sphynx. All colours and patterns are now available in the breed. Although it is not currently accepted in Britain, it has a firm following in North America and is gaining popularity in Europe.

♦ BELOW
This Blue shows the remarkable, sleek bodyline of the breed. The cats are lithe and muscular, with accompanying energy and playfulness.

Non-Pedigreed Cats

A cat does not have to have an impressive pedigree to bring feline quality into our lives. Non-pedigreed cats with unknown parentage can have just as much grace and beauty as the finest show specimens. However, as there are endless possible combinations of sire and dam in a non-pedigreed ancestry, the appearance and character of what emerges is something of a lottery.

◆ FACING PAGE
An ordinary ginger tom looks
perfectly contented with his
non-pedigreed lineage, and is probably
allowed more freedom to roam than
his high-bred equivalent would be.

◆ ABOVE
It may not win any prizes for
symmetry of fur pattern, but this
black and white non-pedigree could
be entered in the household pet
category of a cat show.

AN ORDINARY CAT

Non-pedigreed cats – also known as household pets, domestic cats or random-bred – are the most common cats kept as pets. Fewer than five per cent of pet cats have a pedigree.

Acquiring a non-pedigree is far easier and cheaper than buying a purebred cat. Rescue organizations and humane societies are overflowing with animals all ready to make ideal companions, and some are as beautiful as their purebred equivalents. It is unlikely that such a cat will cost more than a donation to the society and the cost of vaccinations.

The disadvantage of having a non-pedigreed animal is that you invariably do not know what you are getting, whereas a quality guarantee comes with a pedigree. Because of their mixed ancestry, non-pedigrees are usually intelligent and affectionate, but a bad character gene could slip in.

COMMON HERITAGE

Both pedigreed and pet cats have common ancestors in the

◆ BELOW
If your bank balance cannot stretch to the cost of a Maine Coon Cat or Norwegian Forest Cat, this well-whiskered, soft ginger semi-longhair might suffice.

domesticated cat. However, the pedigree has evolved as a result of selective breeding, while the pet cat conforms to no special standards except those dictated by evolutionary pressures and the need to survive.

Non-pedigreed cats may have coats of any length and in a range of colours that are usually plain, blotched, striped or patched. Cats of one colour are less common than tabbies, bi-colours and tortoiseshells, and may indicate an unplanned mating with a pedigreed partner. Eyes are usually green or yellow and the majority of non-pedigreed noses are fairly long.

OFF-THE-STREET OPTIONS

You could, literally, pick your non-pedigree up off the street. Non-neutered (unaltered) mongrel cats roam all over the place, breeding prolifically. The resulting unwanted litters add to a population of feral cats – those that have been born in the wild or that have reverted to the wild state. Some, like those found by the hundred on Greek islands, tread a fine line between wildness and domesticity. Such cats present enormous problems for rescue organizations (if they exist), but have the potential for providing all the qualities looked for in the pet cat. They can be socialized, but the owner has to spend as much time with the cat as possible, particularly during

◆ BELOW
It looks as if there is a touch of Persian in this short-nosed, cobby ginger, and he seems to have inherited some of the Persian placidity as well.

the first few weeks. Medical examination and inoculations are also particularly important.

NEAR MISSES

For something a little more refined, you could go for a cat that only just misses being a pedigree. In one tiny, isolated community, there was only one local unneutered (unaltered) tom – which was clearly the sire of a litter produced by a neighbouring purebred Lilac Point Siamese queen. Four of her kittens were lilac-pointed (albeit with slightly longer, coarser hair than their pedigreed mother), and the fifth looked like a Black Oriental Shorthair. Nonetheless, they were all non-pedigree. Fortunately, they had inherited the best of their mother's oriental looks and their father's robust health and character.

Other non-pedigrees have known ancestry too. Farm cats may have bred for generations. Some kittens would be selected and kept because they were prettier, more intelligent, or had better mouse-catching potential than others. If the owners kept a record of the these kittens' parentage, they would be founding a written pedigree. That is how the pedigree system began.

SHOW STANDARD PETS

Many cat shows have Non-pedigree or Household Pet classes. There are no set standards of hair length, colour or conformation as there are with the pedigreed breeds. The cats are judged on their general appeal – their friendliness, beauty and condition.

◆ LEFT
Any coat length and colour combination is possible in the non-pedigreed range. What these two shorthairs lack in irregular coat pattern they make up for in alertness and pretty, balanced features.

◆ RIGHT
A well-defined blaze, chest and paws would be desirable in a pedigreed bi-colour, but with this non-pedigree, character would be a more important factor if it were to be entered in a show.

Breeding from Your Cat

The vast majority of people are quite content to own a cat, or cats, and leave it at that. Their animals are neutered (altered) and live the life of non-reproductive felines that simply grace the lives and homes of their owner. There are other people who become deeply involved in breeding cats as a hobby – it is rarely a profitable business. The amateur cat breeder may be rewarded by a handful of exquisite and charming kittens that may or may not be perfect pedigrees, but he or she is also taking on an expensive, time-absorbing, and often frustrating commitment.

◆ FACING PAGE
A Singapura mother and her kitten demonstrate the rewards of breeding in their beauty and character. The breed was developed from the "drain cats" of Singapore.

◆ ABOVE
A pale coat combined with darker points at ears, nose, tail and paws – seen to great effect in the Siamese – is known in breeding circles as the "Himalayan factor".

THE REWARDS OF BREEDING

♦ BELOW
The ultimate reward for a breeder is to produce a pedigreed cat of such perfection of type and temperament that it becomes a national Supreme Grand Champion like the Cream Colourpoint Longhair, Rosjoy Rambo.

Think carefully of the implications before you decide to let your cat have kittens. Whether you are giving your non-pedigree a chance to be a mother before having her neutered (altered), or planning to propagate a pedigree line, the process can be both time-consuming and expensive. Perhaps the most important consideration of all is to be sure that you will be able to find good homes for the kittens. If not, or if the prospective buyers change their minds, you must be prepared to give them a permanent home yourself.

Most people who breed from their cats are dealing with pedigrees rather than random-bred animals, with a view to continuing or improving on pure-bred lines. For the cat lover, the pedigree cat world is one of absorbing interest and beauty. It is also a stimulating environment where you will learn a great deal; your rivals will often become your best friends.

THE COMMITMENT

Those who go into breeding pedigrees thinking they are going to earn a lot of money from selling them are going to be disappointed. Even the most experienced and reputable breeders are lucky to break even over the course of any financial year. There are veterinary bills to pay for both mother and offspring, stud fees, special diets for the pregnant and nursing mother, heating for the kittens, veterinary testing and inoculation, and registration and advertising costs.

A heavily pregnant and nursing cat needs attention. The queen may not deliver her kittens at a convenient time and place during the day. This may happen in the early hours of the morning, and she may need some help from you, especially if it is her first litter. There may be deaths to deal with, especially in a first litter, which will be extremely distressing for everyone concerned.

Kittens may be lovable and cute, but they can also be destructive and get in the way. They need to be watched and cared for, and prepared for going out into the world. You should raise a pedigree litter for love and interest rather than money, and preferably when you already have some experience as an owner.

HOW IT ALL BEGAN

Breeding pedigreed cats on a serious level did not take place until the 1800s. The first cat show, held in London in 1871, set a trend for exhibiting, which in turn led to a more calculated approach to breeding. The organizer, an artist and author called Harrison Weir, set guidelines for breeding which became the basis for standards throughout the world, although different countries set their own rules. Most of the cats in the early shows were domestic shorthairs and Persians.

♦ BELOW
After a particularly awful day, with kittens into everything and apparently multiplying, many a cat breeder wonders, "Why am I doing this?" One look at this trio of bi-colours would probably answer the question.

◆ BELOW
Diminutive yet powerful Singapuras are the pedigreed version of the Singapore alley cat. The best examples were selected and bred to produce a pedigree which is increasing in popularity.

◆ BELOW
If your breeding programme produces a line-up of six week-old Blue and Cream Persians, like this one, you should have no difficulty finding a home for them.

It was not until the 1880s that Asian breeds were introduced to western Europe. The first Siamese cats were exhibited in Britain in 1885. By this time, breeders in Europe and America were setting up their own breeding programmes. They drew from the best British pedigreed stock and their own indigenous cats. The first American cat show was in New York in 1895.

A NEW BREED

There are now more than fifty internationally recognized breeds, and several others that are recognized as established and distinct breeds in some countries but not in others. The purpose of breeding may go beyond a desire to produce kittens for show or for sale, or even to keep a pedigree line going. Careful and well-informed selection of the queen and the stud can improve the type. Instead of waiting for the natural processes of evolution to select the fittest of a species, a breeder can speed up the process. Picking the healthiest and most well-formed examples of indigenous street cats, and mating them, for example, led to the development of standard types of British, American and European shorthairs. Breeders can also try to create a new variety of cat – a new colour variation of an established breed, or a new breed altogether. However, this is an area that should be left to the experts who have built up an in-depth knowledge of feline genetics, for mutations do sometimes occur. To establish a new breed takes many years. Only after several matings can a breed be proved to produce healthy offspring of consistent type, and only then be officially registered.

ACQUIRING A QUEEN

Choosing the breed and pedigree line you are going to use to found your breeding programme requires preparation and in-depth research. Gather as much information as you can about your chosen breed and study the genetics of breeding from specialist books and magazines, and from the individual breed clubs.

Unless you are going to breed with a cat you already own, it is sensible to look for suitably pedigreed parents and book a female kitten from their next litter. This kitten will, after all, be the foundation of your breeding line. She should be of the best standard and pedigree that you can afford.

AIMING HIGH

In any event, you should not select a kitten you are planning to breed from until it is at least three months old. By this time you will be able to assess its personality, and the colouring and patterns of its coat. The national cat-registering bodies, such as the Governing Council of the Cat Fancy in the United Kingdom and the Cat Fanciers' Association in the United States, publish set standards of perfection for each registered breed. These not only help you identify suitable parents for your own breeding female, but give you, as a breeder, clear guidelines to aim for.

Individual breed clubs have lists of breeders from whom you can buy your female. Visit cat shows, too – either those for individual breeds or large national shows where the whole range of registered breeds can be seen. Many championship and specialist breed shows take place throughout the year. You can obtain

details of shows from the breed clubs and national registering organizations. Breeders and exhibitors at cat shows are usually delighted to talk about their animals.

The early contacts you make at clubs and shows are vital first steps in joining the cat-breeding network. You may find not only the breeder from whom you will acquire your own potential queen, but also the one who might provide the stud she will mate with. The breeder of your choice may

◆ ABOVE
The majority of breeders in the United Kingdom keep their breeding queens as family pets.

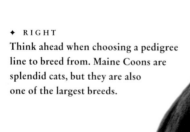

◆ RIGHT
Think ahead when choosing a pedigree line to breed from. Maine Coons are splendid cats, but they are also one of the largest breeds.

not have any kittens at the time you want one, but is likely to know of someone else who does.

BEYOND APPEARANCES

You will initially be attracted by the outward physical appearance of a particular breed or cat. However, when you are considering breeding, it is particularly important to look for animals with responsive and outgoing yet calm natures. This generally indicates that they have been reared in a household where cuddles and good food are considered important, and that they have good character genes to pass on to their offspring.

If you are lucky, the cats you have marked out at a cat show will also be the ones the judges like. The parents of your kitten queen-to-be may be top show winners with great personalities, splendid condition and a helpful breeder/owner.

HOME CHARMS

Before you commit yourself, visit the mother of your queen-to-be in its home, as this is very different from seeing her in the restricted atmosphere of a show. If other cats are there, such as her parents or siblings, you will be able to see how they interact with each other. These are the blood relations of your breeding queen.

Ask detailed questions about their pedigrees and breeding records. It is far better, for example, to acquire a female for breeding which comes from a long line of successful mothers that rear strong litters with no fatalities, than to go for a line of top-winning cats with only a marginally successful breeding record. Responsible breeders will also be assessing you as a future

◆ RIGHT
A Siamese demonstrates how to be a good mother. When you are choosing a kitten to found your breeding line, it is important to look at her mother, and how she reacts with her offspring. Good relationships can have a knock-on effect through the generations.

breeder in your own right, and note how their cats respond to you. Before releasing a kitten, they may even ask for references from your vet.

COMING HOME

Finally, you have the new kitten; you have joined the breed club. The period between now and when she is ready for her first mating is a key preparation time. Your queen-to-be must have the best possible diet as recommended by her breeder. She must be played with and exercised until her muscular condition is superb, and generally handled with love and tenderness so that she bonds with you. When the time comes for her to have her kittens, she will then do so in the confident knowledge of the support of her owners.

◆ LEFT
An adventurous four-week-old Ocicat kitten is ready to explore, but mother is keeping close.

READY FOR MATING?

It is quite obvious when a female is ready for mating. She starts what is known as "calling" – although this can be more like shrieking or wailing in some breeds, such as Siamese. Some Persians content themselves with dainty little mews and miaows. The female displays some brazen behaviour, rolling and dragging herself around the floor, flicking her tail and raising her rump to expose the slightly reddened area beneath. She may also lose interest in her food. If her behaviour fools you into thinking she is unwell, try picking her up by her neck folds (as an interested tom would do) and stroke along her back. If she responds with pleasure, pads her feet and raises her tail, she is definitely in season.

The average age of sexual maturity in a female is around six months, but cats of oriental origin such as Siamese and Burmese can be as early as fourteen or sixteen weeks. British Shorthairs and Persians do not start calling much before ten months. Generally, tom cats become sexually mature a month or two later than females of the same breed. The time of year also has an

+ ABOVE
A Siamese female in season rolls around and thrashes her tail. Siamese are notorious for announcing their sexual readiness with loud and strident calling.

+ BELOW
A Bi-colour Seal Point Ragdoll tom has taken a fancy to a Ragdoll and Turkish Van cross. If they mate successfully, their kittens will be very pretty, but they will not be pedigreed stock.

When selecting a stud, always look for the best example. While this Red Persian is a little out of coat, his type is superb, and he will no doubt father excellent kittens.

effect on the first call. If due in autumn or winter, it may be delayed until the warmer months of spring.

The cycle is approximately 21 days and females may come into oestrus (on call) for about three to ten days. They continue to be fertile until at least fourteen years of age.

It is best to let the young queen run through the first couple of cycles – until she is at least a year old – rather than put her to stud immediately. This gets the system going and reduces the risk of problems at birth.

CHOOSING THE MALE

Many breed clubs publish a stud list of proven males, but the breeder from whom you bought the female is likely to know of suitable mates. An experienced breeder is also likely to know about genetically compatible lines, and even if you have some ideas of your own, it is important to take expert advice.

If you go to a show to look for potential partners, do not be tempted to go for the stunning new male Grand Champion. Other breeders may be clamouring to use him, but the wiser choice would be his father. Not only has he proved himself to be the sire of outstanding stock, but with a

maiden queen it is wiser to use an experienced stud for the first mating.

RENDEZVOUS

Before committing yourself to a particular stud, visit the breeder to check the conditions in which the maiden queen is to be kept. This is an opportunity also to ask vital questions about the number and the supervision of matings. Documentation on the participating animals that needs to be exchanged varies according to the conditions for entry to stud, but for your female include the following:
♦ pedigree
♦ registration and/or transfer
♦ up-to-date vaccination certificate
♦ current test certificates showing negative status for both feline infectious leukaemia and feline immunodeficiency virus (FIV).

The stud owner may require the tests to have been carried out within the last 24 hours, although others accept tests within the past five to seven days. The conditions and fees should be agreed before taking the queen to the stud. Conditions of the mating might include an agreement that no males from a resulting litter will be used for

Whatever the breed, it is important that the male is neither monorchid (one testicled) nor cryptorchid (hidden testicled): this Korat is fully endowed!

breeding, or for the pick of the litter to be substituted in lieu of a mating fee. It is usual for there to be another free mating should the queen fail to become pregnant.

On a more informal level, the stud owner should want to know the pet name of the cat and the diet she is used to.

The ideal Tabby stud should not only be of first-class type, but have clear, well-defined markings.

THE MATING

When the young queen starts to call, contact the stud owner. Both animals must be in good health, and have their nails clipped beforehand.

The journey to the stud usually takes place on the second or third day of the call. The stud's owner prepares for the arrival of the queen by thoroughly disinfecting the entire stud run and the queen's quarters. The queen is settled in her quarters within the stud run, where the stud can "talk" to her. This enables the queen to become accustomed to the stud's presence, and prepares her for mating.

At a quiet moment, the stud's owner releases the queen from her quarters. If all goes to plan, she crouches ready to receive the male; he grasps her by the scruff with his teeth, and taps her rump with one of his back legs until she raises it and flicks her tail over. The first entry of the male induces ovulation in the female and may result in fertilization, though subsequent matings are more likely to do so. (Note that your queen is likely to remain fertile for several days, so keep her in when she returns home.)

When sexual climax is reached, the female utters a strange cry that is only ever heard at this time. As soon as he withdraws from the female, the male moves away as the female turns on him with tooth and claw. She then rolls around, washing furiously for a couple of minutes. Only after she has done this is she calm again. Several matings need to take place over two or three days to try to ensure that the female becomes pregnant.

The stud owner supervises matings so that no harm comes to either stud or queen, but, in many cases, the male and female soon develop a bond. They are then allowed to run together and mating can take place freely. It is very common for the queen to take over the stud's bed and to assume matriarchal dominance. At the end of her stay, the stud owner will provide a certificate giving details of:

✦ the stud's pedigree
✦ number of matings observed
✦ dates of matings
✦ expected date of litter arrival
✦ the agreed stud fee and conditions

✦ BELOW
The queen and tom go through preparatory rituals before mating takes place, but once the male has ejaculated, he moves out of the way to avoid a sharp cuff from his partner.

✦ TOP
A female does not ovulate (release her eggs) until the moment of mating. One of the triggers is the male taking hold of the queen's neck fur; this also has the practical effect of keeping her in one place.

THE PREGNANCY

The average gestation period for cats is between 63 and 68 days. Occasionally, healthy kittens are produced even at 61 days. Kittens produced at or before this time usually require very specialized nursing, as key systems have not fully developed. Some females carry their kittens for as long as 70 days. In this event, the kittens may be larger than normal.

SIGNS OF PREGNANCY

The first indication that a cat is pregnant (or in kitten) is when she does not come on heat two or three weeks after mating. Soon after this, there will be visible signs of pregnancy: the nipples become rather swollen and take on a deep coral-pink tone, a process that is called pinking up. Very experienced breeders may know a cat is in kitten a few days in advance of this, as there is sometimes a ridging of the muscles of the cat's stomach. A vet is able to confirm a pregnancy by feeling the cat's abdomen after three or four weeks.

ANTENATAL CARE

A pregnant cat should be encouraged to maintain a normal lifestyle. You can increase the amount of food you give her from about the fifth week of pregnancy, and introduce a vitamin supplement. In a feral state, a cat gorges itself as it does not know where the next meal is coming from. Your cat will let you know how much food she wants. Seek veterinary advice if you are in any doubt.

Climbing, jumping, running – and hunting if the cat is free-range – are all normal physical activities, even for a pregnant pedigree. Do remember, however, that allowing a pregnant

female free range may expose her to other dangers. She may slow down a bit towards the end of her term, but activity ensures that good, strong muscle tone is maintained. This is essential for a natural, successful birth.

After about four weeks, the queen's stomach starts to distend, the nipples become very prominent, and she begins to look pregnant. By around 28 days, all the kittens' internal organs have formed, and the embryos are about 2.5cm (1in) long. The skeleton develops from about 40 days, and at

50 days, the kittens quicken – show signs of movement. Look for rippling, sliding motions along the mother's flank; they are most noticeable when she is resting.

About a week before the birth, the queen starts looking for a nesting place. It is a good idea to prepare a cardboard-box house for the queen with lots of plain paper inside for her to tear up. If this is not done, she will do her best to get into wardrobes (closets), drawers, airing cupboards – anywhere warm and draught-free.

♦ LEFT
Given a choice, your queen would probably nest in a most inconvenient spot. A kittening box is ideal for both mother and owner, but do make sure the cat is used to and comfortable with both the box and its location well before the birth.

THE KITTENING

Birth is an exciting but messy business, which is why there should be a lot of padding in the kittening box and the area beneath and around the box should be easy to clean and disinfect without disturbing the inmates too much.

About 24 hours before the actual birth, the queen enters the first stage of labour. Outward physical signs are very few. There may be the odd faint ripple along the flank of the cat, and experienced breeders will note that her breathing through the nose has become shallow and rapid on occasion. Close examination reveals a flickering of the nostrils during these early, very faint contractions. Towards the end of this process, a small mucous plug may be found in the bedding, or adhering to the hair close to the cat's vulva.

The next stage can take quite a long time, depending on the number of kittens. It is important not to panic: as long as the queen shows no signs of physical distress, all is going well. During this second stage, the classic signs of major contractions are clearly visible. The queen is breathing deeply and her whole abdomen seems to shudder and ripple downwards.

Eventually, a membrane sac containing a kitten and fluid starts to emerge from the queen's vulva and it may be possible to see the kitten's head within the sac. Sometimes the sac will burst at this point when it is said

♦ ABOVE LEFT
A newborn kitten has just emerged and broken free from the protective sac of amniotic fluid.

♦ ABOVE RIGHT
Mother's first task is to take her newborn kitten and wash it thoroughly, especially around the nose and mouth to clear respiratory passages so that it can breathe – and utter its first cries.

MIDWIFE EQUIPMENT

- ♦ disinfected, blunt-ended scissors
- ♦ sterile surgical gloves
- ♦ kitchen towels
- ♦ hot water
- ♦ ordinary towels
- ♦ towelling face cloths
- ♦ water-based lubricant

that the waters have broken. Often, the birth is so rapid that the kitten is born before the sac bursts.

The queen clears the sac from around the kitten and immediately washes the newborn, particularly around the nose and mouth. This prompts the kitten to get rid of any amniotic residue from its respiratory system and it will often begin to cry. By this time secondary contractions have expelled the placenta (afterbirth), which the queen will instinctively eat. In a feral state, this would provide her with food and nutrients during the first couple of days after kittening when she needs to recover. Hormones in the placenta promote milk secretion, and also help the uterus to contract, preventing a haemorrhage, which is a normal occurence after every birth. In the wild, such haemorrhaging could lead a predator to the kittens' nest. The queen also chews through the umbilical cord. In a straightforward birth, the queen, even a maiden queen,

♦ LEFT
One week old, blind, deaf, hungry – and not at all domesticated.

◆ BELOW
Three weeks old: eyes are open and mobility is
improving. The kitten can now try some finely
chopped cooked meat or kitten food to
supplement the milk from its mother.

◆ BELOW
A non-pedigreed litter has settled down after
the trials of birth.

repeat the process. Generally, once the
hips have emerged, the queen can do
the rest by herself.

In the case of a rump or tail breech
birth, you may need to gently insert a
lubricated finger beside the kitten and
hold it as a hook. But it must be
emphasized that, in most cases, the
queen knows what is best and can
manage by herself.

will usually cope with everything.
However, it may be that you will
have to assist on occasions. For this, a
range of equipment should be within
easy reach.

BREECH BIRTH

It is normal for some kittens to be
born backwards, with hind feet being
presented first. If the rump and tail
rather than the stretched-out hind feet
are presented first, this is a breech
birth and can be a problem. It is so
easy to become impatient and want to
get your hands in the nest to help out,
but the real need to do this should be
very carefully weighed up.

If the queen is contracting strongly,
it is likely that she will be able to birth
the kitten quite normally. This way
round is just a little more difficult, as
the head is not widening the birth
passage so that the rest of the body
can slide through. However, if the
waters have burst and the kitten is
taking a very long time to be born,
there is a risk of brain damage or still-
birth and the kitten should be helped
out as quickly as possible.

If the legs are coming first, quickly
slip on the surgical gloves and smear a
little of the lubrication around the
vulva. Never pull on any part of the
kitten – it is an extremely delicate

organism capable of being very easily
damaged. As the queen's contractions
push the legs further out of the vulva,
use index and middle finger to
"scissor" the legs right next to the
opening of the vulva. As the
contractions cease, the natural effect
is for the legs to be drawn back into
the vulva. The breeder's fingers will
hold the legs in position until the next
set of contractions. Then as more of
the legs appear, use the index and
middle fingers of the other hand to

APPARENT STILL-BIRTH

Sometimes a kitten will be born
apparently lifeless. This may not be
the case; it may not be breathing and
be in a state of shock. If the queen
does not immediately rasp away at the
kitten's face, it is your job to do it. To
clear any excess fluid from the nose
and lungs, hold the kitten in your
hand with index finger going over and
supporting its head. Gently swing the
kitten downwards two or three times
and then wipe and stimulate the face

◆ BELOW
The mother and her kittens need to be watched
carefully at first, in case any complications arise.
However, usually the mother is quite capable of
looking after and training her kittens on her own.

around the nose and nostrils. At the
same time, rub its little body
vigorously. In most cases this will get
it going but you may have to resort to
mouth-to-mouth resuscitation.

It may be that the kitten has
suffered some form of foetal distress
during the birth process and has, in
fact, died. The cause may be more
serious, and a dead kitten should be
laid aside carefully for a post-mortem
examination to establish the cause.

QUEEN DISTRESS

Even very experienced queens may
become distressed and unable to birth
their kittens. Because of this possibility
it is wise to let your veterinarian know
when the kittens are due. The most
common form of distress is the lack of

strong contractions. The vet may inject
the queen with oxytocin, a hormone to
improve contractions. If this does not
work, birth by Caesarean section may
be the only option. This is done very
rapidly and with the minimum amount
of anaesthetic, so that the queen is well
able to look after her kittens.

One of the reasons why it is
essential to examine the breeding
record of the bloodline from which
a queen is obtained is to check for
any predisposition to the need for
Caesarean sections.

POST-NATAL CARE

While it is rare for a healthy queen to
encounter problems after pregnancy,
a close watch should always be kept for
the following conditions:

◆ Pyometra: an infection of the
uterus characterized by a thick, off-
white discharge. This condition is
not serious if caught quickly and
treated with antibiotics. In a serious
form it will mean that the queen
will have to be spayed.
◆ Eclampsia (milk fever): caused by
a dramatic fall in calcium levels in
the queen who will begin to
convulse. An immediate intra-
muscular or intravenous injection
of calcium from the vet brings
immediate recovery.
◆ Mastitis: the queen's mammary
glands become hard, lumpy and hot
due to an infection. Treatment is
with antibiotics. Temporary relief
can be given by the use of warm
compresses on the affected area.
◆ Lack of milk: the queen's milk can
dry up if she doesn't have
sufficient wholesome food and
drink; or the kittens are not
suckling vigorously enough; or
through mastitis. A homeopathic
remedy such as Lachesis or
hormone treatment may result in a
return of the milk supply. If not,
the kittens may have to be hand-
fed until they are weaned. This
means two-hourly feeds with a
commercially available substitute
milk. The vet may know of
breeders who are specialists in the
techniques of hand-feeding.

ABNORMALITIES

Defects are rare. They include:
◆ cleft palate or hare-lip
◆ lack of eyes
◆ heart defects including hole
in the heart
◆ umbilical hernia
◆ intestines on the outside

GROWING UP

If the litter is strong and healthy, the queen will require no assistance from you for the first two to three weeks. However, do change the bedding regularly (provided this does not upset the mother) and make sure the mother has plenty to eat: she may need three times as much as usual. The kittens' eyes open at around a week old and they will stop hissing at you every time you pick them up.

It is important to handle the kittens from the start. Encourage them to become used to the human voice and contact by picking them up and stroking them gently and regularly, and crooning to them. Experts used to advise that queens and their newborn kittens should be kept in a warm, dark, secluded place. However, this is just about the best way to make kittens nervous of people and activity. Once the kittens are weaned they can be introduced into the wider home environment and visitors, even if this is from within the sanctuary of a kitten pen. Social contact increases their confidence to tackle new situations when they leave home at twelve to sixteen weeks of age.

EATING HABITS

The mother guides her kittens to her teats. They knead the teats with their paws and then start to suckle. The colostrum milk of the first few days is rich in the mother's antibodies and nutrients which protect the newborn kittens from infection. The kittens should be gradually weaned off their mother's milk. There is no specific time when this starts to happen, though they may begin to eat their mother's food at three to four weeks. It is not unusual for a kitten to remain

◆ BELOW
Seven weeks old: these three look harmless enough, but at this age they will be learning to hunt and fend for themselves through play.

on mother's milk for the first five weeks. Kittens must be fully weaned by 12 weeks, when they are ready to go to a new owner. They are actually capable of lapping water and of being on a solid diet by about six weeks.

The first solid food should be high-quality canned kitten food, finely

◆ BELOW
Nine weeks old: active, strong and independent enough to venture outside – but not until it has had its first vaccinations.

minced cooked meat or poultry, or flaked white fish. Variety will encourage broad taste and good habits in later life as well as a balanced diet. Avoid dried food at this stage, and feed the kittens small quantities four to six times daily at three to four weeks of age, gradually reducing to three or four times daily from then on.

Until they begin eating solid foods, the kittens do not need to use the litter tray (pan). The mother cleans them herself. You may find that the kittens simply copy their mother and use the tray

♦ LEFT
A Siamese mother shows her kitten exactly where, when and how to use the litter tray (pan). It is unlikely that the kitten will need any extra training from its owner.

♦ BELOW
Some are more interested than others in the prospect of solid food. One of these Siamese kittens may be reflecting on the warmth and comfort of its mother's breast.

without any help from you. If not, you can try placing the kittens in the tray immediately after each feed. The tray should be in a quiet spot where the floor and surroundings can be easily cleaned and disinfected. From this moment until the kittens leave to go to their new homes, your

management of the environment is extremely important. Where there is a lack of hygiene, there is a risk of disease and infection. The kittens may also form bad habits which they will carry with them to a new home. Such a situation would be a poor advertisement for a breeder.

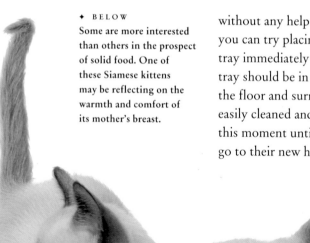

THE BASICS OF INHERITANCE

Before you begin to breed from your cat, it is important to investigate her genetic inheritance and that of the stud you are mating her with. She is the product of a vast number of generations of maybe 50 or more years of recorded breeding. A catalogue of cat show successes may also indicate a healthy genetic coding that she will pass on to her offspring. You can discover just how she acquired her particular colouring and characteristics, and work out what her kittens are likely to have.

Quite how characteristics such as colour or pattern passed from one generation of cats to another was not

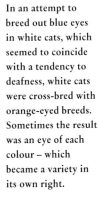

◆ LEFT
In an attempt to breed out blue eyes in white cats, which seemed to coincide with a tendency to deafness, white cats were cross-bred with orange-eyed breeds. Sometimes the result was an eye of each colour – which became a variety in its own right.

◆ BELOW
The blue colouring in a proud father – a Persian Blue Bi-colour – has diluted to lilac in his kitten.

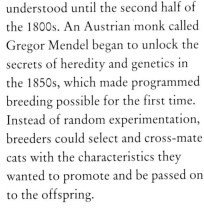

understood until the second half of the 1800s. An Austrian monk called Gregor Mendel began to unlock the secrets of heredity and genetics in the 1850s, which made programmed breeding possible for the first time. Instead of random experimentation, breeders could select and cross-mate cats with the characteristics they wanted to promote and be passed on to the offspring.

THE POWER OF THE GENE

The instrument of inheritance which controls particular features or behavioural traits is the gene. Genes are responsible for all inherited characteristics, from coat colour and pattern, length of tail or shape of ears, to health and character. A kitten inherits half of its genes from its mother and half from its father. The arrangement of genes is different for each kitten in a litter, so each one is genetically unique.

There are certain genes carrying specific characteristics, such as the red gene, that can only be passed down through the generations by either a male or a female, but not both. These sex-linked genes are the reason why, for example, tortoiseshells are

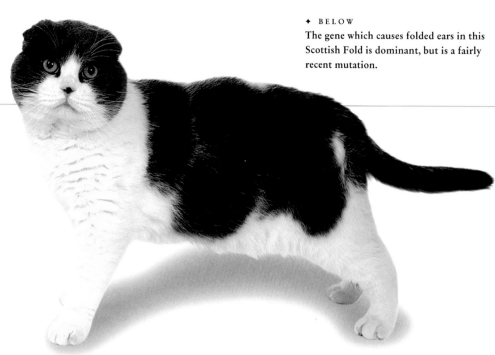

♦ BELOW
The gene which causes folded ears in this Scottish Fold is dominant, but is a fairly recent mutation.

patterns such as blue or self. That is why two black parents may produce a blue or chocolate kitten and why two tabby parents may produce a Self kitten.

Sometimes the fundamental character of a gene is altered by an outside factor, such as radiation or other environmental situations. Japanese Bobtails and Manx cats both developed in isolated island communities which meant that they were forced to interbreed. A mutation gene occurred that resulted in the lack of a tail – which is, in fact, a malformation of the spine similar to spina bifida in humans. Some breeders have taken advantage of such mutations and developed new breeds from them.

always female. A normal male cat cannot inherit both the red and the "not red" gene.

Some genes are more powerful than others and are called dominant genes. If one dominant colour gene and one recessive colour gene occur in a newly fertilized egg, the dominant gene determines the colour of the kitten. The recessive gene, however, could be passed on through several generations without coming out, or being expressed. Then, if it met up with a matching recessive gene, from the other parent, its particular gene characteristic would be expressed. What this means in cat terms is that there are certain dominant colour or pattern genes such as black or tabby, that override recessive colours and

♦ RIGHT
Natural mutation has taken place in Manx breeds, probably as a result of enforced interbreeding on an island – in this case, the Isle of Man off the west coast of England.

♦ ABOVE
Polydactylism (excess number of toes) in this cream kitten is caused by a dominant gene. It is not permitted in any pedigree breeds.

THE ART OF SELECTION

◆ LEFT
Cinnamon is a recessive gene to black and is carried on the same gene locus as chocolate.

The colour range in a litter is determined by genes inherited from the parents, and whether those genes are dominant or recessive. Each kitten will inherit genes from both parents, but in a unique combination.

Genes are found in pairs. Black is dominant to chocolate and cinnamon, so a cat with one black gene will be black, whereas if it has no black genes it will be chocolate or cinnamon. Within this same pair, chocolate is dominant to cinnamon, so a cinnamon cat must have two cinnamon genes (a cat with one gene for chocolate and one for cinnamon will be chocolate in colour). The dilute gene, which dilutes the pigment of a cat from black to blue, chocolate to lilac, cinnamon to fawn, or red to cream, is recessive. In order for a cat to be a dilute colour it must have two dilute genes.

A tabby pattern is carried by the agouti gene which gives each hair a dark tip and alternate bands of light and dark colour. A non-agouti gene blocks the production of the light band in each hair, so producing a solid-coloured coat. White fur is the product of a gene which carries no pigmentation at all.

◆ ABOVE RIGHT
The lineage of this Blue Abyssinian would have included two dilute recessive genes and a black gene.

◆ RIGHT
This Exotic Shorthair must be female as she is a tortoiseshell – a colour produced by the presence of one red and one 'not red' gene.

COLOUR MUTATIONS

Black The first colour recessive mutation from the ancestral grey/brown agouti. Produces an extremely dark, solid colour perceived as black

Chocolate Recessive gene to black creating a dark brown

Cinnamon Recessive gene to black and chocolate. Carried on the same gene locus as chocolate, producing a light-brown colour with a warm (almost red-tinted) tone

Orange Sex-linked gene (carried on the X chromosome, so females XX can have two such genes, males XY can have only one).This alters black, chocolate and cinnamon to an orange (red, auburn, ginger) colour. Females are not sterile

Dilution Very often known as the "blue" gene as the presence of the recessive dilution with black creates a grey (lavender-blue) individual. Also affects other colours. Alters the

structure of the pigment cells
Dilution + black = blue
Dilution + chocolate = lilac
Dilution + cinnamon = fawn
Dilution + orange = cream

Tortoiseshell The presence of the orange gene plus black and its recessive colours of chocolate and cinnamon creates the two-coloured tortoiseshell female, i.e. black, chocolate and cinnamon tortoiseshells. In combination with the dilution gene the pastel blue-cream, lilac-cream and fawn-cream are created. The rare occurrence of the tortoiseshell male is probably due to the presence of an extra X chromosome. The males are usually sterile

Inhibitor Dominant and, as its name suggests, inhibiting – this gene reduces ground colour, e.g. the rufous colour of the brown tabby to the pewter ground of the silver tabby, or converting a self cat to a smoke

Dilute modifier Dominant gene, the presence of which is still disputed. Creates a rather dull brownish-grey colour known as caramel. It has no effect on the dominant colours black, chocolate, cinnamon or red. Probably originated in Chinchilla Persian stock and is to be found in several breeds of pedigreed cat

Full colour and its recessives Recessives to full colour are Burmese, Siamese, and blue-eyed and pink-eyed Albinos.

Burmese affects black, reducing it to a lustrous brown, or sable.

In the Siamese cat, black becomes a warm-toned seal.

Albinos are almost completely lacking in pigmentation (the blue-eyed version) or entirely without pigmentation (the pink-eyed version). Both may be completely or incompletely light-sensitive. Extremely rare in cats, although a race of Albino Siamese was discovered in America

PATTERN MUTATIONS

Agouti The dominant ancestral pattern of the domestic cat in which the individual hairs of the coat are banded with colour. Normally light or grey at the roots of the hair with the darkest colour at the tip

Tabby A range of pattern genes which is not seen unless in conjunction with the agouti gene or the orange gene:

The mackerel tabby has thinly striped markings like those along the sides of the mackerel fish.

The spotted tabby, in which the thin lines are broken down into clearly defined spots, may be a recessive to the mackerel tabby or created as the result of the effects of polygenes.

Abyssinian or ticked tabby markings are reduced almost entirely or restricted to face, legs and tail. This is the dominant pattern.

Blotched, marble or classic tabby markings include a bulls-eye on each flank and further marbling of colour on an agouti-based ground colour. The gene causing this is recessive to the other forms of tabby marking

Tipping or shading It seems likely that the fairly recently discovered wide band gene combined with the agouti gene, affects the degree of colour shown towards the tip of each hair. The effect of the gene varies from the lightest of tipping, as seen in the chinchilla, to quite heavy shading, where as much as half the hair may be dark. This effect may be mimicked by a very heavily silvered smoke, although never to the lightness seen in the chinchilla. The presence of the wide band gene appears to be confirmed by the existence of the golden chinchilla or shaded cat, which is rufous with dark tips to the hair. The ground colour has not been inhibited

White Dominant gene which covers all other colours in an "overcoat" effect to create an all-white coat. In its pure form, in which all offspring produced are white, blue-eyed or odd-eyed cats may well suffer from hearing loss, either partial or total. This is less likely to happen where one parent is white and the other coloured

White spotting A dominant gene that results in areas of colour being suppressed by areas of white, creating the bi- or tri-coloured cat. White spotting can range from a few white hairs creating a chest mark or a spot on the belly, to an almost complete absence of colour. The van pattern suppresses colour to form flashes on the head and a solid-coloured tail, whereas the harlequin shows a more spotted pattern of colour on the body and legs as well

Himalayan or Siamese A recessive gene in which the colour is restricted to the "points" of the cat, these being the face (mask), legs and tail. This pattern is usually associated with intense blue eyes

Burmese A recessive gene to full colour, but incompletely dominant to Siamese. The body appears to be a solid colour, though of reduced intensity

Tonkinese A slightly pointed hybrid pattern created by a cross between Burmese and Siamese cats

✦ RIGHT
An Oriental Classic Tabby has tabby markings on an agouti background.

✦ ABOVE
Maine Coon Black Smoke. This colour is produced by a combination of self black plus the inhibitor gene, giving a silver undercoat.

✦ RIGHT
A Siamese Blue Point has one black, two dilute and two Siamese genes. Selective breeding has reduced the incidence of squints and kinks in Siamese tails.

✦ **BELOW**
The recessive gene for hairlessness has been discovered and lost many times. When a hairless kitten was born in Canada, in 1966, breeders started to develop the breed known as Sphynx.

✦ **BELOW**
A longhaired coat needs two recessive genes for long hair, but in Persians generations of selective breeding have lengthened the coat of the non-pedigreed longhair to the magnificent coat seen here.

✦ **RIGHT**
A strange, curly kitten from Oregon proved, on first mating, to have a previously unknown dominant gene which gave it and its kittens curly hair.

COAT QUALITY AND LENGTH

Shorthair Dominant gene restricting coat length. Strong guardhairs give impression of a crispness or sleekness of texture

Semi-longhair Recessive gene basically producing a long-coated cat but with more noticeable length on neck, chest, rear legs and tail. Coat generally self-maintaining

Longhair Produced by the same recessive gene as the semi-longhair, but bred to produce a coat of extreme length, softness/silkiness of texture and requiring much human intervention to maintain it

Wirehair Dominant gene producing crimped, wiry, upstanding coat

Rexed coat Recessive group of genes, not always genetically compatible, producing a mostly tightly curled, soft-textured coat

Selkirk Rex coat Dominant gene which is the exception to the general Rex group, producing a shaggy, plush-coated cat

Sphynx Recessive gene officially designated hairless but, in fact, producing a peach-skin-like coat which is quite different in quality from the truly hairless individuals still sometimes produced in Devon Rex cats. A hairless cat produced by a dominant gene is seen in Russia

Showing your Cat

A cat has no particular interest in whether it goes to a show or not, but its owner can gain a great deal of satisfaction from having a prize-winning animal and become part of the sociable cat-showing circuit. Shows provide an arena for the serious cat breeder or committed owner of pedigreed animals to display their stock. However, there are often more relaxed classes for ordinary household pets as well.

✦ FACING PAGE
A winner of several Best in Show awards, a Supreme Grand Premier sits with its rosettes and prizes. The kudos for the owner exceeds any real financial gain.

✦ ABOVE
A Persian's coat is carefully groomed before a show.

THE REWARDS OF SHOWING

Showing your cat is an expensive business, even if the animal has championship potential. The rewards are likely to be pride in your – and your cat's – achievements, a rosette and perhaps a silver cup or a supply of commercial cat food rather than prize money. Apart from the cost and maintenance of your pedigreed cat, there are equipment and travelling costs as well as high entry fees to consider. However, for the committed cat fancier – the person who is interested in breeding and showing pedigree cats – there are many other rewards. Cat shows present the ideal opportunity to find out about the various breeds. You can make valuable contacts with breeders and look out for your next new kitten, or for suitable mates for your queen. You will become part of the cat fanciers' network, check out the latest breeds and commercial cat products, make friends and fill in your social calendar with cat-related events. Whether your

◆ LEFT
A White Persian at an American cat show sits with its rosettes in a decorated pen.

◆ BELOW LEFT
Cat shows provide an opportunity for like-minded people to compare notes and make friends.

cat actively enjoys the show or not is debatable. Most cats are so adaptable they will tolerate being confined to a pen for the best part of a day. Others may have a shy or timid nature, or may be particularly active; in either case it would not be fair to subject them to the show scene. If you introduce a kitten to showing at an early age, it is more likely to adapt. Some cats even appear to relish the attention and admiration from passers-by. If you are taking a cat to its first show, keep a close eye on it; if it is unhappy, it will let you know.

QUALITY CONTROL
It is through being judged at shows that new breeds gain acceptance and established breeds keep up to scratch. If a new breed does not make it through the various levels of judging, from local show to national championship, it is unlikely to survive. When judges study a cat, they are making sure that it conforms with the standards set for that breed. If they spot signs of, say, an aggressive temperament, or a deformity in an up-and-coming breed, they can disqualify the cat and stipulate that it should not be used for breeding.

◆ ABOVE
The whole family can be involved – and may prevent the cat from becoming too bored.

◆ LEFT
It may be very boring and rather noisy to sit in a small pen at a cat show all day, but the impressive display of rosettes suggest that this cat is worth breeding from.

A New Craze for Cats

A growing interest in the selective breeding of pedigreed animals and the arrival of exotic cats such as Persians and Turkish Angoras in the West led to the first official cat show in London in 1871. There is a record of a show being held in Winchester, England in 1598, but the London event had the cats in show pens, 25 classes for different breeds, and judging benches. Domestic shorthairs and Persians dominated the early shows, although there were some foreign introductions. The first benched cat show in America was held at Madison Square Garden, New York in 1895, in which Maine Coon Cats featured strongly.

These early events spawned a whole new leisure activity, and the breeding and showing bug soon spread to most parts of the world. Today, scarcely a day, and certainly not a weekend, goes by without a cat show being held somewhere, whether it is organized by a breed club for their specific breed, or for all breeds at local, as well as area and national levels.

THE ORGANIZERS

Throughout the world, organizations register pedigrees and stipulate rules for running shows. Individual breed clubs and area clubs are affiliated to one or other of these authorities.

In the United Kingdom, the Governing Council of the Cat Fancy (GCCF), formed in 1910, is the main regulatory body. The Governing Council of the Cat Fancy in Ireland (GCCFI) licenses shows in the same way as the GCCF, although it is not affiliated to it, and has a close liaison with the GCCF. The Cat Association of Britain (CA), formed in the early

1980s, also registers pedigree cats; it is affiliated to the European *Fédération Internationale Féline* (Fifé) and runs shows under European rules.

Fifé, founded in 1949, is not just a European organization, but has member countries throughout the world (though not the major cat-fancying countries of the United States and Canada, Australia and New Zealand or Japan). The many independent clubs in Europe work as autonomous federations with their own registries, but many liaise with each other. Recently, more shows have been judged by both Fifé and independent judges. Organizational

problems are shared, and judges from both systems can meet and discuss ideas and standards.

In the United States, the largest nationwide registering bodies are the Cat Fanciers' Association (CFA) and The International Cat Association (TICA), although there are many other organizations spread the length and breadth of North America. Some of them are regionally based, such as the American Cat Association (ACA) in California.

Your first step in showing is to contact your area or national organization for their schedule of shows, and show rules.

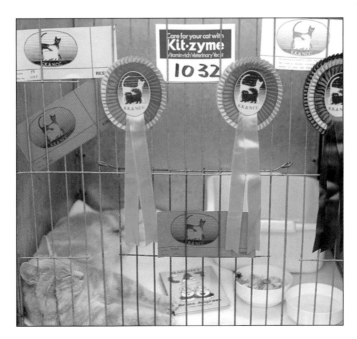

✦ ABOVE
The early cat shows at the end of the 1800s were dominated by Persians and domestic shorthairs in the United Kingdom.

✦ LEFT
Now all that prodding and poking is over, and the rosettes are up, maybe a chap can have a nap.

ENTERING A SHOW

First go to a show without your cat; it will be much easier if you have a clear idea of noise level, numbers, conditions and how the events are run.

The organizing bodies usually publish an annual list of the shows under their jurisdiction, which you can buy for a small fee. These publications should have the name and address of a contact for each show to whom you can then apply for a schedule – allow about three months before the event. The schedule contains the rules under which the show is operating, the classes that can be entered, and qualification requirements for each. It is essential to read the rules carefully and go through the relevant class details before you proceed any further. You also need to check in your rules for such qualifications as the lowest age of entry for a kitten (usually fourteen weeks), at what stage your animal should join an adult class (usually nine months), and what the restrictions are for neutered and

entire animals. Any household pets over the age of nine months, for example, must be neutered.

There will also be an entry form with instructions on how to complete it, as well as details of the entry fees charged and how to pay them. Read it all meticulously. If you get something wrong, you could be refused entry on the day. If you are uncertain about any aspect, contact the show management.

If you are showing a pedigreed cat, you will need to refer to its registration

✦ BELOW
Grooming does not just take place on the day of a show; the health and maintenance programme has to start weeks before to ensure the cat is in peak condition, even if it is a non-pedigree.

✦ BELOW
Some all-breed shows are enormous events with up to 1,500 entrants and thousands of visitors. This is the National Cat Club Show in Britain.

CAT KIT FOR A SHOW

- ✦ Vaccination certificates
- ✦ Grooming equipment
- ✦ Blanket (white, if UK show)
- ✦ Food and water bowls (white, if UK show)
- ✦ Food and water (for the cat)
- ✦ Litter tray/pan (white, if UK show)
- ✦ Litter
- ✦ White ribbon (for the identification label)
- ✦ Cleaning materials
- ✦ Disinfectant (suitable to clean the cat's pen)
- ✦ String and scissors (to secure pen if necessary)
- ✦ Toy
- ✦ Decorations on a theme (if appropriate)

details (obtained from the original breeder), and know its breed number, date of birth, parentage and breeder. Your breeder may be able to advise on which classes to enter if you are unsure.

PREPARING FOR A SHOW
Preparing your cat for a show will take more than just a quick comb through. Longhaired varieties need to be bathed and groomed intensively for weeks preceding the show. Even shorthaired cats need in-depth preparation to ensure that they look and feel perfect to the touch.

On the day of the show, make sure you have all the equipment you will need neatly assembled – keep it all together in a cat bag – and leave in good time. Many European shows last two days, the panel of judges taking different classes on each day. American and Canadian shows may even extend to three days, and therefore need a great deal of careful extra thought and preparation.

WHAT HAPPENS AT A SHOW?

Show style and rules vary from country to country, and according to the size of the show. Individual breed clubs organize their own events, which tend to be small-scale, informal, friendly occasions. Others may be organized by major registering bodies, or may be compound affairs, with a number of separate shows running concurrently for different breeds or classes, each one presided over by a separate judge or team of judges.

Three months before the show date, send off your entry form and fee. When you receive confirmation, and possibly a copy of your cat's entry in the show catalogue, check this as soon as possible. If there is anything wrong, however small, inform the organizer who will check the details against the initial entry form. If you have made a major mistake in your application, you run the risk of disqualification unless the official catalogue is corrected.

When you arrive with your cat at a European show, including all British shows, you will probably have to queue so that your cat can be checked by a vet (vetted-in); in some countries it is left to trust that your cat is in good health and has all the necessary inoculations. For vetting-in you need to have the cat's up-to-date certificates of vaccination ready, as the vet will want to see them. Just before your turn with the vet, a show official will give you a pen number, an identification label to attach to the cat, a veterinary pass card and a check card for the classes entered, with which you claim rosettes or prize money later on. However, if the vaccination certificates are not in order, or there is any suspicion of parasitic infestation, or anything else is wrong, the vet will not allow the cat in. Once through the vetting-in, find the allocated pen. This is where the cat will stay for the duration of the show, apart from when it is taken out to be judged.

LAST-MINUTE ATTENTION

When you find your allotted pen, it is a good idea to clean it with the cat-compatible disinfectant you have brought with you. Check the security on the cage and make sure there are no loose or jagged ends. Attach the identification label (known as a tally) to some thin ribbon or shirring elastic and tie it loosely round the cat's neck. If it objects, as it almost certainly will, do not insist, especially if the cat is in a pen by itself; tie the label to the outside of the cage.

Setting the cat in the cage is termed benching, and all the information you need about this is in the show rules, including what you can and cannot put

✦ LEFT
There may be time for a last-minute groom before the judges arrive.

into the pen with the cat. You must have water in the bowl at all times – some people bring their own bottled still water – and check the cat regularly. The rules even state when you are allowed to place food in the cat's pen. Toys are often only allowed after judging has finished.

Depending on the individual show style, either the judges go around the pens or the cats are taken to a judging arena where they are assessed. In Britain, the owners often have to

leave their animals while they are judged. In Europe and America, however, owners remain in an inner showing square formed by the cat pens, and can be quite close to the judging table, while the rest of the public mill around outside the square.

The winners of each class are either announced or posted on a results board. At many shows the best cat in show is selected from the class winners by a panel of judges.

Finally, it is time to make a fuss of your long-suffering animal – whether it has won anything or not – and then head for home.

✦ TOP
Pens can be rather austere, but you can put in a favourite blanket, a litter tray (pan), and most important of all, a bowl of water.

✦ ABOVE FAR LEFT
Neighbourly relations can sometimes become a little strained in the confined conditions at a cat show.

✦ ABOVE LEFT
An owner visits her cat after judging to keep it company. You should check your cat regularly during the course of the show.

✦ LEFT
Judges take the cats on to a judging table. They wipe their hands with disinfectant between handling each animal, to make sure germs are not carried from one animal to the other.

WHAT THE JUDGES LOOK FOR

The judges check each pedigreed cat against the standard of points for its breed that have been set by the show's governing body. (These standards of points are published and can be bought from the relevant organizations.) A maximum mark is set for each aspect of the cat to be judged, such as the head, tail or coat. This will vary according to the breed and will often differ slightly between one registering body and another. For example, a perfectly textured and coloured coat of an Abyssinian cat could earn 40 points and ideal eyes 5 points, whereas on a Siamese the eyes rate more highly at 20 points, and the coat is worth 35 points. If you want to ask a judge about your cat, it is fine to approach them on the day after judging has finished. Judges are almost certainly very successful breeders in their own right and have a lot of sound advice to give; don't dismiss them just because they have not given a high award to your cat. Contrary to popular belief, judges hate down-marking exhibits.

♦ BELOW
Here is an example of what judges would be looking for in a Blue-mitted Ragdoll under GCCF standards. They will also check the coat colour and pattern against the particular requirements for the breed, which in this case are worth 20 points.

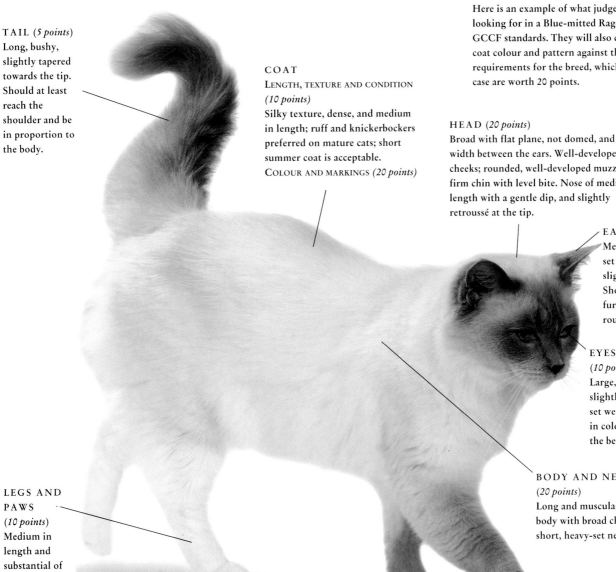

TAIL (*5 points*)
Long, bushy, slightly tapered towards the tip. Should at least reach the shoulder and be in proportion to the body.

COAT
LENGTH, TEXTURE AND CONDITION (*10 points*)
Silky texture, dense, and medium in length; ruff and knickerbockers preferred on mature cats; short summer coat is acceptable.
COLOUR AND MARKINGS (*20 points*)

HEAD (*20 points*)
Broad with flat plane, not domed, and width between the ears. Well-developed cheeks; rounded, well-developed muzzle; firm chin with level bite. Nose of medium length with a gentle dip, and slightly retroussé at the tip.

EARS (*5 points*)
Medium in size, set wide with a slight tilt forward. Should be well furnished and rounded at the tip.

EYES
(*10 points*)
Large, well opened, slightly oblique and set well apart. Blue in colour, the deeper the better.

BODY AND NECK
(*20 points*)
Long and muscular body with broad chest; short, heavy-set neck.

LEGS AND PAWS
(*10 points*)
Medium in length and substantial of bone; paws large, round, firm and tufted.

THE BRITISH SHOW SCENE

Anonymity is carefully guarded in the United Kingdom; there is little of the conviviality of the European or North American judging arenas, or the flamboyance of the decorated pens. At judging time, the owners are banished from the show hall and the judges visit each cat in turn. No identifying features are allowed on the pens, and all visible equipment in the pen must be white—the blankets, the water and food bowls, the litter tray (pan) (even the litter itself, if you are a perfectionist). Results are pinned on a line of hoardings, which becomes the most crowded part of the show for the rest of the day.

There are three levels of show in Britain. Exemption shows are usually run by individual clubs. They are relatively informal and friendly. There are no major qualifying awards available, and some of the Governing Council for the Cat Fancy (GCCF)

◆ LEFT
The equipment inside a pen at a British show must be white, from the cat's blanket to the litter tray (pan). However, now this Oriental Shorthair has been judged, he is allowed to have a toy in his pen.

rules are relaxed. Sanction shows are run according to the rules but no major awards are available. These are also organized by clubs but non-members can enter, and they are a good starting point for new exhibits.

Championship shows are strictly regulated and licensed by the GCCF. This is where qualifying awards, such as challenge certificates, for the

country's top cat show, the Supreme, can be gained. To be awarded a challenge certificate, a cat – which must be an un-neutered adult over nine months old – must win its open class and then be "challenged" against the set standard of points to see if it is good enough for the certificate to be awarded. A cat awarded three challenge certificates from three different judges qualifies for championship status and can enter classes for champions only. There is a parallel process for neutered adult cats aiming for premier certificates and premier status.

At shows run under the rules of the GCCF, judges make notes on every cat in the more important classes, including the open class, and write full reports, which are published in the specialist cat magazine, *Cats*.

At most shows the best adult, kitten and neuter of each breed is awarded Best of Breed. At some

◆ LEFT
At the GCCF Supreme Show the cats are penned in decorated pens, but taken to plain pens in judging rings, as shown, in order to be judged. These pens are disinfected thoroughly between cats.

◆ BELOW
The British owners have to take evidence
of their awards and collect their rosettes
from the rosette bench.

shows, especially the smaller specialist
breed shows, Best in Show is held.
Judges each nominate their best adult,
kitten and neuter, and those
nominated cats are judged against each
other to select the Best in Show Adult,
Kitten and Neuter and, often, the Best
Exhibit in Show. When Best in Show is
held at an all-breed show, the "Bests"
are selected in each section – Longhair,
Semi-longhair, British, Foreign,
Burmese, Oriental and Siamese. The
non-pedigreed cats also have their own
Best in Show, but never compete
against the pedigreed cats.

Open classes are open to all cats of
a particular breed, regardless of
whether they have previously won or
not. They are split into male and
female sections, neutered and entire
cats, and kittens and adults.

There are also various miscellaneous
classes for: cats bred by the exhibitor,
cats under or over two years old, cats
which have not yet won a first prize,
and so on. Whether fun or serious,
these classes give every exhibitor,
however experienced, the opportunity
to measure an exhibit's worth against
the best of the rest; crucial if a serious
show campaign is being planned. Most
shows also have a section for non-
pedigree cats.

If competition is not the aim, there
is the possibility of placing the cat on
exhibition. Here, the cat reclines in a
splendidly decorated pen all day
surrounded by evidence of past show
glories. Often the full pedigree is on
display and the cat does not have to
face the indignity of being hauled out
of the pen periodically.

The highest accolades for a British
cat are won at the annual Supreme Cat
Show. Here, judges provide a written

◆ BELOW
A pair of Persian Bi-colour youngsters destined
for the show circuit.

resumé that the owners can see on the
day. Only winners at lower-level
championship shows are eligible to
enter. The ultimate titles – Supreme
Adult, Supreme Kitten and Supreme –
are held for life. All three then
compete for Supreme Exhibit.

SHOWING IN EIRE
Shows in the Republic of Ireland
follow a similar style to that of the
United Kingdom. The governing
body is the Governing Council of
the Cat Fancy in Ireland (GCCFI).
Most judges are from the United
Kingdom. Titles awarded to individual
animals are ratified by the British
organization. If a cat becomes a
champion with both GCCF and
GCCFI, it is granted the title
International Champion.

EUROPEAN STYLE

Many European Shows last two days, as many exhibitors travel from other countries or even continents. The judges usually take different classes on the second day, so that wins gained on the first day are not duplicated on the second.

When quarantine regulations are relaxed, it may be possible for animals to have access to the full range of European cat shows, but they will have to be suitably vaccinated and micro-chipped. Certain differences in show style between Britain and the rest of Europe, however, will probably continue.

European shows are generally organized either by Fifé (*Fédération Internationale Féline*) or one of the independent clubs. Fifé, founded in 1949, is not just a European organization but has member states throughout the world, excluding, however, the United States, Canada, Australia, New Zealand and Japan.

There has traditionally been a sound working relationship between Fifé and the British GCCF, although each organization continues to retain much of its independence in decision-making and rules. Europe's numerous independent cat clubs operate as autonomous federations with their own registries, but cooperate and usually accept exhibitors from other clubs at their shows.

Some of the shows run by independent clubs have two different judging methods going on at the same time. After vetting-in, the cats are penned, sometimes with other entries from the same household, in a large show pen which may be sumptuously decorated with pedigrees, photographs, previous wins and cattery cards on display. The show pens are often arranged in squares, with the exhibitors inside the square having access to the animals, and the outward-facing side protected with perspex or heavy polythene so that the animals cannot be touched by the visitors on the outside of the square. Within the square of pens it is common for tables to be set up and laden with food and drink, so that the exhibitors can have a good day with their friends. It is very convivial.

Every cat is given a written report on how it conforms to the standard on that day, with the following ratings:

♦ *Excellent:* indicates that the animal has no physical defects; it conforms to standard; and is worthy of being bred from.

♦ *Very good:* indicates a cat of lesser quality relative to its standard of points, which is not good enough to gain a certificate.

♦ *Good:* indicates several defects or falling short of required standard.

All the cats are then judged for each award or qualification, and finally, Best in Section and Best in Show awards are decided.

♦ ABOVE
In European and North American shows, pens can be elaborately decorated, although at British shows, only cats "on exhibition" or at the Supreme Show, as shown, can rest in splendour such as this.

♦ LEFT
European Shorthairs have to reach the desired general standards of points rather than display a full pedigree to be eligible.

SHOWING IN AMERICA

♦ LEFT
Maine Coon Cats were major competitors at the very first American cat show held in Madison Square Garden, New York, in 1895.

Most shows in the United States, Mexico and Canada are full weekend occasions; some may even extend to three days. There may not be a preliminary vetting, on the assumption that no honourable exhibitor would take a sick animal to a show.

The holding pens at an American show are arranged like those in Europe, within a square (known as the ring) enclosed by the cages of the exhibitors. The owners can stay within the ring with their cats, and be fairly close to the judges when they give their verdict. The general public is on the outside of the square, and the outward-facing sides of the pens are usually protected from poking hands by heavy plastic sheets.

The judges remove each cat entrant in turn from its pen, to make an assessment against the required standards, accompanied by a simultaneous commentary. In virtually all North American associations, the judge is able to comment only on the favourable aspects of the animal, and not the negative points. Apart from brief notes for personal use, the judges make no written assessment of the cats.

At the end of the show, the ten top kittens, adults and neuters in the Longhair, Shorthair and All Breed sections are taken to the ring for the Best Cat award. The placements are announced starting at tenth and working upwards. They are important, for promotion to championship status in the American system depends not only on points scored in class wins, but on how many top five placements in the Best Cat stakes have been gained. It is not unknown, though rare, for a cat to become a Grand Champion at its very first show. There are classes for

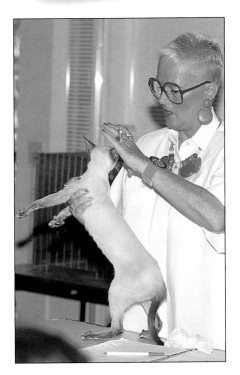

unaltered, pedigreed cats over eight months old, kitten competitions for animals of four to eight months, and provisional classes for breeds that have not been granted championship status (that is, registered as a distinct breed) by the registering association.

Various associations in North America promote the "campaigning" of the very top cats. Exhibitors fly and drive huge distances to attend the shows where the greatest concentration of top cats will be found. Points are scored at every show attended in pursuit of championship or premiership status. The ultimate award is that of National Top Cat. Even to get into the National Top Twenty-five is a remarkable achievement.

♦ ABOVE
American judges often keep up a running commentary on the good points of each cat as they are assessing the animals.

♦ RIGHT
This mixed breed Dilute Calico Van is a top award-winning American cat. Most shows have classes for non-pedigrees. The cats are judged on general appearance, condition and temperament rather than on specific points.

GLOSSARY

*Terms in **heavy type** within the main text refer to separate entries.*

adult a cat of over nine months old that has not been neutered (altered).

agouti a coat pattern where each individual hair is banded with two or three colours.

albino a genetic term referring to a lack of pigmentation in the skin and hair, resulting in an abnormally white animal with pink eyes.

altering American term for neutering.

applehead describes a flattened head shape, usually referring to the old-fashioned Siamese.

back-cross the process of mating a cat to one of its own forebears, including its parent.

bi-colour a white cat with solid patches of another colour in its coat.

breed a particular and consistent type, colour and size of cat that is officially registered by one of the cat associations.

brindled where there are hairs of a different colour, usually white, in a solid coloured part of the coat. This can be very noticeable on the mask of a Seal Point Siamese.

calico American term for a tortoiseshell and white cat.

calling when a female cat is ready to be mated; so termed because of the noise she makes.

cameo describes a white or silver coat subtly **tipped** with red, cream or tortoiseshell.

castration the removal of the male reproductive organs.

Cat Fancy the selective breeding and exhibiting of cats.

CFA the Cat Fanciers' Association, the main registration body for cats in the United States.

chinchilla a white cat whose coat has the lightest form of **tipping**, with dark tips at the very top of each hair shaft.

chintz another term for a **calico** or tortoiseshell and white cat.

cobby describes a short-legged, sturdy-bodied build.

Colourpoint longhaired cat of Persian type with a restricted **Himalayan** coat pattern. The American term for the Colourpoint Persian is **Himalayan**.

colourpointed any breed of cat, other than Siamese and Colourpoint Persian (Himalayan) that displays the restricted **Himalayan** points.

declawing the practice of surgically removing a cat's claws to prevent damage to people and furnishings. It is illegal in some countries unless for necessary veterinary treatment following an accident, for example.

dilute a genetic term referring to a paler version of a basic, **dominant** dark coat colour, for example, the

dilute version of black is blue.

dominant 1. the base colour of a breed, usually black or brown; 2. genetic term for a gene that over-rides another, so that its particular characteristics are expressed in the offspring.

feral a once-domesticated cat that has been left to wander and has reverted to its wild nature.

Fifé *Fédération Internationale Féline,* the major cat registration body in Europe.

Flehman Reaction the sneer-like action that makes use of the taste- and smell-sensitive Jacobson's organ in the roof of a cat's mouth. It is a means of receiving messages from other cats.

Foreign a term to describe a cat of more elongated type compared to cobby British or Persian type.

GCCF the Governing Council of the Cat Fancier's Association, the major registration body for cats in the United Kingdom.

gene pool the variety of genes available within a breed after several generations of breeding. If all cats within a breed are descended from a single mating, with no further outcrosses, the breed has a very limited gene pool.

genotype the genetic make-up of a cat, as distinct from the outward appearance (see also **phenotype**).

gestation the period taken from conception to kittening, most usually 65 days.

guardhairs the topcoat of fur over the awn (undercoat) and soft down hairs. Not all cats have all three levels.

haws see **nictitating membrane**.

heat see **oestrus**.

Himalayan 1. the American term for a Colourpoint Persian; 2. a genetic characteristic expressed in dark points on ears, face, legs and tail on an otherwise pale-coated cat.

kitten a young cat of less than nine months of age.

mask the facial marking of a cat.

nictitating membrane a membrane that is also known as the haw or third eyelid (nictitating means blinking). It moves horizontally and is most usually seen when a cat is ill or has a foreign body in the eye, and is therefore a cause for concern.

nose leather the leather-like nose area.

oestrus the state of a female cat on heat or in season, when she is sexually receptive.

Oriental cats typified by long limbs, svelte bodies, a wedge-shaped face, almond eyes and pointed ears.

parti-colour one or more colours or patterns on a white coat, as in tortoiseshell and white.

paw pads the leathery underparts of the paws.

pedigree a written record of a cat's ancestry, showing its parentage over several generations.

peke-faced an American term used to describe a Persian Longhair with a very short-nosed, flat face.

Persian longhaired cat of Persian type, quite distinct from the members of the semi-longhaired group.

phenotype the outward, physical appearance of a cat, as distinct from the genetic make-up, or **genotype**, which is often quite different.

points the cat's face, ears, lower legs and tail, which may be a darker colour than the main body as in the **Colourpoint** or Siamese.

prefix a name registered by a breeder and placed before any

particular name of the cat, denoting the breeding line of the cattery.

queen a female cat, over nine months of age, that has not been **spayed** and is capable of breeding when she is in **oestrus** or on heat.

recessive gene a gene that, on its own, is usually over-ridden by the **dominant** gene and therefore not expressed in physical characteristics. Two such genes, one from each parent, must be present in a kitten for the characteristic caused by this gene to be displayed. Examples of recessive genes are those for blue or chocolate coat colour.

rex a coat that is curled or crinkled, as seen in the Cornish Rex and Devon Rex breeds.

ruff the distinctive longer fur as seen around the neck of many semi-longhaired cats.

self a solid-coloured cat with no pattern or shading in the coat.

shaded a **tipped** coat, midway between the **chinchilla** and the **smoke**.

smoke the effect of the inhibitor (silver) gene on a non-agouti coat. Each hair is dark for 30–60 per cent of its length and silver at the base.

solid see **self**.

spaying the removal of the reproductive organs of a female cat.

spraying territorial marking of home and garden with urine.

standard of points the standards of size, colouring, markings and other characteristics for pedigreed breeds that are laid down by the cat-registrating bodies. Judges assess each cat against the standard of points for its particular breed.

stud an entire male cat that has not been neutered (altered).

tabby striped, blotched, spotted or ticked markings that in the wild give the optical illusion of breaking up body shape for camouflage.

ticked 1. when applied to hairs, another term for **agouti**. 2. when applied to pattern, the tabby pattern as seen in an Abyssian cat.

tipped the colouring of a cat's fur at the very tip of each hair shaft, the remainder of the fur being pale.

torbie an abbreviation for tortoiseshell-tabby.

tortie an abbreviation for tortoiseshell.

tri-colour another term for **calico**, **chintz** or tortoiseshell and white.

type the ideal head and body shape of a cat as laid down in the **standard of points**.

van a type of coat pattern consisting of a white body with a coloured tail and coloured spots on the head.

zoonoses infections that can be transferred from animal to human and vice versa, such as rabies and ringworm.

INDEX

Page numbers in *italics* refer to illustrations

ACKNOWLEDGEMENTS

The publishers would like to thank Paddy Cutts for her invaluable help.

The photographer and publishers would like to thank the following for their assistance with the photography:
Alison Hay, S. and R. Badger, S. Bagley, G. Black, V. Dyer, C. Fry, Wade and Kirby Heames, H. Hewitt, B. Hollandt, J. and D. Johnson, R. Lowen, B. and L. Riddy, Pampered Pets, Colin Clark veterinary practice, Burntwood boarding cattery, Weycolour Ltd.
Persian: S. McHale, Isabella Bans, Lynn Lincoln, Jo and Nick Bolton, Maxine Fothergill, Carol Gainsbury, Rose Lovelidge.
Turkish Van: T. Burnstone, Joyce Johnson. **Somali:** Jane Bean, Celestine Hanley, Rosie Lowen. **Maine Coon Cat:** Mr and Mrs Badger, Daphne Butters, Sue Deane, Bill Griffiths, Jackie Huddlestone. **Norwegian Forest Cat:** Ginny Black, Pete and Ann Bowler, Pat Stewart. **Balinese:** Mrs P. Browning, Mr and Mrs Cleland, Luisa Jones, Mr and Mrs Meerings, Mrs Pinnington.
British Angora: Ian Connerton.
Ragdoll: Belinda Bright, Dawn Davies, Janet Edwards, Dianne Mackey. **Tiffanie:** Cindy Matthews, Jennifer Ray.
Cymric: A. and J. Beresford.
Exotic: Mr and Mrs J. Clark, Rosemary Fisher, Maxine Fothergill, Carol Gainsbury,

Shelagh Heavens. **British Shorthair:** Brenda Hollandt, Paulette Larmour, Celia Leighton. **European Shorthair:** Stephanie Cole. **Oriental Shorthair:** Carolyn Fry, Mr and Mrs Funnell, Monica Harcourt, Sheena Manchline, Betty Winyard. **Siamese:** E. Corps, Sheena Manchline, Lynn Studer, B. Reece. **Snowshoe:** Mrs M. Shackell. **Seychellois:** Barbara Lambert. **Abyssinian:** Cindy Bailey, Ann Curtis, Mrs H. Hewitt, Heather Reay. **Russian Blue:** Val Price. **Korat:** Judith Jewkes, Jen Lacey. **Burmese:** Maria Chapman, Dr. Kim Jarvis, Naomi Johnson, Mrs Marriott Power, Mr and Mrs P. Webb, S. Williams-Ellis. **Burmilla:** Mrs C. Clarke. **Asian:** Mrs P. Impson, Deborah Laugher, Jennie Quiddington, Michelle Robinson. **Bengal:** Sandra Bush, Helen Hewitt. **Tonkinese:** Hazel Forshore, Carol Poole, Linda Vousden. **Singapura:** Debbie van

den Berg. **Ocicat:** L. Abbs, R. Caunter, V. Phillips. **Manx:** A. and J. Beresford. **Cornish Rex:** S. Luxford Watts. **Devon Rex:** Stephanie Cole, Chris Franks. **Sphynx:** Maureen Roddick. **Non-pedigree:** Monica Harcourt.

The publishers acknowledge reference to the Standard of Points booklet published by The Governing Council of the Cat Fancy, 4-6 Penel Orlieu, Bridgwater, TA6 3PG.

ADDITIONAL PHOTOGRAPHY
t=top; b=bottom; l=left; r=right; c=centre
AKG: 12 b. **Animals Unlimited:** 18 t; 24 t; 31 t; 36 t; 44 t, bl; 45 br; 46 t; 51 b; 52 b; 54 t, b; 60 t; 62 b; 64 c; 69 tr; 68 c, b; 73 c; 75t; 78 t, c; 84 t; 85 br; 89 c; 103 br; 124; 132; 134 bl, br; 137 b; 138 c, b; 139 t, c; 140 t, bl; 141 t; 143 t, b; 144 b; 145 t; 161c; 169 b; 170 c, b; 172 c; t; 196 b; 203 t,

205 t; 217 t, b; 220 t; 221 t, b; 222 t; 225 c; 239; 240 bl; 241 t; 242 t, b; 244 b; 247 b; 248 t. **Bridgeman Art Library:** 13 b. e.t. Archive: 12 c. 13 t. **Janet Boswell:** 47 br; 50 br; 55 b; 60 b. **Gilly Cameron Cooper:** 19 c; 23 t; 34 br; 45 bl; 62 t; 83 c; 85 tr; 99 tl; 112 br; 240 c, br; 244 cr; 246 t; 247 t. **Chanan Photography,** C.A.: 53 c; 55 t; 56 b; 101 b; 151 t, bl; 173 b; 175; 176–77 all; 179 b; 183 t; 209 c, b; 210 t, tr, b; 211 tl, tr; 240 t; 244 cl; 249 c, b. **FLPA:** 2; 8; 10 b; 11 t; 14 t; 15 c, b; 21 c; 23 b; 47 bc; 48 bl, br; 50 t; 51 t, 57 b; 58; 60 br; 64 t; 65 b; 84 bl; 86 t; 87 bl; 88 br; 90; 96 c; 109 t; 112 tl, tr, bl; 116 b; 118 t; 126 t; 134 t; 135 t; 138 t; 146; 164; 175; 178 b; 179 t; 202 t, b; 211 b; 212 t; 214; 229 b; 248 b. **Marc Henrie:** 16; 19 t; 92 c; 139 b; 140 cl, br; 141b; 142b; 151br; 162b; 171c; 179 t, c; 184 b; 205 b; 216 t, b; 218; 234 t; 235 t; 237 bl; 241 b. **Mac on Mac Design:** 30 b; 49 t; 50 bl. **Papilio Photographic:** 9 tl, c, br. **Planet Earth:** 9 bl;11 b. **Warren Photographic:** 6; 18 b; 22t; 25; 26 t;28; 29 t, c; 31 b; 40 t, br; 41 b; 42; 44 cr; 45 t; 47 t, bl; 48 t; 49 b; 60 c; 63 tl, r; 65 t; 67 bl, br; 68 t; 69 br; 70; 72 t, bl, br; 74 b;78 bl, br; 79 tr, c, b; 83 bl; 85 tl; 87 tr; 88 t, bl; 89 tr, b; 92 t; 94 t, bl, br;95 t, b; 96 bl; 98 t, b; 101 t; 102 t, bl, br; 103 tr, bl; 104; 109 b; 114; 115; 118 b;120 bl; 121 bl, br; 122; 123; 125; 224 b; 225 b; 230; 233 t, b; 234 bl.